STIEG
LARSSON

STIEG LARSSON

THE REAL STORY OF THE MAN WHO PLAYED WITH FIRE

JAN-ERIK PETTERSSON

Translated from the Swedish by Tom Geddes

CAMILLUS

STERLING
New York

STERLING
New York

An Imprint of Sterling Publishing
387 Park Avenue South
New York, NY 10016

© 2009 by Jan-Erik Pettersson and Telegram Bokforlag
English translation © 2011 by Tom Geddes
Originally published in Sweden as *Stieg* in 2009; first US edition
published by Sterling in 2011.

ISBN 978-1-4027-8940-3 (hardcover)
ISBN 978-1-4027-8968-7 (ebook)

Library of Congress Cataloging-in-Publication Data

Pettersson, Jan-Erik.
  [Stieg Larsson. English]
  Stieg Larsson : the real story of the man who played with fire / Jan-Erik Pettersson ; translated from the
Swedish by Tom Geddes. -- 1st U.S. ed.
     p. cm.
  Summary: "Stieg Larsson's former publisher reveals the real man behind the mega-bestselling Millennium
Trilogy--a man who fought heroically for human rights, and who brought that same political and moral passion
to his writing. Until the trilogy's posthumous publication, Larsson was best known for his devotion to left-wing
causes and as a tireless anti-fascist activist. Horrified by the rise of far-right extremism in Sweden, he dedicated
himself to exposing these often shadowy and violent groups--at great personal risk--gaining international respect
for the depth of his commitment and knowledge. Jan-Erik Pettersson shows how Stieg's energetic championing
of social justice and women's rights characterized his life as well as his work, finally animating the Millennium
Trilogy and particularly the character of the unforgettable Lisbeth Salander. Throughout the book Pettersson
explores the issues, people, and places who inspired Larsson's portrayal of Salander and her champion, journalist
Michael Blomkvist."-- Provided by publisher.
  Includes bibliographical references and index.
  ISBN 978-1-4027-8940-3
  1. Larsson, Stieg, 1954-2004. 2. Authors, Swedish--20th century--Biography. 3. Journalists--Sweden--Biog-
raphy. I. Geddes, Tom. II. Title.
  PT9876.22.A6933Z8513 2011
  839.73'8--dc23
  [B]

                                    2011019903

Distributed in Canada by Sterling Publishing
^{c}/o Canadian Manda Group, 165 Dufferin Street
Toronto, Ontario, Canada M6K 3H6

Picture Credits:
SCANPIX-US/SIPA —1: Leif Blom / Scanpix/Sipa Press; 2: Per Jarl / Expo /Scanpix/Sipa Press/0909041551; 3: Per
Jarl/Expo/SCANPIX/Sipa Press/1102072325; 4: Per Jarl/Scanpix/Sipa Press/0810222205; 5: Monica Schmidtz/Scan-
pix/Sipa Press/0806181906; 6–7: Associated Press; 8 (top): s51/s51/ZUMA Press/Newscom
8: PATRICK KOVARIK/AFP/Getty Images

For information about custom editions, special sales, and premium
and corporate purchases, please contact Sterling Special Sales at 800-805-5489
or specialsales@sterlingpublishing.com

CONTENTS

FOREWORD

STIEG WAS NOT ALWAYS RIGHT. In the five years we worked together on *Expo* magazine we argued frequently yet amicably. He had his ideas on how *Expo* should develop and what articles we should publish, I had mine. Sometimes I won, sometimes he did. They were always productive discussions.

On one matter he was certainly proved right: his books were a success. I remember an evening at Stieg and Eva's when the other guests had either left or dropped out of the conversation. The whisky was on the table, and for some reason we started talking about pensions. Stieg was not exactly known as a financial genius. Now that he had left his press agency job, I wondered how he would manage financially and whether he had made any provision for the future. He declared confidently that he was going to write a few crime novels that would make him a multimillionaire. I hardly gave his intentions a second thought after that night, but when he showed me his publisher's contract I realized he could well be right.

Today the Millennium Trilogy is known more or less all over the world. The argumentative and anecdotic northern Swede has suddenly become a superstar. It is unreal, gratifying and at the same time a little sad.

Stieg was so much more than his crime novels. All of us who lived and worked with him know that he was motivated by neither money nor fame. With this publishing success behind him he would have been in an admirable position as an independent and outspoken social commentator. But it was not to be. All I can do is remind the millions of readers who have been hooked by his plots and his characters that there was another side to Stieg.

It is no coincidence that his crime novels embody trenchant social criticism. Stieg was a political animal. He was a fervent advocate of women's rights. He was an anti-fascist. Despite the runaway success of his thrillers, I have always considered his articles about Swedish and international right-wing extremism more interesting – and more important.

But all are linked. Stieg's novels would never have covered the ground they do without his social commitment. For those who want to understand the gestation of the misadventures of Lisbeth Salander and Mikael Blomkvist, the answers are in Stieg's published articles, investigations and surveys; they are in the setting up of the *Expo* Foundation; they are in his lectures, stories and biography.

They are in this book.

Mikael Ekman
Mellerud, April 2010

AUTHOR'S PREFACE

THIS IS NOT A BIOGRAPHY IN THE CONVENTIONAL SENSE. It is a book about the public persona of Stieg Larsson, about his work and his writing, about the interplay between his life and work and society at large.

The Millennium Trilogy has become a unique phenomenon. No previous Swedish novels have made such an explosive breakthrough on to the international scene or attained such near-mythic status. This phenomenon has not arisen out of nowhere, of course: it has emerged from the broad swell of Swedish crime fiction, which in turn is closely linked to Swedish society, its values and the social and political changes that have so strenuously tested its ideals. Developments in the book trade in recent years, both in Sweden and internationally, have also played their part.

But irrespective of all this, and of whether Stieg Larsson's novels will still be read in ten or twenty years' time, Mikael Blomkvist and above all Lisbeth Salander will certainly be found in future international handbooks of famous fictional characters.

And the battle against the forces that refuse to regard all human beings as fundamentally equal will continue, whatever the future might bring.

I would like to take this opportunity to thank those who agreed to be interviewed for the book. A special note of gratitude to my editor, Agnete Danneberg, for all her help; and my warmest thanks also to Annika Seward Jensen, publisher at Telegram Förlag, and to *Expo*.

ACTIVIST

"Bjursele was like a poster for the Västerbotten country village. It consisted of about twenty houses set relatively close together in a semicircle at one end of a lake. In the centre of the village was a crossroads with an arrow pointing towards Hemmingen, 11km, and another pointing towards Bastuträsk, 17km. Near the crossroads was a small bridge with a creek that Blomkvist assumed was the water, the *sel*. Now at the height of summer, it was as pretty as a postcard."

—Stieg Larsson,
The Girl with the Dragon Tattoo

STIEG LARSSON'S NOVELS are set mainly on the streets and squares of Stockholm, in the editorial offices and cafés of the metropolis. Mikael Blomkvist the journalist is at home there, it is his base, and he makes trips further afield when the task in hand requires. It was on one such job that he ended up in this picture-postcard idyll. In the first book of the Millennium Trilogy, *The Girl with the Dragon Tattoo* (published in its original Swedish as *Men Who Hate Women*), he travels up to the landscapes of northern Sweden that the author himself knew well from his childhood. A world away from the urban heart of Stockholm: a village, a lake, a cottage, deep in the rural hinterland of Västerbotten.

Excursion to Bjursele

I AM ON MY WAY FROM UMEÅ up towards Norsjö and Bjursele, driven by Erland Larsson, Stieg's father. It is difficult to believe that this quiet road cutting through the coastal landscape can be the European E4 highway.

Västerbotten comprises coast, fields and meadows, deep forests, bogs and fells, and covers a seventh of the total area of Sweden. Rivers and streams in parallel sequence cross the country in a south-easterly direction on their way from the mountains to the sea. There are hundreds of lakes, but they are all small, most of them with names ending in *träsk* (marshy lake).

What we today call Västerbotten was first settled in the fifteenth century along the coast, where the soil is fertile and the summers often surprisingly warm. Then people moved further up the river valleys, and the poorest – or the most adventurous – continued northwards into the interior and colonized the great silent wastes.

As we leave Umeå Erland points out where he and Stieg's mother, Vivianne, used to join other participants to prepare for the May Day demonstrations. As he was a graphic artist and decorator, he was the one who had to paint all the placards, since it was the simplest and quickest way of getting it done. He and his wife used to march in the Social Democrat procession.

But not their elder son. Stieg marched beneath more militant banners with his comrades in the Communist Workers' Party.

Even as early as the turbulent year of 1968, when he was only fourteen years old, he was politically committed. He wore a round purple badge with a gold star, the symbol of the Vietnam NLF (National Front for the Liberation of South Vietnam) movement, on his chest. He was comparatively young to be so fervently engaged in politics. Most activists were in their twenties. But he was already extremely independent and spent much of his time in a room of his own in the basement, reading, writing or having discussions with his political friends.

Political debate at his parents' home was becoming increasingly heated, not least because of the Vietnam War. Erland says that was when he first lost an argument with his son. He thinks it was because left-wing groups were actually taught how to argue their case.

Politics formed an integral part of their family life, something that Stieg was accustomed to from his earliest childhood with his maternal grandfather, Severin Boström, who was a loyal Communist. Erland and Vivianne were both Social Democrats, and active in the Federation of Retail Employees. Vivianne was also involved in local politics, a member of the municipal council and its committee for the disabled, and a founder member of the first equal opportunities committee in Umeå.

So it was only natural for Stieg and his parents to discuss what was happening in Sweden and the world, and furious arguments would often break out round the kitchen table. For Stieg, the socialists – in other words, his parents – were reactionaries and betrayers of social-ism's ideals.

It was of course important to challenge the parental generation in every possible sphere, not just the political. On one occasion, not long before Stieg's eighteenth birthday, Erland came home from his evening job as a cinema commissionaire and found Vivianne in tears at the kitchen sink. 'You've got to talk to Stieg,' she said. Stieg was holding a piece of paper that he wanted his parents to sign requesting his withdrawal from the Swedish Church. Erland thought it was no great problem, since Stieg would be eighteen in a few months and could request his own withdrawal anyway. (In Sweden one is automatically a member of the Established Church unless application is made to leave it.) 'Yet they had quarrelled over it for three hours, which shows just how fraught such issues were in those days,' Erland said.

Stieg later tried hard to persuade his brother Joakim to leave the Church, which he actually did in his thirties. 'Then after Stieg's death we wondered whether it was acceptable to have a church funeral if he wasn't a member of the Established Church,' says Joakim. 'But it turned out that he still was. He had never bothered to apply to leave it. I felt as if he was laughing at me from his heaven.'

WE ARE NOW LEAVING UMEÅ, Erland Larsson and I, and continuing northwards towards Bjursele. We are driving through the Västerbotten coastal landscape, where the land rises in stages from the sea up to the coastal plain, with its mix of fir and deciduous forest, its fields and pastures. A thriving area still.

We pass Lövånger, with its medieval church and picturesque parish village, and a few miles on Erland we turn off the main highway and begin heading east. We arrive almost immediately in Önnesmark, where Erland has a summer cottage which he and Vivianne bought in 1987. Stieg often came up here when he wanted to write and be left in peace. Erland used to bring him, since Stieg could not drive. Parts of the Millennium Trilogy were written in the cottage in Önnesmark.

On the way back to the main road we call on the nearest neighbours, Gunnar Nilsson (whose namesake was Mikael Blomkvist's neighbour on Hedeby Island) and his partner, Birgit Granlund. You can't just drive by without stopping to say hello. When you do, you're immediately invited in for coffee, with home-made unleavened bread and thin slices of meat from an elk that Gunnar himself shot.

Gunnar is over eighty and says he is hale and hearty now. He was worse before he had his bypass operation. He speaks a strong local country dialect which is not always easy to understand. They are flourishing but the village isn't. The old folk are dying off and there are no new people moving in.

Now we are back on the E4, heading north towards Skellefteå. Just before Bureå we turn inland towards Hjoggböle. We're going to take a look at what Erland calls Grandad's place, a farm where his own father lived as a child. We drive on to Sjöbotten and Ersmyrliden. It's somewhat tricky to locate and feels isolated, despite the fact that we're quite close to Skellefteå airport.

Eventually we find the red cottage down by the lake. Only one house is visible from it, a ramshackle yellow building on the opposite side of the road. Erland was here frequently as a child and he remembers sometimes playing with a tall, thin boy known by his initials P. O., the grandchild in the neighbouring house. In later life P. O. was to become a top-class high-jumper in Sweden and later an author and playwright, increasingly successful over the years and eventually world-famous.

So this little piece of land has its place in the history of Swedish literature. P. O. Enquist has reflected on it and the two houses in his autobiography, *Ett annat liv* (Another Life). Writing of himself in the third person, he says:

> His grandmother lives four miles away at Bjursjön. The house stands on its own by the lake, though a hundred yards further on is a smaller house at the edge of the forest. There are only those two: the Old House and Larssons. In Larssons, a hundred yards from his grandmother Johanna, lives the father of the young Stieg, who will go on to write crime fiction. The fact that the two houses in the forest produce two writers is statistically normal hereabouts, everyone thinks; writers are more plentiful than cow udders in these villages. In Hjoggböle, which is bigger, we'll soon have five. Every village has its writer.

Erland Larsson believes that Enquist confused the two houses and that the Old House was actually the name of his own father's childhood home. But perhaps that is not important. The remarkable thing is all these authors who emerged from the soil of this sparsely populated and desolate landscape.

Åke Lundgren, an author from Kågedalen, writes about the literary miracle which is Västerbotten in the Swedish Tourist Association's Yearbook for 2001, which is devoted to the province. He calculates the number of living, established authors born there as a total of fifty. He also provides a map showing their birthplaces. Oddly enough, most of the writers do not come from the south, the university city of Umeå, but from the sparse settlements to the north and west of the industrial town of Skellefteå. And not only the majority but also the best known. Three of the unequivocally greatest names in modern Swedish literature – Sara Lidman, Torgny Lindgren and P. O. Enquist – come from the Skellefteå region. But the most commercially successful Swedish author of all time – Stieg Larsson – is not even counted, because when that yearbook was published there were only a few fragments of his first novels on his Apple Mac.

There must be something special in this soil; something that fosters writers, however unlikely that may seem. Perhaps it is the language, that peculiar dialect with its abrupt and expressive phrasing, or all the reading, the Bible study, in these villages of devout nonconformist religiosity. Or simply the isolated and uneventful life, which means that people suddenly feel the urge to tell a story or listen to someone telling one. As Åke Lundgren writes: 'I didn't know what an author was, and yet they were everywhere. They were the pedlars who sold underclothes and brought us news into the bargain. They were the preachers who distributed gaudy magazines and claimed that the end was nigh but that Paradise awaited us.' Or there is the starkly simple explanation given by P. O. Enquist: 'Inbreeding!' Everyone is related to everyone else in these parts. And ultimately everyone is related to Ol'Zackri, an eighteenth-century peasant by the name of Nils Zachrisson who was forefather to some of the best-known preachers in Västerbotten.

Erland Larsson, a keen genealogist, has not been able to discover evidence of such connections. But he has found traces of links to another well-known Västerbotten family, the Bure clan. Its most prominent figure was Johannes Bureus, head of the National Board of Antiquities, medievalist and one of the giants of Swedish academic life in the Great Power period of the seventeenth century.

WE COME TO SKELLEFTEÅ, the town where both of Stieg's parents grew up. As a native of Småland in the south myself, I find something very familiar about this town, with its numerous nonconformist churches, its local patriotism, its proliferation of societies, its many small businesses. We drive through the town and turn inland. From Skellefteå the roads go to Boliden, Jörn, Bastuträsk and Norsjö. Autumn has arrived and we can see the first of the snow on the fields. It's a little worrying, because Erland still has summer tyres on the car.

The forests are getting denser. These are the forests that have played such a major role in the region's history and economy.

There was never any shortage of trees, so the Swedish state could easily afford to give substantial acreages to those who wanted to colonize the land. But then, in the nineteenth century, the forests suddenly became valuable and the export-driven industry really took off. Sawmills sprang up all along the coast, and timber barons and trading houses cheated the farmers of their forests. The felling turned into devastation. It soon came to be known as *Baggböleri*, after a village not far inland from Umeå, the site of a sawmill involved in a famous lawsuit about over-exploitation.

A few became very rich in no time at all; others were ruined. One of those who speculated in forestry at the end of the nineteenth century, as the construction of the railways was beginning, was Erik Lidman, the grandfather of Sara Lidman on whom she modelled one of the characters in her 1970s series of historical novels focusing on conditions in northern Sweden and the coming of the railways. He fared badly in those years of investment and speculation, was forced into bankruptcy with enormous debts and then jailed for having embezzled state-aid money while chairman of the local council. The family had to move 'up-country' and settled in Missenträsk, the village north of Jörn which his grandchild Sara was to place on the literary map of Sweden.

But the sparsely populated region west of Skellefteå does not consist solely of forest. Nor does the area around Boliden. Westwards and upstream beside the Skellefteälven river lies the Skellefteå ore-field, one of the most mineral-rich in the world. In the early years of the twentieth century times were hard in Västerbotten. The timber industry was in crisis and there was massive unemployment, not least in the immediate vicinity of Skellefteå. But in the period 1918–24 an intensive programme of prospecting led to promising finds of minerals along the river. There was a lot of copper in the ore located, but unfortunately not of high enough quality to justify mining it. Then in 1924 the Boliden deposits were found, proving to be almost literally worth their weight in gold. The discovery of gold-bearing ore led to the setting up of Boliden Aktiebolag, the enterprise that went on to become so dominant in the region. This was ore of a complex composition, containing not only gold and silver but also sulphite and arsenic. But developments in metallurgical technology meant that the ore did not now need to be exported, and an enormous smelting works was built on two islands on the coast just to the east of Skellefteå.

Thus was born the giant industrial concern Rönnskärsverken. It was here that the ore could now be refined within Sweden, creating huge numbers of jobs for an underemployed population. This was where the farm boys from the entire district could come and easily find work. A whole new settlement, Skelleftehamn, grew up here, with modern workers' apartments of two rooms, kitchen and bathroom. In the 1930s people would travel for many miles just to see what it felt like to have an indoor toilet.

Up until the Second World War gold production was munificently profitable, but when Sweden was closed off from the rest of the world during the war years production fell. Instead there was increased demand for lead and copper and also aluminium. After the war, Rönnskär invested heavily in modernizing and replacing worn-out machinery. Ore was imported from abroad, the firm continued to expand and by the middle of the twentieth century it had come to be an ever more dominant industry in the region.

ERLAND MET VIVIANNE BOSTRÖM, a girl of his own age, at a dance in 1953. He was about to do his military service in Solna, but when he was back home in Skellefteå on harvest leave in the autumn he and Vivianne saw one another again and started, as he put it, 'going out'. Vivianne soon became pregnant and Erland had to get himself a job pretty quickly. The choice at the time was fairly obvious: Rönnskär. Erland's father, no longer alive, had worked there, as had Vivianne's father, Severin Boström.

Severin helped the young couple and through contacts found them somewhere to live in Skelleftehamn, right by Rönnskär, in the residential development that had been built for workers and staff at the big industrial complex. On 15 August 1954 Vivianne gave birth to a boy who was christened Karl Stig-Erland.

So Stieg Larsson's birthplace was Skelleftehamn, and the first Millennium film had its premiere in this community, which now comprises some 3,000 inhabitants, a shadow of its former self.

The life that awaited the Larsson family was no bed of roses. They lived in cramped and old-fashioned conditions. The house had no central heating and when the chill of autumn arrived Erland would have to get up early and lay a fire in the tiled stove, and then Vivianne would get up, put the porridge on and change Stieg's nappy.

The Rönnskär factory was also widely reputed to be the dirtiest workplace in Sweden. The wages were regarded as high, but so was the price the workers had to pay in ill-health. Its poor environmental conditions were immediately apparent from the smell. As luck would have it, the wind was mostly offshore; otherwise, it was generally agreed, it would have been hard to live in the district at all. But those inside the factory could not escape it. They were exposed on a daily basis to all the gases produced in the smelting process and all the dust in the atmosphere. Arsenic, lead and other toxic substances were all handled here. It was said that when a true Rönnskär man blew his nose, there was blood on the handkerchief. Gases and dust particles eroded the mucous membrane and could even destroy the septum. Many succumbed to cancer of the throat, sinuses and lungs. There was also a saying that if you lived to draw your pension you hadn't got long to go, because your body was so accustomed to the toxins that it would collapse without its daily dose. Yet the works had taken on a central role for the area. A constant question on people's lips was what would happen if Rönnskär were to close down. And everyone knew the answer.

'It was a depressing place,' says Erland. 'On the five o'clock train into town you'd meet old men who'd been there for ages. Some of them had lost all the cartilage in their nostrils because of the arsenic.'

Erland's own health broke down early on, possibly because of the arsenic, and he decided to quit. But there was not much else by way of employment locally for people with no specialist training or education. He was told that if he went to Stockholm he could enrol at the Retail Institute and train as an interior decorator, something which appealed to his aesthetic leanings.

There was a severe housing shortage in Sweden in the 1950s and Stockholm was worst affected of all. Erland and Vivianne could not even begin to think of getting an apartment. Rented rooms were the most that they, like so many others, could hope for. But there were plenty of these available, because of people's need to subsidize their own accommodation by renting out. Through one of Vivianne's relations they managed to obtain a room in Enskede, sharing a kitchen and bathroom with the landlord. The three of them moved in and lived there for a few months before they came to the conclusion that it was unsatisfactory.

'There was nothing exactly wrong with it, but it was no way to live with a child,' Erland says.

They talked over the impossible housing situation with Vivianne's parents, Tekla and Severin, who were then living in Ursviken, between Skellefteå and Skelleftehamn. The older couple thought they could easily take care of the little boy for a while, until his parents had organized something better. Severin worked during the day, but Tekla was a housewife.

So the matter was decided. There seem not to have been any lengthy deliberations.

'A lot of people have been surprised that we sent Stieg away,' Erland says. 'But there was nothing unusual about it in those days. Severin himself lived with a relative's family when he was a child.'

After a period in Stockholm Erland took a job in Uppsala with

11

the Tempo retail chain, but he and Vivianne really wanted to return to the north, where their son and family were. So when the opportunity arose to work as an interior designer for Åhlens department store in Umeå, there was no reason to hesitate. It was not Skellefteå, but at least it was the right part of the country. As always, arranging accommodation was more difficult, and they had to make do with yet another rented room, which they moved into just before the Christmas of 1956. Again, it was too small for a family with children. Vivianne later found employment in a shop in the town.

NORSJÖ, WHERE WE ARRIVE NEXT, is about fifty miles due west of Skellefteå, in the land of lakes and midges. It was in this parish, more precisely in the village of Raggsjö, that Torgny Lindgren was born. An author much loved by his Västerbotten readership, he is a big name not only throughout Sweden but also internationally, a member of the Swedish Academy and recipient of the renowned French Prix Fémina. His first major success was the novel *The Way of a Serpent*, set in Raggsjö and based partly on a story the author had heard as a child. A man called Isak had recounted how he and his parents and siblings had once long ago been driven out of their home, which was owned by the local shopkeeper. They could not afford to pay the rent and woke up one morning to hear noises on the roof: the shopkeeper and his assistant were starting to demolish the house. The family had to take refuge in a hut in the forest.

Torgny Lindgren writes of these Västerbotten villages in a language strong on dialect, with biblical imagery and phraseology. It is rusticity in a highly literary form.

Norsjö today is a relatively lively place with a population of about 7,000. Mikael Blomkvist comes here on his search for somebody who might have worked in a joinery business and could have been the person who took the amateur photographs he is trying to trace. He finds that the workshop was closed down some twenty years previously.

There may be no joinery in Norsjö any longer, but the high street has an array of shops, banks and a state liquor store. The restaurant is shut, so we try the hot-dog stall near the bus stop, where Blomkvist bought himself a hamburger. Erland was here six months ago with a French TV crew, who were surprised that the hamburger cook turned out to speak French. The cook is still there and remembers the Frenchmen, but he has never heard of Stieg Larsson.

'What about the film, then, *The Girl Who Played with Fire?*'

'No, sorry. Never heard of it.'

It was in Norsjö that Blomkvist eventually unearthed a clue; he finds someone who used to work at the mysterious joinery business, a retired carpenter who exclaims, 'It's Assar Brännlund's boy!' The subject himself turns out to have died in an industrial accident at the Rönnskär factory, but his wife is still alive and living in Bjursele.

We go there too, just as Blomkvist did, heading from Norsjö back towards Skellefteå, and a dozen miles before Bastuträsk we come to the village of Bjursele. This is the location of the red house, the third after the bridge, where Blomkvist tracked down the woman who had taken the photo in Hedestad. He parked in the space outside the former grocer's shop, but there was no one at home in the house. His second attempt was more successful, and he managed to obtain another photograph which turned out to be decisive in solving the mystery.

This very spot in front of the grocer's shop, although not mentioned in the novel, was well known to Stieg Larsson. His grandfather Severin Boström had his workshop in the long, low building next to it.

Severin, who had worked in the copper smelting plant for many years, was far from healthy in the mid-1950s (Erland is sure this was due to the fumes from the factory). He left his job in 1957 and moved with Tekla and their grandchild, Stieg, to Bjursele, which was Tekla's home village. He had already been taking on repairs, of cycles, motorbikes, chainsaws and the like, as well as doing his full-time job. They bought an old property just outside the village, at a place called Måggliden.

We leave the car by the road and walk up the path leading to Måggliden. As with so many other buildings, it is at the top of a hill. People often built on raised ground up here so that the frost wouldn't take the potatoes and other crops. It's a pretty place, with an uninterrupted view out over the lake below. But it didn't use to look like that, says Erland. The trees have all been thinned out; there was thick forest before.

Måggliden actually consists of just two houses. The older, bigger one where Severin, Tekla and Stieg lived is in a poor state of repair and leaning alarmingly. The newer one is in better condition and seems to be a summer cottage now. There are towels still hanging on the clothes line, as if the residents had simply got tired of the summer one day and left.

ERLAND AND VIVIANNE LARSSON visited Måggliden frequently. After they moved to Umeå it was not so far to come. With some help from Erland's employer, they had been able to get a proper apartment in the Sandbacka district, at 36 Hagbergsvägen. In 1957 Stieg acquired a younger brother, Joakim. Erland and Vivianne wanted Stieg to return to them now that their situation was at last a bit more satisfactory. But it was not to be.

'Stieg had put down roots with his grandparents and we didn't want to pull him in different directions,' explains Erland.

So Stieg stayed in the country with his grandmother and grandfather. Umeå had to wait.

It was a free and easy life up at Måggliden, and there were a lot of other children around to play with. He was much indulged by Grandma and Grandad, and the rules as to what was and was not allowed were far from rigorous.

After Stieg's death his partner, Eva Gabrielsson, told the newspaper *Norra Västerbotten*:

> His grandfather had once been a factory worker. Now he provided for his wife and Stieg by repairing small appliances and cycles, taking on odd jobs in the area, plus some fishing and hunting. After having been interned in the 1940s in Storsien concentration camp in Norrbotten, redesignated a work camp after the war, he and the other prisoners found it difficult to regain acceptance in society. The incomprehensible silence that surrounded them then is still the same today. Stieg's grandfather chose to move away. That was the burden Stieg carried: to defend people's equal rights, to fight for democracy and freedom of expression and ensure that what happened to his grandfather would never be repeated in Sweden.

Storsien near Piteå was one of a total of eight so-called work companies comprising 300 men eligible for call-up but classified as being 'of unreliable patriotism' – principally Communists but also a small number of Syndicalists and Social Democrats who were interned. The inmates themselves regarded it as a mild form of concentration camp. The real danger from their point of view was, of course, a German invasion and occupation of Sweden, which seemed quite likely at that time in the war. Had that happened, things would have indubitably gone badly for them.

The work companies were in existence for quite a short period in 1939–40, but Olof Thörnell, supreme commander of the Swedish armed forces, had well-advanced plans to extend the system so that many thousands of Communists could be interned. However, the government put a stop to it when they learned of his intentions.

Erland insists it was not true that Severin was interned at Storsien. 'He was certainly a Communist, in fact without a doubt a Stalinist, but so was everyone else at Rönnskär then. But he never went to any internment camp, I'm sure of that.'

Unfortunately, it seems more or less impossible now to get to the truth of the matter, since the declassified documents in the Military Archives do not include a comprehensive list of all the internees at Storsien. Severin Boström's name certainly does not appear on the lists still extant. On his call-up card it is noted that he had deferment of service in the conscriptions of 1939, 1940 and 1941, and that he was called up in January–April 1942. Whatever the facts may be, the memory of his grandfather and his political attitudes had a long-lasting effect on Stieg. Later in life for instance, he would use the name Severin as his pseudonym when writing for the Trotskyist paper *Internationalen*.

STIEG LIVED WITH HIS GRANDPARENTS near Bjursele from 1957 to 1962. He started school in 1961, at the age of seven. If you follow the winding road a little way from Måggliden you come to a village called Pjäsörn, where the school was. The building is still there but seems nowadays to be used as some sort of meeting house.

Only a year or so after starting school, his rural life in Bjursele came to an end. One morning in the summer of 1962 Severin Boström was found dead in his bed. He had died of a heart attack, at the age of fifty-six. So it was decided that Stieg should go to live with his mother and father in Umeå. His grandmother went too, initially also living with them.

❖

Umeå

Stieg was eight when he arrived in Umeå. He spoke a broad rural dialect and came from an environment that was completely unlike the town.

'He had lived as a free spirit up in Bjursele, doing more or less what he liked. But life was a bit stricter here at home in Umeå,' says Erland.

In a newspaper interview his childhood friend Bosse Lindh, who lived in the same street, has described his first meeting with Stieg: 'He came running into our flat speaking a language I'd never heard before. He didn't even knock. I thought it was very odd. I'd never even seen him before.'

What's more, he no longer got the swigs of coffee he was used to up in Bjursele. His grandmother and grandfather drank a lot of coffee and Stieg was always given some. He said himself much later that after arriving in Umeå he was totally deprived of caffeine.

He started in Year 3 at Haga school in Umeå. He was an able boy but not outstanding. One classmate remembers him as being slightly different and as someone who stuck up for the weak. 'If there was anyone being bullied or victimized he would step in and try to resolve the problem. Not by fighting – there were others who did that – but by talking.'

At high school, he would answer back the teachers he didn't like. He got into an argument with his civics teacher, because he thought she was marking him too low, and threatened to report her to the Education Committee. The teacher was the daughter of a former member of the extreme right-wing Lappo movement in Finland and they were diametrically opposed on political matters. But his marks were raised.

His favourite subjects were drawing and essay writing. His Swedish teacher Manne Lidén had modern ideas and let the pupils do joint projects and compile their own newspapers, which Stieg enjoyed.

He had a keen interest in the sciences and new technology as well. Everything to do with space fascinated him. At a friend's house he read *Allers* magazine, stories of encounters with the unknown, about spaceships and flying saucers.

When Erland was going through a cardboard box of Stieg's effects he found a telescope and detailed charts of the stars and their positions. He remembered that Stieg had even got permission to borrow the school keys so that he and his friend Bosse could go in at night and use the telescope there. Stieg had considerable powers of persuasion. 'He inherited that ability from his mother,' Erland thinks. 'She was a saleswoman to her fingertips.'

Stieg was an enthusiastic radio ham, and was involved in something called DX-ing, which at that period, the mid-1960s, was a popular hobby among teenage boys. Radio listeners generally want to hear popular programmes with as good a reception as possible, but for DX-ers it was quite the reverse. They tried to find the most distant and inaudible radio stations they could, mostly on short-wave. The DX-er would then send in a listener report to the station broadcasting and would hope to receive what was called a QSL card in response. It was easiest to get postcards from the Eastern Bloc: the Soviet Union, Poland and East Germany.

Stieg's brother Joakim used to be a radio enthusiast too, but mainly because his elder brother was. 'It was Stieg who started it and I just tagged along. I did everything he did,' Joakim Larsson remembers.

Stieg and Joakim loved going to the cinema and they had plenty of opportunity to do so because of their father's extra job as a cinema commissionaire. Stieg's interest in film was to continue and in the late 1960s and 1970s he began collecting film music. His favourite film of all was Stanley Kubrick's *2001: A Space Odyssey*, based on the novel by the American sci-fi writer Arthur C. Clarke.

Stieg and Joakim shared a room when they were at Hagmarksvägen. The boys slept in bunk beds, Stieg in the upper and Joakim in the lower. Stieg, a night owl even as a child, used to keep his little brother awake by making up adventure stories. He went on doing it even after they moved to a new and larger apartment on Ersmarksgatan.

He sometimes wrote his stories down. He set one of his handwritten boys' detective stories in the USA, though every stone and every bend of the road can be recognized on the way down to the sea at Nydala. At some point after that, when Stieg was twelve, Vivianne and Erland decided to buy him a typewriter. And very soon the persistent clattering of keys could be heard from the boys' room at all hours of the day and night.

Stieg preferred to write in the late evening and into the small hours, so, to save Joakim from being disturbed too much, his parents rented a former club room in the basement where he could be by himself and read, write or listen to short-wave radio.

AT THE BEGINNING OF THE 1960s US President John F. Kennedy declared that the USA would put a man on the moon before the decade was over. The Apollo programme, as it was called, seemed to be the spearhead of all that was new, technological and future-orientated. It was a boy's dream, a sci-fi magazine come true.

Stieg Larsson sat in his basement room listening to radio stations from around the world and knew precisely what was going on. But, like all Swedes at the time, he was living in a bubble: the bubble of unlimited economic growth and belief in the future. Swedes had a special position both in their own eyes and in the eyes of the wider world. Sweden was 'the middle way', neither truly capitalist nor truly socialist, but a country where a socialist party had been in government for decades, seemingly invincible, almost as if it were the natural order of things.

The real debate was over. What was there to look forward to? More technological progress and continuing expansion of welfare provision? A glittering future, but not an inspiring one. It was hard to imagine anything new, anything radically different. Or was that the wrong way of looking at it?

Perhaps technical developments themselves would reveal unknown worlds. Perhaps technology and the imagination were connected.

Isaac Asimov, a Russian-born professor of chemistry in the USA and one of the biggest names in science fiction, had published his famous Foundation Trilogy in the 1950s, to great acclaim from readers for its depth of ideas. Asimov plotted his books with a complexity which delights some readers and drives others to distraction. The trilogy is set in a Galactic Empire comprising thousands of inhabited planets on the verge of collapse as the story begins. The hero of the novels, Hari Seldon, metaphorically rides out into the galaxy to save the world, or rather worlds, by means of an encyclopedic knowledge bank and a mathematical theory which facilitates the explanation and prediction of everything that happens in the universe.

Asimov's books are informed by a profound rationalism: reason can and must prevail; but belief in reason is in some way transformed into religion and mysticism. However, there is another side to Asimov that differentiates him from the more hard-boiled, technology-obsessed proponents of science fiction. His writing embodies a kind of homage to the outsider. Hari Seldon does not want to put himself centre stage with his concept of the power of knowledge. He chooses to transpose what he calls the Foundation to a planet far away at the edge of the Empire. He is striving not for imperial power, but rather to create an oasis for the collation of knowledge where wisdom and mental faculties are more valuable than technology.

Asimov's books became cult reading for Stieg and other sci-fi fans when they were eventually translated into Swedish some twenty years after their original appearance. By then Stieg had already started at high school and was often to be found sitting in the Konditori Mekka on Rådhusesplanaden in Umeå. That was where he and his friend Rune Forsgren planned their Asimov-inspired stencilled fanzine, which they called *Sfären* (The Sphere). The print run was tiny, only twenty or thirty copies, but that didn't matter. What was important was that they made contact with other sci-fi enthusiasts and became part of that world. There were perhaps a few hundred in the country who were very active, publishing their own magazines, contributing to each other's and attending science fiction conventions. *Sfären* was short-lived. Stieg and his friend abandoned the project after four issues, though Stieg was to remain an active member of sci-fi circles even after he moved to Stockholm; he was chairman of the Scandinavian Science Fiction Association for a year in 1980 and editor of its journal.

Vietnam

IN 1970, WHEN HE WAS SIXTEEN, Stieg took a further step towards independence and moved to his own rented room. It was his parents who rented it for him and it was diagonally opposite their apartment on Ersmarksgatan. Stieg used to go home for meals, but otherwise he mostly looked after himself.

If his parents went out on to their balcony late in the evening they could see whether he had gone to bed. More often than not, he hadn't.

Stieg had chosen to specialize in the social sciences at high school and was already something of a veteran of the anti-Vietnam War movement, having been actively involved since 1968. His schoolfriend Ingela Mattsson-Löfbom says that part of his class read a book by

Vilhelm Moberg in their study group, a task they rounded off with a visit to Kittelfjäll. During the day everyone went out skiing – except Stieg, who sat indoors tapping away on his typewriter. He was writing about the student uprising in Paris in 1968.

He was a thin boy with round spectacles, black leather jacket and shoulder bag. He dressed the way many did at the time. He was politically committed, eager for discussion, but always relaxed and sociable. His typewriter was his constant companion. He got to know Eva Gabrielsson through the NLF movement. She was also from the Skellefteå area and they became an item almost immediately. They didn't just share an interest in politics – Eva also loved writing, read science fiction and contributed texts to Stieg's publication.

THE AMERICAN MANNED MOON LANDING took place, exactly as predicted, before the end of the 1960s: on 20 July 1969. The entire Larsson family watched it together on TV. But it was not the triumph Kennedy had expected. The crowds who gathered that year in front of US embassies all round the world were not there to glorify and celebrate that magical technological feat. No, they were shaking their fists and yelling in rage at the barricaded embassy buildings.

An incredible amount had happened in a few years from the middle of the decade. A new, younger generation had discovered that the structure of society was not what they had been brought up to believe. The world as they knew it was faltering and an empire was on the ropes – not the Galactic Empire but the dominant one of our own world.

The older generation thought Vietnam was just another great-power conflict and too far away for us to understand, so the best approach to adopt was neutrality. The young saw it quite differently. Many of them recognized something they had experienced in the school playground: a stronger pupil beating up a weaker one and everybody else just standing around watching – or pretending they hadn't seen what was going on.

It was by no means the majority of Swedish youth who joined the protest movement against the American war in Vietnam, but it was a significant number and the commitment was sustained by a profound passion for justice and anger that the atrocities were being perpetrated with the consent of Western democratic leaders.

Soon young activists were to be seen on duty outside the state liquor store in Umeå and in every other town of any size. With one hand they proffered the *Vietnam Bulletin* and with the other a collection box in the red, blue and yellow colours of the NLF movement. Stieg Larsson was among them. Today scarcely anyone would even raise an eyebrow at the sight of a pamphleteer or money collector, but in those days the mood was different and clearly hostile to the young anti-Vietnam War activists. Irate words were often exchanged, people spat and there was even physical violence. The working class, who were the prime target for the activists, were not always very receptive, even though many workers believed at heart that the Americans should go home immediately and leave the Vietnamese people in peace. But the slogan 'Tage and Geijer – Lyndon's lackeys' (Tage Erlander was prime minister, Arne Geijer was chairman of the Trade Union Federation and Lyndon Johnson was US president) that was so prominent in all the demonstrations had an effect that the demonstrators had not anticipated. It alienated hundreds of thousands of loyal supporters of the Social Democratic Party and was frequently the only thing people remembered from the early Vietnam demonstrations.

It was obvious that the slogans and leaflets were also directed at Sweden's Social Democrats, the party that had given Sweden its superb welfare state. The Vietnam movement had grown from the struggle against the Establishment, and what could be more Establishment than the Social Democratic Party? The raised voices round the Larssons' kitchen table bore witness to this. Stieg thought his parents were betraying the principles of socialism.

But if politicians and the parental generation had failed, there were new authorities calling for attention. It was writers, artists and actors who now became the idols of the young. People saw and heard Sara Lidman's public appearances. Slight and slim, with short cropped hair, she was a flaming beacon with her calls for the right of the Vietnamese people to defend themselves. And she was well known in Västerbotten: our Sara from Missenträsk near Skellefteå, famous for her novels. Nor was she content to restrict herself to watching the conflict from Swedish horizons. She went to Vietnam herself in the mid-1960s and in 1966 published a book entitled *Samtal i Hanoi* (Conversations in Hanoi). This brought the distant conflict down to a human level and allowed Swedish readers to meet 'the people of Vietnam', that abstraction about which so much had been spoken and written in the media and the publications of the anti-Vietnam War movement.

UP UNTIL THE LATE 1960s the left-wing movement in Sweden had concerned itself primarily with international solidarity, but quite suddenly this focus was shifted by a strike in the Norrbotten iron-ore mines just before Christmas 1969. Thirty-five workers from the Leveäniemi mine in Svappavaara, which was owned by the state enterprise LKAB, downed tools on 9 December. Their grievances were not just to do with wages but also with their working environment, the constant supervision, stringent cutbacks, and time-and-motion studies. The strike quickly spread to all the LKAB mines in Norrbotten and at its height involved some 5,000 people. Strike meetings were held in a sports hall in Kiruna and the Swedish media were there in force to broadcast direct from the volatile gatherings. Sara Lidman was on the barricades again and speaking for the workers, having two years previously published a book of interviews describing their conditions: *Gruva* (The Mine).

It was a highly unusual situation. Sweden was the country of institutionalized and peaceful industrial negotiations, regulated by centralized bargaining and national contracts. Ever since the great strike of 1945 in the steel industry calm had reigned over the labour market, with the majority of Swedish workers loyal to the Social Democratic Party and the national Trade Union Federation. Now all this seemed to be hanging in the balance, such was the shock effect of the miners' strike. Perhaps the drastic restructuring of industry in the 1960s had created a ferment of dissatisfaction over which no one had any control but which was now about to burst forth in more strikes and protest actions, especially in heavy industry.

For the various groups on the Left, the events at the mines fitted in all too well with their analysis of the direction in which society was heading. They were convinced that the working class would rise up at any moment in order to bring in socialism, not just in poor countries but also in Europe and the USA. Reformist welfare states like Sweden were not seen as an exception. The miners' strike and the wildcat strikes that followed set off feverish political activity.

These new left-wing groups included the Maoist KFML (Marxist-Leninist Communist Association), which had a powerful hold on the anti-Vietnam War movement through the front organization De förenade FNL-grupperna (United NLF Groups). KFML had been founded as a breakaway group from the established parliamentary party VPK (Vänsterpartiet Kommunisterna, Left-Wing Communist Party) and consisted of a mix of older orthodox Communists and young Vietnam activists. Even further to the left were a number of groupings, including the Trotskyists, who were new to Sweden and known as the Revolutionära Marxisters Förbund (Revolutionary Marxists' Association).

Trotskyism drew its inspiration from Leon Trotsky, the foremost leader of the Russian Revolution after Lenin. Following Stalin's assumption of power, Trotsky was expelled from Russia, but even while in exile he continued his unremitting verbal attack on Stalinist policies. Not surprisingly, Trotsky was the most detested figure in the Soviet Union at the time. To be accused of Trotskyism could amount to a death sentence. And Stalin eventually succeeded in having Trotsky killed, dispatching an assassin who had been guaranteed immunity to murder him, which he did with an ice pick in Mexico in 1940.

Trotskyism had played only a minor role in Sweden prior to the 1970s, though it had some significance on the Continent. In the Republican period in Spain and the ensuing Civil War the Trotskyist and anarchist groups had enormous influence initially, but the Communists loyal to Moscow saw these parties as agents provocateurs and adventurers and vehemently opposed them – so vehemently, in fact, that it led to outright civil war among the forces of the Left themselves in Barcelona in May 1937.

During the May uprising in Paris in 1968 the French Trotskyist party, La Ligue Communiste, made an impression on many young people with their militant style. There were a number of Trotskyist groups in Britain, with a leading spokesman in the person of Tariq Ali, from Pakistan, who was both an intellectual orator and an icon for the militant activists of the New Left. He was the Street Fighting Man the Rolling Stones sang about and he almost turned John Lennon into a Trotskyist, certainly persuading him to compose a song about the need for popular revolt: 'Power to the People'.

IN THE EARLY 1970S THE TROTSKYISTS managed to gain a foothold in various places where the KFML grip was weaker, including Umeå. Stieg Larsson was an ordinary Vietnam activist who sold the *Vietnam Bulletin* and read the KFML paper *Gnistan* (The Spark). But the former was soon joined and later replaced by the Trotskyist paper *Mullvaden* (The Mole), the organ of the Revolutionary Marxists' Association. When it started up, in 1970, there were already a few people in Umeå drawn to Trotskyist ideas, mainly from the Social Democratic Youth Organization, which was in the process of radicalization, rather than from the NLF movement. The year 1972 marked the formation of the Umeå Red Group, as a first step towards affiliation to the national Trotskyist organization in Sweden.

It might seem surprising that Stieg should join the Trotskyist movement so early on. His beloved grandfather Severin was an orthodox Moscow Communist and both his parents were Social Democratic Party members. But Stieg was essentially a contrary individual, someone perpetually striving for independence and making his own decisions. So it was entirely consistent that he should choose to become involved with an organization that was very critical of both these directions within the Labour movement.

The 1970s were a period of intense activity as the Trotskyists expanded through organized study circles and well-attended meetings. There was an election forum in 1976 that exceeded all the other left-wing groups together in size and one of their biggest events was a meeting addressed by the legendary Peruvian peasants' leader and Trotskyist Hugo Blanco which attracted an audience of 700.

In Umeå there is still a nucleus of activists from the 1970s in the Socialist Party. Erik Pettersson, Jan Olof Carlsson and Stig Eriksson all remember Stieg Larsson as a young Trotskyist activist alongside themselves. They can think of three reasons that may have been deci-sive for his adoption of Trotskyism.

Firstly, since Stieg did not have much time for state socialism, he saw Trotskyism primarily as the obvious alternative, a form of liberated socialism. Secondly for him came its emphasis on internationalism. Thirdly, Trotskyists were more open to culture than most left-wing groups were.

Stieg did not approve of political correctness, classic social realism or the concept of a 'popular culture' as defined by the Maoist Left. He was far more interested in the subversive element in popular culture, how books and films dealt with social trends.

He had his enthusiasm for science fiction and was an admirer of Robert Heinlein, author of a number of controversial novels in the genre. Heinlein had begun as an adherent of the Left but gradually gained the reputation of being a reactionary thinker. For Stieg, however, he was an important and fascinating writer whose books were often critical of existing power structures.

Stieg was also an ardent fan of cinema and enjoyed films which were anathema to the Left. Sam Peckinpah's *The Wild Ones*, for instance, with its Expressionistic scenes of brutality, and even Sergio Leone's Italian films, deprecatingly called 'spaghetti westerns'. Leone was then rather an object of ridicule in the American movie industry and his films were mostly given their initial run outside the USA; the new star he introduced, Clint Eastwood, was much more popular to begin with in Europe than in his own country. But he was later to become increasingly appreciated as one of the precursors of what were called the revisionist westerns that gave a deromanticized, naturalistic portrayal of the epoch.

Stieg's affection for the films of Peckinpah and Leone is easy to understand. When Peckinpah shows violence in horrifying detail, it is both to deromanticize an American myth and to remind us of the other savagery that was going on every day in a far-off country in East Asia. Both Leone and Peckinpah bring opposing value systems into conflict in their films and they depict human beings in a cynical society where no one can rely on anyone else any more, and where in the end the hero has to strike out on his own if he is to maintain his moral position.

IN 1975–6 STIEG DID HIS MILITARY SERVICE IN UMEÅ. Many on the Left have an instinctive dislike of everything military and large numbers were opting out as conscientious objectors at the time. But Stieg had no misgivings about being called up. He was no pacifist and regarded force as in some circumstances justified or necessary. To defend oneself against an oppressor was the right thing to do. There was, of course, no doubt that the higher ranks in a country like Sweden were on the side of the upper classes, but one could imagine that in an extreme situation the foot soldiers might well turn their weapons on their leadership.

In the 1970s the Trotskyists tried to foment disaffection in Stieg's regiment in Umeå. They agitated in support of various rank-and-file demands for improvements, the most significant of which was that everyone should be given 1,000 kronor on call-up. Their campaign caused serious concern in both the military and the security police, who saw it as undermining national security.

Stieg Larsson was among those who covertly sold the Trotskyist national service newspaper Röd Soldat (Red Soldier) in barracks – without being caught.

A year or so earlier, in October 1974, the Umeå police had raided the Trotskyist bookshop the Red Room and confiscated all copies of Röd Soldat, because it carried an article advocating the mass taking of sick leave in order to push through the 1,000-kronor demand. The confiscated papers were shortly returned with a hole in one page. The police had actually sat down and cut out the offending article in every single copy.

WHEN STIEG MOVED TO STOCKHOLM about a year after this, his contacts with the Umeå Trotskyists decreased, although he remained a member and went on writing for their magazine *Internationalen*. He left the Socialist Party in the late 1980s. It was an undramatic break: he simply stopped paying his membership subscription.

But he continued to meet his old party comrades whenever he visited Umeå.

'It was apparent that he still read *Internationalen* and felt respect for the work we were doing, and that he still even felt allied to our cause. I think that if he had returned to party politics he would have ended up where he started,' opines Jan Olof Carlsson.

Media attention suddenly focused on the Socialist Party again after Stieg Larsson died, when it turned out that just before a trip abroad he had drawn up an unwitnessed will in which he stated that in the event of his death his estate should go to the Communist Workers' Association, as the party was then called.

The Umeå Socialist Party had no idea that there was such a bequest. But since Stieg was no longer a member they felt the morally correct course was not to lodge any claim to the money.

IT WAS PROBABLY AT SOME POINT IN 1973, during his high school years, that Stig became Stieg.

There was another Stig Larsson in Umeå of about the same age, also from Skellefteå and also a left-wing activist, but a member of the even more revolutionary KFML(r). It was inevitable that their paths would cross in a small town like Umeå. Their mail was frequently delivered to the wrong address and their mothers came to know each other as a result. In 1973 Stig was one of the exhibitors in a photographic exhibition in Umeå which was reported in the newspapers, and many attributed the photographs to Stieg. It must have been then that he tired of the constant confusion and decided to alter the spelling of his name.

There is an oft-repeated tale that they got together and tossed a coin to decide which of them should change name. That may well be one of Stieg's anecdotes, since Stig Larsson has no recollection of any such meeting and thinks Stieg changed it of his own volition.

'He could have called himself Karl,' muses Erland Larsson, who had never been keen on the new name. 'There'd have been nothing wrong with Karl Larsson.'

At the time there was only one well-known Stieg in Sweden and he, strangely enough, was also a crime writer: Stieg Trenter. He was not christened Stieg either, but was originally Stig Johansson. It would be reasonable to assume that Stieg Larsson, as a voracious reader of crime fiction, knew of Stieg Trenter, but there is no evidence that Trenter was among his favourite authors.

The other Stig Larsson soon gave up politics and turned to art and theatre. He trained as a director at Dramatiska Institutet (University College of Film, Radio, Television and Theatre) in Stockholm and later, together with Horace Engdahl and Anders Olsson (now both members of the Swedish Academy), founded the literary journal *Kris* (Crisis), which was very influential in Sweden, introducing theoreticians of postmodernism such as Derrida, de Man and Blanchot. His debut novel, *Autisterna* (The Autistics), brought him immediate success and for some years he was one of the most acclaimed writers in the country.

When *Le Nouvel Observateur* in 1989 included Stig Larsson in a list of the hundred people in the world they thought would be particularly significant for European culture in the 1990s, Stieg Larsson was still a totally unknown press agency employee and anti-racist activist.

Out into the World

IN 1972 THE INTERRAIL CARD was introduced. For a fixed price anyone under twenty-one could have unlimited travel for a month in a score of European countries. It was the birth of a whole new interrailing generation. But of course there was a limit: you couldn't use the card outside Europe. And for many of the generation of 1968 long-distance travel was the goal. It was far-off countries that beckoned, those that had come to be called the Third World. The periphery was to be the centre; that was where the future was taking shape, often in violently dramatic form.

Even while still at high school Stieg was determined to get out into the wider world and he took on all sorts of casual jobs to make money. He delivered newspapers, washed up in restaurants and worked in a locksmith's shop.

His first attempt at travel ended ignominiously. He hitchhiked down to Stockholm, went into a café and had his wallet stolen, with all his travel money, amounting to nearly 1,000 kronor.

In 1972 it was time to try again. His journey took him to France and Spain and on to Algeria. There he met a group of people who were on their way down to the Sahara by lorry and motorbike. Crossing the Sahara Desert by motor vehicle and getting across to Niger and black Africa via the Hoggar Mountains and the Tuaregs' fabled oasis of Tamanrasset counted as one of the great adventures of the era. But in Stieg's case the trip was never completed. The lorry broke down and the person who was entrusted with money to ride the motorbike to Oran and buy spare parts never returned. So the sorry party had to trudge back to the city on foot. Stieg sold his new leather jacket there to raise money for food. They hitchhiked back through Morocco and across Europe, and Stieg arrived home gaunt and miserable, in cobweb-thin jeans.

UMEÅ WAS A UNIVERSITY CITY; it was even known as 'the red university'. What would have been more natural than for Stieg to apply for a place there? But he never did. 'Taking the academic path', up until then regarded as the desirable thing to do, no longer had such prestige, especially for a young Trotskyist for whom a factory worker had higher status than an academic. The only further study that had any appeal for him was journalism, so he applied to the College of Journalism, but he failed the entrance exam and was not accepted.

In any case, the world was now one big university which was opening its doors to those with confidence and enquiring minds. The generation that had grown up during the Second World War was a stay-at-home generation – of necessity, since borders were closed. And most of those who were young then could not afford to travel anyway. But a new age had dawned and the world was becoming accessible again; the young could see foreign countries in moving pictures on TV and now they wanted to explore them in reality.

After his military service, Stieg started work at Hörnefors pulp mill and then took a job with the Post Office. He moved out of his room and began earning plenty of money. But his ultimate aim was still to make his way out into the world.

It was at this stage that he began to take an interest in the north-eastern corner of Africa. In 1973 frightful images of starving people in Ethiopia were broadcast on television. The country had been afflicted by severe drought, and the isolation and ineffectual nature of the regime meant that outside aid only sporadically got through to those in need. The newspapers were writing about a war of liberation in the northern region, in the province of Eritrea. In 1977 Stieg decided to set off there himself. Through some Eritreans, he made contact with the Marxist EPLF, and was also commissioned to deliver documents and money to the organization in Eritrea.

He made a will before he left, the only one he ever wrote, and it was definitely not a joke. Travelling to Algeria, later so notorious for its brutality, was not especially hazardous in the 1970s. But the situation in Eritrea and Ethiopia was quite different. Right then it was a very dangerous place to be.

THE CONFLICT BETWEEN ETHIOPIA and Eritrea was a long-standing one, a hangover from the days of colonialism. What we now call Ethiopia is one of the world's oldest kingdoms, formerly known by the name of Abyssinia. But the history of modern Ethiopia can be said to have begun in 1930, when a young chieftain, Ras Tafari Makonnen, was declared a true emperor of Ethiopia, directly descended from King Solomon and the Queen of Sheba. On assuming the throne he took the name of Haile Selassie I.

Italy had had colonial interests in this area since the late nineteenth century and had taken control of the province of Eritrea. In the mid-1930s fascist Italy mobilized nearly the entire male population of the province for an attack on Ethiopia.

When the invasion came, Selassie, who had begged in vain for help from the League of Nations, led the resistance, but was forced to give up and take flight. When the British ejected the Italians in 1941, however, he was able to return in triumph with the reputation of being a defender of liberty in Africa. In fact, Ethiopia then became feudal, an increasingly despotic autocracy with military ambitions and a recipient of massive American military aid.

Ethiopia regarded Eritrea as historically part of its own country. The Eritreans did not regard themselves thus, but they were nevertheless compelled into a federation with Ethiopia, as recommended by the United Nations, which soon brought Eritrean independence to an end. In the view of the Eritreans, the world stood idly by as Ethiopia swallowed them up, so they formed their own resistance through the ELP movement. This was challenged in the early 1970s by a new organization with a younger membership, EPLF, which in the spirit of the period was Marxist in orientation – and as a natural consequence it gained the backing of various solidarity groups in the West.

Meanwhile, internal criticism of Haile Selassie was growing, especially in the army, into which he had poured vast resources. His regime had turned rotten from within and the coup was easy to carry out when it took place in September 1974. The emperor was simply driven away in a little Volkswagen and put under a kind of house arrest, where he died in mysterious circumstances. The remains of 'His Imperial Majesty, King of Kings, Lion of Judah' were buried in an anonymous pit that was sealed with concrete and over which a urinal was subsequently built.

WHEN STIEG ARRIVED IN ETHIOPIA, the military were in power. A previously unknown general, Mengistu Haile Mariam, had taken over in 1977 by eliminating his principal opponents. Mengistu purported to be a radical reformer of his country, declaring himself a Marxist-Leninist and breaking off the old connections with the USA immediately.

But it was a strange form of socialism that came in military attire and was led by a faceless organization called Dergen, not unlike the mystical Angka of the Khmer Rouge, at that very moment subjecting Cambodia to a reign of terror.

And exactly as in the case of the Khmer Rouge, Mengistu set about an immediate extermination of all dissidents and those who were merely suspected of being so. The events that unfolded over the course of almost a year went under the ominous name of the Red Terror. Thousands of alleged opponents, mostly young people, to a great extent left-wing activists, were seized, tortured, summarily executed and their corpses often left out openly in the streets to instil fear into the populace.

Thousands of young Eritreans had joined the liberation struggle, now entirely dominated by the EPLF. The Ethiopian army was in retreat and victory seemed within their grasp. But the celebrations were premature. Mengistu the Marxist decided to bring all his forces to bear to crush the similarly Marxist guerrillas of Eritrea.

If Stieg Larsson had any qualms about undertaking this trip, they did not deter him. He went via Moscow, flying on to Sudan and from there to Addis Ababa. He travelled around the country by bus in the company of a New Zealand girl and saw large military convoys on the roads. Back in Addis he was suddenly picked up by British intelligence services and driven to the British consulate on the edge of the city. They wanted him to tell them what he had seen of military build-up on the roads. But he refused. So he was thrown out and had to walk all the way back to his hotel.

He then managed to get to Asmara in Eritrea, establish contact with the guerrillas and be taken to one of their bases in the mountains. There he met a group of female guerrilla soldiers whom he taught to use mortars. It was a skill he had learned while doing his national service and training as an officer in Umeå. Women played an active role in the EPLF guerrilla army, constituting about 30 per cent of its fighting force. Young women can be seen in many photographs of the Eritrean liberation struggle. The EPLF made a conscious effort to involve them in what was otherwise a staunchly patriarchal society and to give them the same responsibilities as the men.

Stieg then fell ill with nephritis and ended up in hospital in Addis Ababa, where conditions were incredibly basic. It could not even be taken for granted that patients would be fed – that was the responsibility of the relatives; but an elderly woman in the hospital took pity on him because he had no parents there and gave him food to assist his recovery. He went back to the hotel, collected his belongings and got on a bus convoy to Kenya. There he was able to make contact with his nearest and dearest, who had not heard from him for some while, and whom he now asked to send money so that he could come home, which he did via Idi Amin's Uganda.

THE YEARS FOLLOWING STIEG'S VISIT were a dire period for both Ethiopia and Eritrea. Mengistu undertook a major offensive against the Eritrean guerrillas and forced them to retreat into the mountains of the north. But despite the Ethiopian army's full-scale assaults, now with the support of the Soviet Union, they were not able to eradicate the resistance.

Ethiopia remained a harsh dictatorship throughout the 1980s and was plagued by enormous internal problems, not least the catastrophic drought of 1984, when a million people starved to death, and when European rock musicians led by Bob Geldof launched their Band Aid initiative to help save the starving. But with Gorbachev in power in the Soviet Union, economic aid to the Ethiopian military soon dried up and the Mengistu regime collapsed. In 1991 rebel troops seized Addis Ababa and the dictator fled to Zimbabwe, where he still lives. In 2006 he was convicted of genocide by an Ethiopian court and later sentenced to death. His fall meant that the guerrillas could at last come down from their hideouts in the mountains. Resistance was now much weaker. The EPLF soon took the capital, Asmara, and a free Eritrea was declared in 1993.

Their leader, Isaias Afewerki, became head of the one and only party and also president. The idea was that the party would rule the country for a transition period before free elections were announced. But no elections were ever held and there was a new and bloody war with Ethiopia. The continuing tension between the two countries was the pretext for jettisoning plans for a multi-party system. Instead, Afewerki's party clamped down on its political opponents. This took place while the media were diverted by the 11 September attack on New York and led to newspapers being closed down and critics of the regime imprisoned. Among them was the Swedish-Eritrean journalist Dawit Isaak, who has been incarcerated without trial or sentence ever since.

Eritrea spent thirty years fighting for its freedom. The leadership that took office was toughened by the experiences of war. The qualities which brought about victory – decisiveness, constant readiness, implacability to opponents – are now what prevents the establishment of the promised democracy.

The story of Stieg Larsson's Eritrean adventure had a remarkable postscript in 2009, when the former head of PR and newspaper editor for the neo-Nazi National Socialist Front, Björn Björkqvist, published an article on the website Newsmill under the headline 'Time to examine Stieg Larsson's benevolence?' Björkqvist said he wrote his article as a result of the award to Stieg's magazine *Expo* of the Dawit Isaak Prize by the Publicistklubben Väst (Journalists' Club West).

'So Stieg Larsson helped train the army that enabled Isaias Afewerki to come to power – the man who has now had Dawit Isaak imprisoned,' Björkqvist writes.

It is somewhat bizarre to suggest that Stieg Larsson could have foretold in 1977 what the Eritrean liberation movement and its leader Afewerki would do some twenty years afterwards. Any more than could the many Eritreans who had previously been members or supporters of the liberation movement but are now languishing in prison or exile.

TT Press Agency

WITH THE COMPLETION OF THE NINETEEN-STOREY office blocks on Sergels torg in the mid-1960s, Stockholm acquired its first skyscrapers. They were seen as a sign that the city was becoming a modern metropolis and were called 'the five trumpet blasts', a name scarcely anyone remembers today. It was here, in the northernmost building, that the very heart of the Swedish news media was housed for many years: TT, Tidningarnas Telegrambyrå, the Press Agency. This was where Stieg Larsson took a job in 1979 that was to be his longest if not his most important.

When he moved to the capital from Umeå at the age of twenty-two and worked for the Post Office, his employer helped him find an apartment in a newly built suburb in south-west Stockholm. This was a time of restructuring, closures and removal vans. The Labour Market Board, AMS (Arbetsmarknadsstyrelsen), was providing financial support for people to relocate and in Norrland the initials were jocularly reputed to stand for All Move South.

Stieg Larsson, together with Eva Gabrielsson, who had also moved to Stockholm, later lived in Rinkeby, one of Stockholm's most multi-cultural suburbs, housing the greatest number of immigrant families.

At TT Stieg began by writing up sports results and the like until, standing in for a colleague, he had a chance to display his talent for illustrating articles with diagrams, boxes and other devices, and this led to the offer of a permanent position. He was to stay with TT for twenty years.

TT was the media's own news bureau, a byword for objectivity and factuality in the Swedish media. It set the standard for how a straight-forward and non-partisan news text should be written. In the mind of the general public it was for decades mostly associated with the radio. TT had the monopoly for news transmissions on Swedish Radio and during the drama of the war years in particular people would crowd round their wireless sets when they heard the magic words 'the News from TT'.

Stieg Larsson had not studied journalism and had not been taken on as a reporter. He had created his own corner – news graphics – where he was something of a pioneer at TT. He had always been interested in drawing and had obtained his highest marks at school for art. His father, Erland, had a similar talent and for a while even had the same profession, graphic illustrator of news articles on the provincial newspaper *Västerbottenskuriren*.

Stieg dealt mainly with urgent jobs for news cables. If an aeroplane had crashed in Guadeloupe, he would draw a map of the area with the crash site marked in.

He worked on his own, producing maps, graphics and diagrams in the form of boxes and circles with his special tools – fine-nibbed pens, transfer letters, a caption machine, a scalpel. It was a real craft, at least until the late 1980s, when Adobe introduced its Illustrator program, which revolutionized the whole of news graphics. His illustrations, which were sold individually to newspapers, were a profitable sales line that brought in several million kronor a year for TT. Stieg developed another lucrative concept too – a folder of maps of the countries of the world that could be updated – which was also a commercial success.

During this period, the early 1980s, he was still active in the Socialist Party and had begun writing for its weekly magazine *Internationalen*. He submitted articles on national service for women, on the New Age movement and superstition; he drew a map of US and Soviet military bases and nuclear weapons facilities throughout the world. At first he frequently used his grandfather's name, Severin, as his pseudonym.

Internationalism was part of his outlook. Kenneth Lewis, who was active in the 1960s in Revolutionära marxisters förbund—an early Trotskyist organization in Uppsala—says that the Maoist tendency on the Left adhered to the so-called focal-point theory that all activity should be concentrated on Vietnam. This resulted in the Trotskyists attracting many left-wing activists who were against such tunnel vision and were interested in other topics and countries, and in liberation movements elsewhere in the world.

This was a fundamental attitude that fitted well with Stieg Larsson's own. When he took up a cause it was more often than not something he had found his own way to and could be well off the beaten track.

It was to be events very remote from Sweden that gave Stieg's dreams of revolution a concrete focus and spurred him on to write more.

Dreams of Revolution

"Lisbeth Salander put her book down on her lap and sipped her iced coffee before reaching for a packet of cigarettes. Without turning her head she shifted her gaze to the horizon. From the pool terrace she could just glimpse the Caribbean through a group of palm trees and the rhododendrons in front of the hotel. A yacht was on its way north towards St Lucia or Dominica. Further off, she could see the outline of a grey freighter heading south in the direction of Guyana or one of its neighbours."

—Stieg Larsson
The Girl Who Played with Fire

IN THE INTRODUCTORY SECTION OF *The Girl Who Played with Fire*, Lisbeth Salander has recently got her hands on a billion Swedish kronor from the undeclared wealth of the villain, Wennerström, and set off to see the world. She has arrived in the Caribbean, more specifically on the island of Grenada. Here she walks on the miles-long Grand Anse beach and wanders the narrow streets of the capital, St George's, partaking of Carib beer and the local fruit, and waiting for a possible catastrophe to strike in the shape of Hurricane Matilda.

She reads about the revolution that began here in 1979 and which 'the guidebook said was inspired by the Communist dictatorships in Cuba and Nicaragua'. But she is given a different version of history by the owner of the guesthouse where she spends her first few days.

NOWADAYS THE CARIBBEAN ISLANDS are marketed as a tourist paradise for affluent Americans and Europeans. History is expunged, the islands' bloody and dramatic stories are forgotten.

The informed description of Grenada and its capital in *The Girl Who Played with Fire* reveals that Stieg Larsson was well acquainted with the island and knew more than the tourist brochures chose to reveal. There is a photograph taken on Barbados in 1981 of a twenty-seven-year-old Stieg, equipped with the obligatory shoulder bag, on his way to Grenada. He and Eva were about to make a study visit in a show of unity with an island that was a symbol for the continuing existence of the dream of solidarity and spirit of revolution, where a party called the New Jewel Movement (NJM) had carried out its own revolution a few years before and set out on the path towards an indigenous variant of socialism.

This revolution was barely reported at all in the mainstream Western press. But the US government had watched events with some concern. In the same year that the NJM seized power on Grenada, the Nicaraguan dictator, Somoza, was toppled by a radical liberation movement.

Conservative circles in the USA exaggerated the situation into a second Cuba sprouting up in their own back yard.

The Swedish guests had a full programme of visits to agricultural cooperatives and women's organizations, meetings with politicians and civil servants. They even met the prime minister himself, Maurice Bishop, and had first-hand experience of his personal charisma.

Stieg wrote an article afterwards in *Internationalen* about Grenada's unknown revolution which brought down an exceedingly corrupt regime and won overwhelming popular support. It also described the new government, which introduced significant changes in key areas of social provision and the economy within a short space of time. All school fees were substantially reduced, the number of doctors doubled and a system of maternity care created that was unique in the region. Grenada was now moving towards comprehensive land reform, as well as closing down the lucrative marijuana cultivation that existed as much here as in so many other islands of the West Indies.

Stieg's impression was that the poor were well on their way to a better life, but government employees, who were used to being able to line their pockets, had had their salaries cut and Bishop himself was driving around in the same old wreck of a car that he had owned before the revolution.

In Sweden Stieg Larsson and Eva Gabrielsson were two of the founder members of the Sweden–Grenada Friendship Association. This meant that Stieg followed the entire dramatic sequence of Grenada's revolution, a remarkable and tragic story of idealism and courage, treachery and fratricide.

GRENADA IN THE GRENADINES IS A PLACE of unusual beauty in the southern Caribbean, surrounded by blue sea and sparkling coral reefs.

The natural landscape is spectacular, with high forested mountains and dormant volcanoes in the hinterland. Gentle trade winds temper the tropical heat, but the forces of nature retaliate at regular intervals with violent hurricanes which almost always cause widespread devastation, but also mobilize the people to help one another in rebuilding what has been razed to the ground.

On Grenada history has been as dramatic and prone to eruption as nature. Long ago the Spanish, English and French sniffed the air and detected the smell of vast profits from the West Indies. In a way it was here that colonialism began, taking on the distinctive form of huge plantations, black slaves and cruel overseers, the whole directed by a relatively small group of administrators who might be from Spain, Britain or France.

The original inhabitants were soon tricked by false promises and broken agreements. But after all they were only heathens and, as Columbus had already asserted, *caribes*, cannibals. There was actually no cannibalism at all on the islands, but that was a minor detail: the main point was to establish the natives' barbaric status.

In fact the original inhabitants were themselves colonizers. They had come from the area of the Orinoco river in what today is Venezuela. They were called *kalinagos* and were quite warlike, and certainly looked intimidating with their tattoos and body paint. They successfully chased off a contingent of Englishmen who came to Grenada in the early seventeenth century in three great ships. So Europeans had to think carefully before settling in these islands – but the potential profits were the deciding factor.

The big money for the colonists lay in setting up plantations, especially for growing sugar cane, which had been so successful on British Barbados. The French, who had managed to establish themselves on this particular island and renamed it La Grenade, also tried their hand at sugar, together with indigo, the small bush from whose leaves a wonderful blue dye could be produced.

The only question was who could be got to work on the plantations. It was quickly realized that the native Indians would not do it. It might be possible to bring over convicts from the home countries, but the real solution came in the form of black slaves from Africa, who were shipped out to the West Indies from the mid-seventeenth century onwards in the holds of vast, hellish ships.

The combination of the slave trade and the cultivation of sugar, cotton and coffee was what brought the colonial synergy effect. Even the more indolent French made a decent profit from Grenada by expanding their slave trade and cultivating an ever greater variety of produce. But in the end it was Britain that won and France that lost the colonial battle. Britannia ruled the waves and Grenada was a tasty morsel when the British decided to seize it in 1762 during the Seven Years' War.

The British were resourceful and powerful and treated their slaves the way it was thought they should be treated: with exceptional savagery. From time to time the slaves would rise up in desperate acts of revenge, which were answered with appropriate repressive measures, such as crushing the rebellious in the sugar mills, or leaving them to die of starvation in iron cages so cramped that it was impossible to move a single limb.

But world history sometimes takes unexpected turns. The most astounding events took place in France towards the end of the eighteenth century – the middle and lower classes made common cause and overthrew the old regime. In August 1789 the newly formed National Constituent Assembly accepted the quite remarkable document entitled *Declaration of the Rights of Man and the Citizen*. The first article stated: 'Men are born and remain free and equal in rights.'

The consequences of such an assertion were far-reaching, to say the least. But the French revolutionaries did not dare, or did not wish, to follow it through to its logical conclusion. That would have meant the abolition of slavery in their own colonies.

Yet the ideas of the French Revolution spread to the four winds and the slaves in the French West Indies soon started taking matters into their own hands. In 1791, on the economically flourishing island of Saint Domingue (now Haiti), a freed slave, Toussaint L'Ouverture, known as the Black General, led hundreds of thousands of slaves to rebel and forced the French to abolish slavery – admittedly only temporarily. Nevertheless, it constituted an astonishing victory when it was possible to declare in 1801: 'There are no slaves in this territory.'

By that date Grenada was British, but since ideas are no respecters of national borders, the same attitudes caught on there. Grenada had also gradually become a much more mixed society, where even some of the freed slaves and mulattos had achieved position and property. Julien Fédon, the son of a Frenchman and a black woman who possessed a not inconsiderable amount of land on the island, with slaves of his own, detested British rule, and the new ideas from France gradually convinced him that a revolution was necessary.

On 2 March 1795 he considered the time was ripe. He led a group of slaves and former slaves who attacked and killed a number of British plantation owners before taking refuge on Fédon's land. He received almost immediate support from sections of the French Catholic population, the number of revolutionaries multiplied and they commandeered ever larger tracts of the island. A bitter war ensued, with extreme cruelty on both sides, lasting for over a year and ending in victory for the British, whose superior resources eventually allowed them to prevail.

The British promptly hanged the instigators of the rebellion, but they never caught Fédon himself. He mysteriously disappeared and was soon transformed into a legend and a ghost who could be seen riding around at night on his white charger. He has lived on in the popular imagination as the patron saint of the blacks on the island right up to the present day.

For a century and a half Grenada continued as a plantation economy, growing nutmegs, coconuts, cotton and coffee. Slavery was abolished but wages remained low and conditions hard for the former slaves and contract workers who laboured on the plantations.

In the early 1950s there came a light at the end of the tunnel in the person of an elegant and powerful black trade union leader, Eric Matthew Gairy. His public image was a mixture of belligerent workers' champion and patriarchal overlord of the poor who signed up with him, and his power grew at breakneck speed when he entered politics. Grenada was still a British colony, but it was heading for independence as the colonial system collapsed bit by bit after the Second World War. The first free elections were held in 1951 and were a resounding victory for Gairy and his party, the Grenada United Labour Party. It was not such an easy ride in subsequent years: Gairy lost office, but when the British banned him from taking part in politics for having disrupted a political opponent's meeting, he was able to turn this to his advantage and re-emerge as the quintessential enemy of the colonial system and protector of the weak. Gairy's party won the election again in 1961, and when the British to all intents and purposes withdrew from the administration in 1967 his power became virtually unlimited.

His exercise of it, however, became increasingly bizarre. He demanded absolute loyalty from his supporters, threatened anyone who showed any inclination to oppose him and built up his image as a great mystic with supernatural abilities. It was said, for instance, that he could walk on water, and he himself became progressively more obsessed by the belief that alien spacecraft had landed on his island.

Opponents who were not cowed into silence might receive unexpected visits, not from extraterrestrials but from Gairy's own police force, called the Mongoose Gang. But it was when this bunch of semi-criminals gave some political activists a whipping that the end hove into sight for Gairy's regime. A new grouping was formed which quickly attracted large numbers of young people and which bore the imaginative name of New Jewel Movement. Jewel was an acronym for Joint Endeavour for Welfare, Education and Liberation. The leading figures were Maurice Bishop and Kendrick Radix, two young lawyers who had studied in England and been inspired by Marxism and Black Power.

The NJM asserted that they were the only ones who could guarantee true freedom and independence now that Britain was about to relinquish its hold on Grenada. Gairy did not share that opinion and let his bloodhounds loose to knock some sense into the young hotheads. The result, however, was not what Gairy had intended; rather the opposite, in fact. All sectors of society turned against him and demanded that the government accept responsibility for the vicious assaults. But even this had no effect on Gairy. He made sure that parliament was convened with diminishing frequency and attacked the free press. As more and more Caribbean leaders abandoned him, he looked for new friends – for example in 1976 Chile's bloodstained dictator Augusto Pinochet came on a state visit.

In March 1979 Gairy visited the USA. Simultaneously, rumours were rife that the entire leadership of the NJM was about to be arrested. But the NJM had other plans. March was an excellent month for political action. It was when Fédon had carried out his revolution nearly 200 years earlier; now they would follow in his footsteps.

The coup was surprisingly simple. The key element seems to have been the takeover of the state radio. On the morning of 13 March the people heard the announcement that they were now listening to Radio Free Grenada, that the leader of the NJM, Maurice Bishop, was the new prime minister and that he had at his side Bernard Coard, a prominent young academic who had returned from abroad in the mid-1970s to work for the NJM.

There was singing and dancing in the streets of St George's on that first day of the revolution: 'Freedom come, Gairy go, Gairy go with UFO.'

The initial phase of the revolution was a period of general mobilization and voluntary work, such as renovating schools and running literacy programmes in rural areas. The government established diplomatic relations with Cuba at an early stage and also received substantial aid from there, which of course was viewed with the utmost irritation in Washington, where Ronald Reagan was then president.

Grenada also received support from groups all over the world, such as the Sweden–Grenada Friendship Association which Stieg Larsson and Eva Gabrielsson helped to set up. Stieg and others saw Grenada as a new phenomenon, a country in step with the mood of the times: a relatively orthodox Marxism, Black Power and a connection to the black traditions of the island, women's liberation and, by no means least, the exultation inspired by such a small country cheekily sticking its fingers up at the superpower USA.

When Stieg Larsson and other sympathizers visited Grenada, it was above all to highlight the positive things that were happening on the island that weren't being reported in the mainstream media, and to defend it against the criticism of displaying totalitarian tendencies. However, this solidarity committee's rose-tinted descriptions were not entirely truthful. Opposition figures on Grenada lived under repression, many politicians and dissidents were jailed and Cuban influence was spreading.

In *Internationalen* a Swedish solidarity group described the spring 1983 anniversary celebration of the revolution on Grenada with its military parades and vibrant calypso music. When the deputy prime minister, Bernard Coard, spoke, the already buoyant mood became ecstatic when he announced that Maurice Bishop had just landed at Grenada's new airport from a trip abroad and would soon be joining the meeting.

What hardly anyone was aware of, including Stieg, was that disagreements within the government had been escalating for some time and had almost reached breaking point. And that Bishop and Coard were already on opposing sides.

There were also tensions beneath the surface in a society that was being propelled by idealism and devotion to the cause but which lacked the economic resources to fulfil all the hopes that had been aroused in the populace. As the criticism gathered pace, the government responded with further repression – for example, by closing down the island's only significant newspaper, The *Torchlight*. Various different cultural and religious groups, including the Rastafarians, who were a significant presence on Jamaica and not insubstantial on Grenada, began to feel uneasy and dispirited. Rastafarians, whose beliefs had always perplexed Westerners with their mix of politics and messianic fervour and worship of Prince Tafari, later Haile Selassie of Ethiopia, had backed the revolution at first but had then increasingly come into conflict with the government, primarily because it wanted to put a stop to the cultivation of marijuana, the ritual smoking of which was widespread among the Rasta sect.

❖

IT WAS MID-OCTOBER 1983 when everything came to a head. The international press spoke of a coup. But what had actually happened?

There was a good deal of confusion among the solidarity groups. But they did have some background knowledge, allowing them to delve a little deeper into events which were difficult to interpret at the beginning.

The three Swedish Grenada activists, Eva Gabrielsson, Roland Eliasson and Stieg Larsson, had direct contact with Swedish aid workers on the island and reported the dramatic events in *Internationalen*. Their accounts revealed the tremendous confusion and desperation, and for that very reason gave a rare sense of immediacy and authenticity.

They relayed news that Prime Minister Maurice Bishop had been put under house arrest by his own colleagues in the government and that he had been freed again by the people to great jubilation. Everyone was on Bishop's side and 10,000 people demonstrated in his support. 'I've never seen anything like it before. No one was prepared to give in, they all wanted to fight,' said one Swedish aid worker.

It was obvious that Bernard Coard, assumed by all to be Bishop's right-hand man and brother in the struggle, was now his principal antagonist. 'Those who spoke in favour of Coard said that Bishop was not sufficiently left wing.'

Bishop was soon seized again, then, 'As the crowds were dispersed, gunfire was heard, and that was probably when Bishop was shot.' So Bishop was dead and the coup within the Marxist government was a fait accompli.

'People I spoke to think that Coard had infiltrated the party and installed his men in various posts. They have no backing whatsoever from the populace. The Military Council consists of fools, twenty-year-old "Marxist-Leninists" coming straight to power.'

'This is all terrible. We still can't understand what kind of regime it is.'

'All we can do is weep.'

The fragmentary depiction of the course of events in Internationalen was on the whole correct, as was proved later when the actual circumstances were eventually reconstructed.

The governing party had split into two factions, one led by Bernard Coard and his wife, Phyllis. Possibly under pressure from Cuba and the Soviet Union, they insisted on policies in line with strict Leninist principles. They accused Bishop of being disorganized and having petit-bourgeois and social-democratic leanings, as had been evident in his opposition to the closure of *The Torchlight*. The Coard faction had demanded a shared leadership between him and Bishop, to which Bishop first gave and then rescinded his agreement. When Bishop returned from a state visit to Eastern Europe on 8 October he was immediately taken into custody. At a meeting of the Central Committee, to which he was brought by force, he was accused of spreading false rumours about Coard. He was expelled from the leadership, and that same evening it was announced that he had resigned and been replaced as prime minister by Bernard Coard. Bishop was coerced into speaking on the radio during the evening to deny all rumours of a split in the Central Committee. No one believed a word of what he said. The next day huge crowds gathered and marched on the Residence, where Bishop was being held under house arrest.

They found him tied to the bed, half naked. He was released and escorted in triumph into town. A reporter heard just one murmur from his lips, 'the crowds, the crowds', as tears ran down his face. He was too weak to give a speech to the assembled masses. Instead he and his adherents holed themselves up in Fort George and prepared to make a radio broadcast to the people. The Coard faction reacted swiftly to the new situation and sent a detachment of soldiers to the fort. There was the sound of shooting. The majority of Bishop's supporters were unarmed and many of them were shot dead in the assault. Bishop surrendered in order to prevent further bloodshed. He and another seven people were led into the yard, where a pre-prepared judgement was read out. They were then lined up facing the wall and summarily executed.

The crowds who had freed Bishop were demoralized and broke up in the face of threats of renewed violence. A 'Revolutionary Military Council' was formed under General Hudson Austin shortly afterwards and a curfew was proclaimed.

Six days later, on the morning of 25 October, the USA invaded Grenada on the pretext that the safety of a thousand American citizens on the island was at risk. The invasion was effected with the cooperation and at the request of a number of other countries in the region. It subsequently emerged that the USA had applied strong pressure to elicit official petitions from them.

The USA defeated Grenada in four days, a not entirely surprising outcome. There was scarcely any resistance from the people, who were incapable of action after the unpopular Bernard Coard coup and Maurice Bishop's death.

INTERNATIONALEN'S REPORTS FROM GRENADA attracted a certain amount of attention. Ulf B. Andersson wrote in *Journalisten*: 'It is remarkable that a little paper like *Internationalen* succeeded more than most of the Swedish media in clarifying the events leading up to the invasion.'

A few weeks later Stieg Larsson wrote about Grenada again in *Internationalen* and his analysis was unequivocal. Not unexpectedly, the USA was the villain of the piece. The Americans had come to regard Cuba, Nicaragua and Grenada as a Soviet triangle and an immediate threat to American interests. Foreign Minister Alexander Haig had commissioned an urgent report in 1980 on the prerequisites for a military invasion of the triangle. In August 1981 the US deployed troops in a war games scenario called Operation Amber on a mountainous island belonging to the Amberdine group. The object was to seize the island for seventeen days and install a new US-friendly regime.

The ultimate aim of the invasion of Grenada, in Stieg Larsson's opinion, was to erase any trace of the revolution, the first in an English-speaking country and one which had been only a stone's throw from the USA.

Stieg did not prove that the USA had staged the coup within the revolutionary government, nor did he seek to do so. But the facts he uncovered point very clearly to there having been military preparations. That it was the revolutionaries themselves who gave the Americans the excuse to intervene was just another tragic irony.

BERNARD COARD AND SIX of his supporters were freed from Richmond Hill jail on Grenada in September 2009. They had been arrested soon after the US took Grenada, but the trial of the sixteen men was not held until 1986. Coard was sentenced to death, but in 1991 had his sentence commuted to life imprisonment.

Shortly before his release from jail, Coard met with Maurice Bishop's daughter Nadia and, according to her account, he expressed his regret for the events of October 1983.

Arriving by air on Grenada today, you land at Maurice Bishop International Airport. It was the site of the American parachute troops' landing in 1983 and was renamed in 2009 in honour of the leader of the revolution at the suggestion of the country's present prime minister, Tillman Thomas, who was himself imprisoned for a while during Bishop's revolutionary period.

Maurice Bishop's remains have never been found and no proper funeral has ever been held.

THE HURRICANE THAT LISBETH SALANDER experiences in the novel struck the island in the autumn of 2004 – though under the name of Ivan. Only a few months before his death, Stieg Larsson emailed his publisher to say that he and some friends were reviving the Grenada Committee so that they could organize aid for those affected by the storm, which had been the worst for many decades.

The rebellion on Grenada in the 1980s was almost a model revolution, in ultra-compact form, in both its hope and its tragedy. There was the mobilization of the people, then the speedy and in many cases successful reforms, the growing external and internal repression, the power struggle and the bloody purges, and finally a classic North American military invasion.

It was of course a period of sorrow and even disillusionment for those who had had such high hopes. But Stieg Larsson's reaction was typical of the man. He refused simply to accept that all attempts to construct a new social order in the Third World were doomed to failure, that the saying that all revolutions devour their own children was true. He wanted to get to the bottom of the circumstances behind the invasion. How had it been prepared, who were those responsible, what forces had been at work?

Feature Writer

STIEG NOW HAD BROADER SCOPE for his writing at the TT Press Agency. In 1983–4 the firm opted for a combination of text, pictures and graphics, creating a department called TT Pictorial (TT Bild). It produced longer feature articles, 'TT Reportage', that could be sold to newspapers, even in the form of finished text. The reporter Kenneth Ahlborn was made head of department.

He soon discovered that Stieg Larsson was someone brimming over with ideas and encouraged him to write. Stieg had an almost encyclopedic knowledge in such fields as politics and history, especially the Second World War. In other spheres which did not interest him – music and sport, for instance – he was quite demonstratively ignorant.

A colleague who worked with Stieg during his early years at TT claimed in a much-cited article in *Dagens Nyheter* in January 2010 that Stieg was a poor writer who could scarcely compose the shortest of articles: 'His style was affected, the word order often unidiomatic, sentence structure too uniform and syntax sometimes completely weird – it was a language that had to be rewritten to fulfil its professional function.'

But Kenneth Ahlborn emphasizes that there was absolutely nothing wrong with Stieg Larsson's writing; his articles needed a certain amount of editing, but no more than those of most other journalists. And it was always so enjoyable talking to Stieg. He knew a lot, but was basically a normal guy – though with tremendous application in everything he undertook.

His feature articles for TT often dealt with slightly offbeat subjects where he could make use of his wide reading. They could include such topics as 'This is how the pyramid of Cheops was built' or 'What is the truth about the Bermuda Triangle?', easily digestible pieces which newspapers were happy to buy. For Stieg they were not just entertainment, but also popular science. This was a time when the new spirituality which had been awakened in the hippie era had become the height of fashion under the appellation New Age and was spreading as lifestyle articles in the press or in trendy management theories. Stieg thought it was all superstition and pseudo-science, and it irritated him. 'You can hardly cross the street without someone tapping you on the shoulder and asking what star sign you're born under,' he wrote in

Internationalen in 1983. For him the New Age phenomenon also represented something completely alien to his whole outlook – the idea that everything was preordained by a higher being, that we could not influence our world by our own actions.

STIEG'S GREAT INTEREST IN CRIME FICTION was another way in for him. He conducted interviews with individual writers and presented surveys of recent books, especially in the run-up to the peak buying periods, summer and Christmas, and the local press were happy to take such material.

Elizabeth George was a real favourite, Kenneth Ahlborn remembers: 'Once when we were discussing some detail in one of her books, Stieg was able to go direct to the horse's mouth. It was quite impressive that he had her telephone number and could ring her up just like that.'

Stieg had been reading detective stories since boyhood. He had avidly consumed the apparently endless series of *Tvillingdetektiverna* (The Detective Twins) by Sivar Ahlrud – a pseudonym for two authors: Sid Roland Rommerud and Ivar Ahlstedt. In fact very few boys born in Sweden in the 1950s or 1960s could have avoided reading at least one book about the ginger-haired twins Klas and Göran Bergendahl, who based their operations in a little village with the Västerbotten-sounding name Vindsele, but travelled all over the country to solve such eternally topical puzzles as *Tunnelbanemysteriet*, *Raketmysteriet* or *Skyskrapemysteriet* (The Tube Train Mystery, The Rocket Mystery, The Skyscraper Mystery).

Kenneth Ahlborn very much shared Stieg's interest in popular culture and obscure subjects, and both delighted in the detective series published by B. Wahlström, with their now classic covers by the illustrator Bertil Hegland. They revelled in memories of the Detective Twins. Ahlborn's favourite was *Skyskrapemysteriet* and Stieg's was

Lördagsmysteriet (*The Saturday Mystery*). On one occasion they started discussing what might have happened to the heroes of all these stories for children and adolescents when they grew up. They flippantly agreed each to write a book to elucidate the matter.

Kenneth Ahlborn thought of opening with a state of emergency where the only option was to call in the Detective Twins, Nils-Olof Franzén's Agaton Sax, Åke Holmberg's Tam Sventon and Astrid Lindgren's Kalle Blomkvist – and we would meet them as they arrived by taxi at the incident room one after another, gout-ridden and hard of hearing, but with their former powers of deduction still intact.

Stieg Larsson was quite determined he would write about a Pippi Longstocking with attention deficit hyperactivity disorder and what befalls her in her twenties in a later era. She would probably not cope very well in modern society, would be diagnosed as disturbed and locked up in an institution, perhaps even be subjected to physical or psychological abuse, and emerge intent on revenge.

In the autumn of 2004 Kenneth Ahlborn bumped into Stieg Larsson, who told him somewhat triumphantly that he had finished his book about Pippi.

'I thought he was joking at first, but then I realized he was serious. He had had the book accepted by a major publisher and it was about to come out.'

IN STIEG'S CASE HIS INSATIABLE APPETITE for crime fiction had continued uninterrupted from his boyhood. The Bergendahl twins had given way to Sam Spade and Philip Marlowe, the tough-guy heroes of Dashiel Hammett and Raymond Chandler novels. Over the course of time he had other favourites, but he clung stubbornly to English-language writers and their mode of storytelling. In more recent years he had been heard to remark: 'The only Swedish thriller writers that are worth having are Sjöwall–Wahlöö – if you read them in English.'

But by now he had discovered the female crime writers. In fact they became almost the only ones he read: Elizabeth George, Sara Paretsky, Sue Grafton, Minette Walters, Patricia Cornwell. His favourites were George and Paretsky. They are of course quite different in style and choice of subject matter, but there is nevertheless a discernible relationship with the novels that Stieg Larsson would himself write. Elizabeth George has long, intricate narratives with many subplots, and portrays the social interplay between the two detectives, Thomas Lynley (Lord Asherton) and his refractory subordinate with the working-class background, Barbara Havers. And Sara Paretsky remoulds the hard-boiled American thriller tradition into feminist social criticism, where the investigations of her protagonist, V. I. Warshawski, lead her to the centres of power, compel her to unravel scandals in both politics and society and confront ruthless big-business interests.

As well as feature articles for TT, Stieg also produced an extensive portfolio of travel writing for the Swedish magazine *Vagabond*. The journal was new on the market then and one of their early ideas was to send a competent writer on the classic train journey from Moscow to Beijing on the Trans-Siberian Railway.

Per J. Andersson, editor of Vagabond, described in a 2008 article how Stieg's friend Per Jarl, who in those days shared their premises and did freelance work for them, immediately expressed an interest in going as a photographer and suggested Stieg as the writer.

'He's a cartographer at TT. And very talented.'

'At maps, maybe, but can he write?'

'No question!' Per Jarl avowed.

Per Andersson remained sceptical about Stieg the map specialist at

TT, but his doubts proved ill-founded when the text arrived, 'typed without a single error on fourteen A4 pages!'

And it really is a piece of reportage which still holds its own, written with pace and subtlety and with just the right amount of detail and factual information.

Stieg describes how travellers on the Trans-Siberian live two parallel lives. There was the little life played out in the cramped compartment among people from different countries, drinking tea, eating substandard food in the restaurant, learning coarse Russian songs, discussing politics and falling in love. They were a mixed crowd:

> There was the woman who opened a nightclub in one of the compartments; a professional traveller from Stockholm whose preparation for the journey had been meticulous in every respect [. . .] There was the conscientious objector from Skåne fleeing to Tibet, and the two Norwegians who intended to fly home as soon as they reached Beijing. And many more. We must have been quite a typical group of Trans-Siberian travellers.

SIMULTANEOUSLY, OUTSIDE THE WINDOW, the great wide world was gliding majestically by 'like a giant Russian videotape'.

For the journey on the Trans-Siberian Railway 'is not just a ride through geography and the magnificence of nature. It is above all a journey through time and place in history to sites that have played their part in the formation of our present, where the sounds of heroic deeds and tragedies still echo.'

The story of this landscape is of convicts' forced labour building the tsar's imperial railways; of the decisive role of the railway in the Russian Revolution; of Kirov, a desolate station on the line which took its name from the party leader in Leningrad who was assassinated in 1934 – by a Trotskyist, it was said of course, which was the pretext for the wave of bloody purges in the Communist Party; of Sverdlovsk, formerly Yekaterinburg, where the last tsar was murdered after the revolution.

Stieg described how China wins its propaganda battle against the Soviet Union by welcoming visitors with tea, cakes, beer and undrinkable whisky and allowing unrestricted photography.

And so they arrived.

'At 6.36 the next morning the final stage is completed and the journey ends as suddenly as it began as we come to a halt in Beijing Central Station. We have 9,001 kilometres of track behind us and are only four minutes behind schedule.'

THE *VAGABOND* ARTICLE WAS REAL PROOF of what Stieg Larsson was capable of achieving when he was allowed free rein to expatiate on something he enjoyed. Nevertheless it was not features and travel articles into which he poured his soul. Kenneth Ahlborn knew full well that Stieg's commitment was directed elsewhere; that when he sometimes arrived for work at TT in the middle of the day, there was good reason for it: 'I knew of course that it wasn't secret drinking, lack of respect for TT or anything like that behind his late appearances, but that he was engaged on a sort of civil defence mission against neo-Nazis and other sinister elements every evening and every night.'

MAPMAKER

IN THE LATE 1970S AND EARLY 1980S Stieg Larsson's interest in conspiracies and the exposure of shady anti-democratic networks led him into alternative realms of journalism, where mapping out a territory was done by methodical infiltration and research, charting a frightening terrain which few knew existed, especially at that time.

In 1973 I was myself witness to a remarkable gathering of Swedish neo-fascists around the statue of Charles XII in Kungsträdgården Park in Stockholm. I was soon to take my final exams at the College of Journalism and part of that last term's work was to produce a group newspaper of our own. A friend and I decided to compile an investigative report on right-wing extremism and neo-Nazism. I can't remember how we arrived at the idea, but it was not an obvious choice of topic. This was at the height of the left-wing vogue and political commitment was mostly manifested in other directions. Sweden was shaken that year by the 'IB Affair', the controversy surrounding Sweden's intelligence services which had been secretly collecting information on individuals regarded as a threat to the state, and the journalists Jan Guillou and Peter Bratt had just been arrested for spying. Earlier that autumn General Augusto Pinochet had toppled Chile's elected left-wing president, Salvador Allende, and placed the country under military dictatorship.

Perhaps we had a feeling that the extreme right-wing groups, however small they might be, had begun to see their opportunity. They were also quite rewarding to write about, since they were so unknown and their story was both fascinating and frightening. Were they serious when they said they believed in a national revolution, the abolition of democracy, the introduction of an authoritarian regime in Sweden?

We had met the lawyer Ulf Hamacher, leader of the revamped Swedish National Association (Sveriges Nationella Förbund, SNF), at his home in Götgatan in Stockholm. He was smoking a cigar and looking expectant. They had big plans for the future, he said. The left-wing tide would soon be turning. The man on the street would soon be desperate for a reversion to norms and authority. And the nationalists were the only ones who had a programme ready for such an eventuality.

In an article in *Expo*, published much later, Stieg Larsson wrote about the development of SNF over the next few years and what Hamacher had been alluding to:

In 1974 SNF began a nationwide campaign to attract new members and activate the old ones. A new programme and new rules were adopted. A youth wing was formed, Swedish National Youth (SNU), with Mikael Kindberg as chairman. It tried infiltrating moderate student associations, but also engaged in 'apolitical' activities through a diving club, a rifle club, a gymnastics, folkdance and folk music group, and study circles to discuss national defence. It also set up an 'internal tribunal' with Ulf Hamacher as chairman.

THIS QUOTATION ILLUSTRATES how the extreme Right were constantly seeking platforms on which to base their activities, because their fundamental position was so tenuous. What filled them with hope were developments abroad, particularly in Latin America, where not only Chile but a number of other countries were then bringing in extreme right-wing dictatorships.

Hamacher himself was a strong sympathizer with Pinochet and a few years later went on to establish himself as chairman of the Swedish-Chilean Society. He even took up residence for a while in his new Utopia.

We had also gone to listen to the foremost opponent of the Left, Christopher Jolin, who expounded his theory as to why things had been better during the Cold War in the 1950s, when there was a general awareness of the Communist threat in all sections of society. Jolin was in some ways the most significant name on the extreme Right. He had published a book in 1972 entitled *Vänstervridningen i Sverige – hot mot demokratin* (The Swing to the Left in Sweden – A Threat to Democracy), in which he asserted that left-wing extremists had infiltrated the country's major media, not least Swedish Radio, which he rechristened 'Swedish Redio'. His book went through several reprints and he himself was much praised in Conservative circles for his groundbreaking efforts. But when he came out of the closet as an actual fascist, many who had supported his views hastily distanced themselves from him. Jolin too joined the Swedish National Association and subsequently worked for Ahmed Rami's anti-Semitic Radio Islam.

So on 30 November 1973 I had taken up position near the statue of Charles XII to watch the neo-fascists assembling. The demonstration was organized by the Swedish National Association and the Narva Association (named after Charles XII's victory over the Russians in 1700). It was an extraordinary sight: elderly men in hats and camelhair overcoats, torches ablaze in the November dusk, and a troupe of young men in period uniforms of Charles XII soldiers. The costumes had been hired, it turned out, from the open-air folk museum, Skansen, where it was assumed they were for a historical festival, a non-political event.

One of the men walked solemnly forward, knelt and laid a wreath on the plinth of the king's statue, then stood and bowed. There was a roll of drums. And with that the show was over.

In a way this performance was symptomatic. The extreme Right as a historical masquerade, something that would soon end up as an exhibit at the Skansen museum together with the Charles XII uniforms.

I would not myself have put money on these people and their organizations having any future. I could never have predicted the violent confrontations that would eventually erupt between large groups of neo-Nazis and young anti-fascists in that very same place around the statue of Charles XII.

Charles XII and White Supremacy

KING CHARLES XII STANDS POINTING TO THE EAST, as he has done for more than 140 years. We think he is pointing out where the enemy lies. That was presumably not the idea when the statue was erected, but today the statue is and will remain, like the king himself, a nationalistic symbol, more charged with meaning than any other bronze figure in the country.

Charles XII was actually an anomaly on the Swedish royal throne: a warmongering autocratic ruler yet a dubious symbol of a greater Swedish unified culture. After the Battle of Poltava, for example, he and his troops took up residence in Turkish Bessarabia, and around his Swedish colony there grew up a multicultural town, Carlopolis (now

Tighina, previously Bendery in Russian, in present-day Moldavia), populated by every ethnic group imaginable – Turks, Cossacks, Armenians, Jews. But that was historical fact. When the romantic image of King Charles as the youthful hero was formed in the nineteenth century and then assigned specific political functions in the twentieth century, that was myth-making.

A CENTURY AGO, ON 29 APRIL 1910, the liberal newspaper *Aftontidningen* published a sensational article. It was by August Strindberg, the first of his acerbic pieces which would provoke the 'Strindberg feud', this one a historico-political polemic which he called 'Pharaoh Worship', a violent attack on King Charles XII: 'The fact that the founder of the kingdom, Gustaf Vasa, with his superlative qualities, should become an object of adulation is only right and proper, but when the nation is gathered round its scourge and notorious destroyer, then there is something decidedly sick, not to say rotten, in the air!'

Within days the press controversy took off. Some 150 contributors carved one another to pieces and the whole debate ran for over a year. Literary Sweden and political Sweden were divided: for or against Strindberg. And this time it was Strindberg who was pointing out the enemy. His chief antagonists were not just anybody, but two of the country's most revered figures: Verner von Heidenstam, member of the Academy and national bard, and the world-famous explorer Sven Hedin.

Thirty years later they were both expressing sympathy for Nazi Germany, Hedin more unambiguously than Heidenstam. The political future was in some way encapsulated in this press polemic.

Among Strindberg's enemies was a professor of politics at Gothenburg University, Rudolf Kjellén. He perceived major principles at stake in the battle between Hedin and Strindberg: a struggle between the olden days, 'the Sweden of fruitless negation and bizarre Utopias', and the new era, represented by men such as Hedin, 'the strong and heroic man of action'.

Kjellén was a Conservative, a member of the Allmänna valmansförbundet (General Electoral Association), the right-wing parliamentary party of the day. But he was a new kind of conservative. He foresaw a war looming, the masses marching under the red banners of the workers' movement instead of the blue and yellow flag of Sweden. He was worried, and concluded that the right wing to which he belonged had to be rejuvenated, and radically so. It was no longer a question of upper class or lower class, workers or bourgeoisie. All had to be accommodated under one roof, feel that they shared the same home. He called it 'the people's home' (*folkhem*) – and so coined a concept that, unbeknown to him, was to play a key role in modern Swedish history. It was not as individuals that people would feel a sense of community but as parts of a larger, almost metaphysical whole: the nation. And the nation in turn must maintain its position, conquer its living space, by force if necessary. 'States are baptized not in ink or print, but in blood.'

Kjellén thought that workers' movement socialism had seen better days, but so had liberalism. In modern society freedom had evolved into self-indulgence; freethinking had come to matter more than right-thinking. Now was the moment to change direction, and the people were already feeling 'a need for something solid to hold on to, a doctrine to believe in, an authority to subject themselves to, a strong man to follow'.

In the autumn of 1910, only a few months after his contribution to the Strindberg feud, Kjellén wrote some oft-quoted lines on 'the idea of socialism': 'Socialism as party politics limits this idea to the working classes. Hence its danger to society. Extend the idea to the entire people – think of national socialism instead of class socialism – and the danger to society becomes the magnificent strength of society!'

Kjellén died in the 1920s, so he was never to experience Hitler's rise to power, but he became a revered thinker in Nazi Germany and his disciple Adrian Molin developed his concepts further in Sweden. Molin was the most important inspiration behind the formation of the Swedish National Youth Association (Sveriges Nationella Ung-domsförbund) in 1915. If Kjellén was one of the world's first national socialists, then the SNU was the nucleus of one of the world's oldest Nazi organizations.

In the 1930s the SNU broke with the traditional right-wing party and went on to form Sveriges Nationella Förbund (Swedish National Association, SNF), which amalgamated with Per Engdahl's fascist party, Nysvenska rörelsen (New Swedish Movement). Engdahl was the cleverest ideologist and the most significant traditionalist within fascism and Nazism in Sweden, but his party never attracted a mass membership, no more than did the groups that called themselves national socialist, led by the Furugård brothers from Värmland or the non-commissioned army officer Sven-Olof Lindholm.

One feature of the extreme Right in Sweden is that, despite the weakness of its popular support, it is remarkably well represented among the elite and ruling classes: among scientists, academics and high-ranking military officers. It was not just theorists like Kjellén and Molin who were in the vanguard in formulating ideas which then became prevalent in the Third Reich. Herman Lundborg, the world's first professor of eugenics, was part of the trend as early as 1910, and founded the Swedish Society for Racial Hygiene. A decade later he managed to get more or less the entire Establishment behind him when he set up a Swedish racial research institute.

The National Eugenics Institute opened in 1921, with Lundborg at its head, and became well known for its large-scale field-research projects on the Swedish people. He and his colleagues travelled all over the country, photographing, measuring and making notes. The subjects of this research, seeing no harm in it, were allocated to racial groups on the basis of their physical constitution, skin colour, hair colour, shape of cranium, cranial circumference and so on. And there were few who doubted its scientific validity. On the strength of his findings, Lundborg pursued a vigorous campaign for an active population policy, including compulsory sterilization of undesirables, such as Lapps, Gypsies and vagrants. If this were not implemented, the fusion of the races would escalate and culture would fall into decline: 'Sexual urges would intensify, immorality, hedonism, vice and crime break out and leave their mark on society. Sooner or later it would lead to discord, dissent, riot and revolution' (according to an article in *Svensk Tidskrift* in 1921).

One reason for the rapid and widespread support for Lundborg's theories was that there had been a deep-seated belief since the mid-nineteenth century that the Germanic peoples of northern Europe were related and that Sweden was their original home. So when the Nazis stepped forward and began talking of restoring the honour of the German nation and defending the Nordic race, many Swedes were willing to listen. And these were not so much Swedish Nazi party members as influential individuals in politics, the civil service, the business world, the military, the police, even the royal family.

Some of the greatest admirers of Germany before and during the Second World War were to be found in the Swedish military. When Hitler celebrated his fiftieth birthday in the spring of 1939, he was congratulated by a Swedish delegation of high-ranking officers led by the future supreme commander Olof Thörnell. They were accompanied by the openly Nazi Carl Ernfrid Carlberg and Henri de Champs as representatives of the Manhem Society (a patriotic Scandinavian association named after Olaus Rudbeck's seventeenth-century book of Gothicist speculations) and the Swedish-German Association, who also presented Hitler with a gift, a statuette of Charles XII, which he is said to have much appreciated.

In the initial phase of the war the Swedish coalition government adopted a far-reaching policy of acceding to German demands, with increased exports of iron ore, the transit of troops by rail and sea, and censorship of any Swedish newspapers which criticized Germany.

Things did not go so well, however, for the official Nazi parties. Generals and colonels would never dream of subordinating themselves to Warrant Officer Lindholm, not even under a German occupation. And the nation it was the intention to unite was not very interested in the constant bickering among the Nazi parties themselves. But there was a common pool of historical ideas and attitudes from which groups and individuals drew their inspiration and which made some hold fast to their fundamental credo – aggressive nationalism, racism, the belief that elites should rule – while other friends of Germany took down their portraits of Hitler and enrolled for correspondence courses in English.

IN THE FIRST VOLUME OF THE MILLENNIUM SERIES, *The Girl with the Dragon Tattoo*, three just such irredeemable Nazis appear in fictional form, the brothers of the industrialist Henrik Vanger: Richard, Harald and Greger. Harald, a doctor, had worked at the National Eugenics Institute and was a leading light in the campaign for the sterilization of undesirable elements in the population and co-author of the book *The People's New Europe*, 'one of the most disgusting books to have been published in the Swedish language', according to Henrik Vanger. Harald joined Per Engdahl's fascist movement, New Sweden, and followed Engdahl through various organizations over the years. Greger concealed his sympathies more successfully, but turned out to have been a significant contributor to the Nordic National Party, a Nazi sect.

Richard Vanger, the eldest of the brothers, is said to have tried out most of the Nazi associations in the country:

> Any sick conspiratorial association that existed, you can be sure his name was on their membership list. In 1933 the Lindholm movement was formed, that is, the National Socialist Workers' Party [...] In 1939 the Second World War began and in 1940 the Winter War in Finland. A large number of the Lindholm movement joined as Finland volunteers. Richard was one of them [...] He was killed in February 1940 – just before the peace treaty with the Soviet Union – and thereby became a martyr in the Nazi movement and had a combat unit named after him. Even now a handful of idiots gather at a cemetery in Stockholm on the anniversary of his death to honour him.

RICHARD VANGER HAS MANIFEST SIMILARITIES to the chief propagandist of the real Lindholmers, Gösta Hallberg-Cuula. He was one of the first Swedish Finland volunteers, then in the Continuation War of 1941 leader of a shock-troop platoon of Swedish Nazis, and after that founder of the extreme right-wing Sveaborg association of front-line soldiers; he was renowned for his view that 'war is a wonderful trade when you get to fight the Russians'. He was eventually killed on the Svir front inside Soviet territory in 1942 and became one of the cult figures of Swedish Nazism, still honoured with speeches and the laying of wreaths.

WHEN THE SECOND WORLD WAR was over and Hitler's Third Reich lay in ruins, the dreams of Swedish Nazis and fascists were also shattered.

It would be reasonable to suppose that it would all be over now, the link broken, Charles XII consigned to the history books. But that is not what happened. While most party members and Nazi sympathizers soon covered their tracks, modified their opinions and became members of democratic parties, there were small pockets of 'hibernators' who kept in contact with one another, distributed simple publications and indulged in strange ceremonies.

These hibernating Nazis did not concern themselves with politics, and especially not extreme right-wing politics. Or at least that was how it was meant to appear. Carl Ernfrid Carlberg, engineer and book publisher, had long been expert at such subterfuge. He had set up the Gymniska Förbundet (Gymnastics Society) in the late 1920s. Many people thought it was a sports association, and in some ways it may have been. But the idea was to form outwardly non-political, but in reality Nazi, school associations that would strive for 'an idealistic lifestyle in an Aryan gymnastic spirit'. He established the Manhem Society, the quasi-medieval Scandinavian association which before and during the war became a forum for Swedish upper-class Nazis and so-called friends of Germany; and then, shortly before he died, the Carlberg Foundation (Carlbergska stiftelsen), which was both a rallying point and financier of the extreme right-wing groups that were endeavouring to re-establish their political direction and support after the war.

A man who had no intention of disguising his opinions was a gardener by the name of Göran Assar Oredsson. He had heard the Nazi message from a few of the old hibernators and decided to set up a new party, from 1961 called Nordiska Rikspartiet (Nordic National Party, NRP), and he even went so far as to make the historical connection plain by marrying the ex-wife of Sven Olof Lindholm.

NRP was the group that initiated the idea of the Charles XII celebration in Stockholm, and really got it off the ground when they joined with the re-established Swedish National Association. In the late 1960s it actually began to attract a few counter-demonstrators, but not in significant numbers. Who could be bothered to fight against hopeless moribund Nazi sects?

Just a few individuals thought otherwise and warned that the beast might reawaken. One was Armas Sastamoinen, a journalist on the Syndicalist newspaper *Arbetaren* (The Worker), who had published a book in 1961 entitled *Nynazism* (Neo-Nazism). 'The resurrection of Nazism, seen in its wider context, is a reality which should never be underestimated [. . .] The business of hatred has a ready ally in every person who has been offended or wronged, and how many of us have not? The battle against this hatred should be part of our daily ablutions,' he wrote in the foreword to his book.

THE AUTUMN OF 1976 brought a shocking political event in Sweden: the Social Democrats, led by Olof Palme, lost the election and went into opposition, after forty-four years of unbroken rule. The following election was lost too, and it was not until 1982 that Palme was to come back in as prime minister. Yet the Sweden of the 1970s is still regarded in the rear-view mirror of history as Palme-land. And in Palme-land right-wing extremism was an utterly marginalized phenomenon.

Neither before nor since has a modern politician been seen and heard as clearly as Olof Palme, nor given Sweden such a distinctive voice of its own on the international stage, nor spoken so much about international solidarity and aid to Third World countries. Even if the activists of the generation of '68 were extremely critical of Palme — and vice versa — there was broad consensus on the basic issues of solidarity and equality.

It has sometimes been said that the 1968 movement was mere surface froth. That may be true, but during and following this revolutionary froth came a left-wing swell that was considerably more powerful, that was palpable in the workplace, that influenced the Swedish trade union congresses and dictated much of the political agenda. The 1970s were not just a time of ideologies; they were also the decade of equality reforms, with the introduction of separate taxation for husbands and wives, with gender-neutral parental benefits and much extended child-care provision. And in the employment sphere there was the law on joint decision-making of 1976 and six years later the law on employment protection, which abolished the unrestricted right of the employer to hire and fire staff.

Yet there was one fundamental problem. The Swedish welfare state had until then been run under the aegis of post-war prosperity. But after the first oil crisis in 1973, the golden age was over. Reforms continued, but in a society where one sector of industry after another was shaken by structural crises and where the national budget deficit was increasing. There was nevertheless no obvious alternative to the Social Democratic model. The Conservative government which came into power in 1976 continued policies which included extensive subsidies to major companies in difficulties.

Both the left-wing surge and the radicalization of Social Democracy gave the business world cause for concern. In 1971 the head of information at the Swedish Employers' Federation, Sture Eskilsson, had written an internal memo proposing that they should take up the ideological battle. They should imitate the Left, he argued, and start up magazines and book publishing houses as platforms for informed debate, win over the intellectuals first and then try to propagate liberal free-market ideas and solutions on a more widespread basis. It was a clever notion and by no means impractical. In fact the Left too had much to gain from a more informed public debate.

Initially Eskilsson's proposals fell on deaf ears. It was not until 1976 when there was a significant shift in the direction taken by the Federation that some life was breathed into the five-year-old document to turn it into reality. But the overall context was now considerably tougher than Eskilsson may have imagined. The classic formula of cooperation between the employers' and employees' organizations – the spirit of the Saltsjöbaden agreement – had to be abandoned, and confrontation was adopted right across the board instead, with the aim of realigning the politico-economic focus of debate.

Perhaps 1976 marked the beginning of the political 1980s. It was the year the neo-liberal political economist Milton Freedman won the Nobel Prize in Economics, and the ideas he represented were to define economic thinking in the West for the next twenty years. Three years later Margaret Thatcher became prime minister of Great Britain on a platform of putting Conservative policy on a neo-liberal course.

The market was given free rein and was sometimes rather like a beast of prey let loose. There was a dangerous glint in the eyes of super-capitalist Gordon Gekko in the Hollywood film *Wall Street* when he hissed, 'It's all about bucks, kid. The rest is conversation.' His real-life counterpart, Ivan Boesky, the 'corporate raider' whose business was 'enhancing shareholder value' – that is to say, buying himself into or taking over companies in order to drive up the share value and sell at the right moment – raised cheers from a whole auditorium of students at the University of California when he declared in 1986 that greed was the new civic virtue.

But Sweden was not the USA. When the Moderates tried to introduce the concept of system change into the electoral campaign of 1985, they suffered a substantial setback. A change of system was nevertheless what was happening in all but name, or rather a change of epoch. The secure post-war world was breaking up; the feeling that everything that had been fixed was now volatile inspired some and frightened others.

The ideological shift was given impetus by the business federations that launched the publishing houses of Timbro and Ratio, the City University and, towards the end of the 1980s, the New Welfare Foundation. They produced their own counterparts to the official government White Papers and called them Citizens' White Papers (*Medborgarnas offentliga utredningar*) – to demonstrate where the real power should lie.

The 1980s were full of contradictions. Democracy was revered, not least in contrast to the repressive, decaying and corrupt Soviet empire, but at the same time distrust of politicians and political solutions was on the increase. Individualism, freedom of choice, nonconformism, hedonism were put in the driving seat. People should at last be able to do as they pleased, after decades of collectivism and regulations. But in contemporary popular culture and in the typical management theories of the day there was a renaissance of the strong man, the leader, hand outstretched, proclaiming the need to play for the team, to pull in the same direction, and intent on ejecting all fifth columnists, which is to say all individualistic nonconformists.

THE FACT THAT THE LEFT-WING SURGE was replaced by a surge to the right did not bring a concomitant upswing for the ultra-Right. The unrelenting battle against the Left and Communism was what had united the various groups, but now that was taken over by mightier forces: by established organizations, economists, international politicians like Margaret Thatcher and Ronald Reagan. Since new recruitment remained slow, right-wing extremism had been transformed into an old folks' mafia and dining club, where the inclination was to sit and dream about the glory days of yore.

But that too was to change. The 1980s turned out to be the decade when everything was happening for the extreme Right in Europe, when the transformation to postmodern fascism came about in organizations like Le Front National in France, Die Republikaner in Germany, Die Freiheitliche Partei Österreichs (the Freedom Party of Austria), the Lega Norte in Italy, the Vlaams Blok in Belgium.

Instead of the marching phalanxes of the 1920s and 1930s paying tribute to a single leader there came the postmodern fascist parties, which were much more politically obscure and much more flexible in their actions. Their slogans were ethnic homogeneity and Western values rather than the biological superiority of the white race; the free market rather than state control and economic corporatism; a general distrust of established politicians rather than explicit antagonism towards the democratic system.

But behind all this there was still the same old vengeful bitterness, the same feeling of abandonment and floundering in a world that was changing much too fast. The same hatred of the weak, the deviant, the foreign, the different.

'The business of hatred has a ready ally in every person who has been offended or wronged,' Armas Sastamoinen had written. And in the 1980s there were plenty of wronged people.

Investigative Anti-Racist

'WHERE THERE ARE FASCISTS THERE ARE ALSO ANTI-FASCISTS,' Stieg Larsson once wrote in an article for *Internationalen*.

Suddenly there were fascists in Britain again. They had reappeared in the 1950s, when the Second World War was only just over. Everyone could still remember standing united in the face of Hitler's bid for supremacy – the fighting, the privations, the endurance even under the worst of the bombings. And no one could have failed to see pictures of the absolute horrors in the liberated concentration camps. So it was unbelievable that anyone would want to wear a Nazi uniform or shout a slogan that might be a reminder of the odious political movements that had driven the world to war.

Yet it happened.

Britain was not the same country after the war that it had been at the beginning of the century. It had been possible then to say that the sun never set on the British Empire. The empire now still existed in fragments and as a historical relic, as pink shading on the map, but in reality it was gone. After the war, decolonization was merely an administrative measure. Country after country demanded and was given its freedom. Most British people accepted this with a sort of lofty equanimity. But there were some who could not bear such dislocation of the world order and the God-given superiority of the white race over people who were, in Kipling's words, 'lesser breeds without the law', and they gathered in small cliques whose formal agenda was to work for the preservation of the empire.

The obverse of these developments was also a cause of concern to them. Not only was Great Britain giving up its colonies; the colonies were now coming to Britain – in the form of spiralling numbers of immigrants who were transforming entire city districts into Indian or Caribbean enclaves.

From the Caribbean in particular there had been large-scale immigration immediately after the Second World War, and a smouldering racism began to rise to the surface, exploding in the autumn of 1958 in Notting Hill, a now fashionable but then run-down and poverty-stricken area of London. The chain of events was triggered by a gang of youths assaulting a Swedish woman, Majbritt Morrison, who was married to a West Indian. It escalated into packs of several hundred whites attacking West Indians on the streets and in their homes.

Many of the assailants were streetwise teddy boys, an early subculture among the youth of Britain. But what made matters worse was that supporters of Sir Oswald Mosley's neo-fascists had already been busy before these riots with anti-immigrant agitation under the slogan 'Keep Britain white'. And there were even more aggressive far-Right extremists in the background. It was in that very same area of Notting Hill that there had previously lived a former colonial army vet, Arnold Leese, who was known for two things: his great expertise on camels and his intense loathing of Jews. After his death his disciple and admirer Colin Jordan moved into his old home and made it a venue for a British Nazism re-emerging from the shadows. He saw this as his big opportunity to win new supporters.

The riots fizzled out in a week, but left a baleful omen: the combination of original undaunted fascism and a youthful xenophobia ready for violent confrontation.

MAURICE LUDMER WAS A SPORTS JOURNALIST from Birmingham who had been politically active in the British Communist Party since his youth. Together with Indian activists, he created the first anti-racism organization in Britain after the Notting Hill riots: the Coordinating Committee against Racial Discrimination.

He was well established in the Labour and trade union movements and was able to mobilize large contingents of workers to demonstrate at racist gatherings. He broke with the Communist Party in the late 1960s because he regarded its position on racial matters as not sufficiently unambiguous. In 1975 he started a magazine, *Searchlight*. There had been an anti-fascist journal of the same title for a few years in the early 1960s, edited by Gerry Gable, who was also involved in this new project. The cover of the first issue bore the proud motto of the Spanish Civil War international brigades: 'They shall not pass. *No pasarán!*' *Searchlight* became something of an institution for keeping far-Right extremism under close scrutiny, and a number of similar magazines were launched in other European countries.

In the early 1980s Stieg Larsson made contact with Gerry Gable and the European editor, Graeme Atkinson, who ran the paper jointly after the death of Maurice Ludmer, and he began writing for them in 1983 as their Scandinavian correspondent. At *Searchlight* he came face to face with a hard-line anti-racism which was somewhat shocking for cautious Swedes used to their moderate popular movements. It was more of a left-wing intelligence service that often had better information on the far Right than did the British security services.

The fascist and Nazi undergrowth was a distorted world, full of conspiracies and gallows humour. *Searchlight* had insight into everything that revolved round the Nazi leaders Jordan and Tyndall, even their rivalry for the affections of the French House of Dior heiress. But it was also a dangerous world of suppressed violence that could flare up at any time.

Searchlight was recognized early on for publishing detailed exposés of the internal workings of fascist groups which the other media could not get near. They achieved this by infiltrating them.

The man who penetrated deepest and longest had originally been a true fascist himself. Ray Hill was born in the late 1930s in a typically working-class area of Lancashire, was frequently unemployed in his youth and felt a failure as a family provider. He believed he could have found a job had it not been for the plethora of immigrants. He decided to emigrate to South Africa, where he joined the Nazi South African National Front, and took part in the expulsion of coloured people from a white area. Shortly afterwards he happened to drive past an Indian family sitting in despair by the roadside. His spontaneous reaction was to help them, which instantly made him realize that he himself bore a share of the guilt for their situation. The experience shook him to such an extent that he changed allegiance: not openly, but staying on in the fascist organization and providing information to Jewish associations, since the Jews were among those most victimized by the antipathy of the SANF.

When he returned to Britain he got in touch with *Searchlight* while still technically a member of the main fascist party, the British National Party. He also contributed the most revelatory sections of a Channel Four TV documentary from a hidden tape recorder he took to closed Nazi meetings, and he leaked details of a plot to detonate a bomb at the popular Notting Hill Carnival, and so averted a catastrophe.

Searchlight was not a magazine which filled its columns with a general political critique of fascism. Its strength was and is in concrete detail, the precise description of developments within extremist organizations and the acts of aggression they have perpetrated. But equally important were its more in-depth studies, background articles explaining the historical alliances between past and present groups and their protagonists.

STIEG LARSSON HAD LONG BEEN INTERESTED in right-wing extremists. Back in the 1970s, when he was living in Umeå, he discovered that there was a group in the town that was affiliated to the Nordic National Party. He was so fascinated by the notion that such a crazy thing as real Nazism still existed in Sweden that he began reading up on the subject. When he wanted to write a school essay on neo-Nazism, his teacher suggested he write about atomic power instead, but Stieg nevertheless followed up his own interest and went to see what there was in the library, finding almost nothing except a couple of books by Armas Sastamoinen.

Frederick Forsyth's book *The Odessa File* had been an early influence on Stieg. It is about a German journalist who decides to try and trace a former SS commandant, Eduard Roschmann, known as the Butcher of Riga. His hunt puts him on the track of the secret organization called Odessa (Organization for Former SS Members) which had assisted many Nazi war criminals to create new identities and flee to Latin America.

In an interview with the journal *Humanisten*, Stieg said, 'For many years I thought I was the only person in Sweden making a systematic study of this subject. But in 1979 a book appeared with the title *Fascism: förtrupp eller eftersläntare* (Fascism: Advance Guard or Stragglers), by the journalist Hans Lindquist. So I realized there must be at least two of us out there who were intrigued by this weird political fringe.'

Contributing to *Searchlight* was like taking a university course in the theory and practice of the ultra-Right. Stieg obtained a comprehensive overview of how the connections functioned between the various groupings and how their ideas had spread over time and between countries. It was a kind of jigsaw puzzle. The more names, organizations and concepts you became familiar with, the more clearly the overall picture was revealed. With all the background facts, it was possible to assess the implications when a new group introduced itself or a previously anonymous figure came to the attention of the media.

Searchlight was also something of a focal point for international cooperation and exchange of information among anti-fascists in Europe and even North America. Graeme Atkinson was the one who coordinated a network of people and organizations who were intent on fighting fascism, and Stieg Larsson became an active member.

What was local was international, and vice versa. So it was interesting for British readers to have Stieg's reports about the referendum on immigration in the little southern Swedish town of Sjöbo in 1988, initiated by the Centre Party councillor Sven-Olle Olsson: an example of how xenophobia can be driven by local opinion and through established democratic parties.

But when he wrote about Ahmed Rami and his community radio station, Radio Islam, it was more about the opposite of this: a person who in the narrow Swedish context could present himself as, and even initially be taken for, an anti-fascist and champion of the oppressed, yet who had far-reaching international contacts with right-wing extremists.

It was obvious to Stieg that Rami was not a radical advocate of freedom and had never been one. On the contrary, he was seeking a platform to publicize opinions which represented the staple fare of anti-Semitic and revisionist networks on the Continent. Rami himself appeared at conferences alongside notorious Holocaust deniers like David Irving and Robert Faurisson – and the latter even travelled to Sweden at Rami's invitation.

Ever since its inception *Searchlight* had been investigating and exposing the sometimes overt, sometimes veiled anti-Semitism of the far Right. They wrote about David Irving, who presented himself as a serious historian and even managed to get his books published by respectable publishers in Europe. They described the ways in which ultra-Right organizations, on the principle that my enemy's enemy is my friend, had sought allies among left-wing nationalists or radical minority groups, not least those connected with Islam. In the 1970s and 1980s they cultivated links with the American Nation of Islam, whose leader, the black preacher Louis Farrakhan, employed his skilful demagoguery to interweave anti-Semitic accusations into his speeches about black self-awareness.

For British anti-fascists the struggle against anti-Semitism was a fact of history. The clashes of the 1920s and 1930s with Oswald Mosley's Blackshirts were still within living memory, especially their march through the Jewish quarter of the East End in 1936, when his opponents mounted a powerful resistance, leading to what was perhaps the most legendary event in the history of British anti-fascism: the Battle of Cable Street. The *Guardian*, in a retrospective article in 2006, quotes an eyewitness:

'There was [*sic*] masses of marching people. Young people, old people, all shouting "*No pasarán!*" Suddenly a barricade was erected there and they put an old lorry in the middle of the road and an old mattress. The people up the top of the flats, mainly Irish Catholic women, were throwing rubbish on to the police. We were all side by side. I was moved to tears to see bearded Jews and Irish Catholic dockers standing up to stop Mosley. I shall never forget that as long as I live, how working-class people could get together to oppose the evil of racism.'

Mosley was not allowed to pass in Cable Street. By the end of the 1930s his reputation and support were steadily crumbling, and he was interned during the Second World War, re-emerging afterwards as an anti-immigration campaigner.

Yet he had once been regarded as a person of stature, the scion of an eminent family of the British landed gentry and elected as a Conservative Member of Parliament at the youthful age of twenty-two. After an interlude in the Labour Party he became increasingly influenced by Mussolini and his theories of a society based on elite government, technocracy and organization of working life in guild-like corporations. Together with his right-hand man A. K. Chesterton, cousin of the writer G. K. Chesterton, he succeeded in uniting the various fascist groups into the Union of

British Fascists. But so much opposition took the sting out of his successes and after the war he became rather a tragic and impotent figure. His disciple Chesterton took cover in the League of Empire Loyalists, an ultra-conservative upper-class clique that fought against the continuing dissolution of the empire.

BY 1970 THAT SAME OLD EMPIRE LOYALIST, Chesterton, had begun to realize that overt anti-Semitism and a uniformed militia would achieve nothing. A fresh start was needed, a new organization. It was given the name National Front and launched as a party that, unlike the Nazis, advocated an apparently moderate and serious-minded critique of immigration. In that way he thought it should be possible both to exploit the xenophobic mood in the hard-pressed industrial centres and to have some influence on the right wing of the Tory Party, where such opinions already had a powerful advocate in the populist public speaker Enoch Powell.

When Stieg Larsson later wrote an account of Keep Sweden Swedish, the faceless grouping that sought to form a Swedish National Front in the early 1980s, not much was known in Sweden about the implications, but for Stieg and others who had been following British developments it was clear enough.

The British National Front is probably less interesting for what it actually achieved than for having provided the seeds of nearly all the ultra-right-wing ideas that would follow. It is an example of how real fascists could make themselves seem acceptable but could also easily revert to an ideology of violence and spread their views to other extremist groups through international contacts.

But with its semi-democratic public profile the British National Front did have its successes: up to a quarter of a million votes in the mid-1970s British elections, a sensational result for an extremist right-wing group at the time. Then towards the end of the decade they began to lose ground dramatically, probably because the tough new Tory leader, Margaret Thatcher, played the anti-immigrant card and spoke openly of ordinary people's fear of the country being swamped by alien cultures.

As usual in a crisis situation, internal struggles broke out in the National Front. A different generation had risen to the top, younger men with academic backgrounds who jettisoned any illusion of a parliamentary path and went back to Nazism, although now in a new guise: an anti-Hitler Nazism, in which they praised the brothers Gregor and Otto Strasser, who had led an apparently anti-capitalist wing of the German Nazi movement. Strasserism was said to be a sort of amalgamation of the workers' movement's ideals of the Left and the nationalism of the Right. They were also in touch with some extremist Italian neo-fascist fugitives from the law who had fled to Britain in the hope of finding a safe haven.

One of the Italians' contacts within the British far Right happened to be Ray Hill, the mole, who of course reported everything to *Searchlight*. There it was soon established that the people who had now turned up in England were the ones who had carried out the frightful bombing of Bologna railway station on 2 August 1980, when eighty-five victims died.

After a tip-off from *Searchlight*, the police apprehended them, and their extradition to Italy was assumed to be a foregone conclusion, but the court rejected the case on technical grounds, and the terrorists were set free to continue their budding cooperation with the British neo-fascists.

The Italians took up with the young Strasserites in the National Front and persuaded them of the theory called 'the third position', meaning that as a party they belonged to neither Left nor Right, that they were against imperialism and in favour of small-scale and ecological thinking, that they rejected a hierarchical division of races but still advocated strict segregation, since racial inter-breeding and multiculturalism constituted the greatest threat to modern society. In the thoroughly corrupted world in which we lived, they argued, there were no suitable conditions for normal political activity; all that could be done was to create an elite of political soldiers to prepare for underground warfare using the methods of terrorism.

The National Front leader Derek Holland outlined the new philosophy in his book *The Political Soldier*, which was to be influential in many quarters, even in Sweden. In contrast to the decadent, apathetic and hedonistic citizen of modern bourgeois society, he posited a different kind of human being: a visionary, poet and musician who is also a soldier in the service of nationalism, someone who is morally pure, irreproachable and as totally dedicated to the cause as were the warriors of Sparta in antiquity.

BEFORE THEY ADOPTED THE EXTREME REVOLUTIONARY APPROACH, the National Front had been set on gaining influence in established right-wing circles. The political atmosphere of the 1980s seemed favourable for such a move.

In 1981 Ronald Reagan became the fortieth president of the United States. Reagan was known at the time for being on the far Right and had, for instance, supported the racist Southern senator Barry Goldwater in his attempt to win the presidency in the 1960s. But although the Ku Klux Klan and other overt racists detected a breath of fresh air, they were to be disappointed. Reagan did not intend to fall into that trap. He certainly wanted to transform the United States, to shift the political agenda to the right, but his programme was primarily economic – though it was pretty obvious that his basic convictions remained unchanged.

At the beginning of his presidency Reagan sent an official letter of thanks to a British anthropologist living in the USA named Roger Pearson, in which he expressed his deep appreciation of Pearson's substantial contribution to maintaining and furthering the ideals and principles America valued.

Those ideals and principles were far from innocuous, as Stieg Larsson pointed out in an article for *Internationalen* in 1984. Through *Searchlight* he knew that the man was not simply a natural scientist with controversial theories but 'one of the central figures in the post-war Nazi semi-underground movement'. Pearson the academic and magazine publisher had also acquired international political influence through his position in the World Anti-Communist League founded in Korea.

The aim of WACL was to fight for democracy and against Communist dictatorship, and that was certainly what many of those who joined the organization believed they were doing. But with Roger Pearson as chairman, WACL was hardly going to be an advocate of democracy. They were disseminated through Pearson's own network, the Northern League, which brought together various figures from the Nazi past, such as Hans Günther, who was known in German as "Rassengünther" (Race Günther), one of the most admired academics of the Nazi period. When Pearson moved to the United States in the sixties, he continued to publish books with titles such as *Eugenics and Race*, and he worked with Willis Carto, a multi-millionare who was one of the most prominent figures of the American ultra-right. He was also associated with *Mankind Quarterly*, a controversial academic journal often criticized for espousing racist views.

For Stieg Larsson, WACL represented an important step in the attempts of the far Right and the neo-Nazis to attain respectability. It was not a matter of forming parties and achieving election successes, but rather of gaining a foothold in the established conservative parties. It nearly succeeded in Pearson's case, but when some alert Tories raised the alarm about his extreme right background, he was dropped from his position as leader of the WACL. However, a few years later the organization acquired a more direct association with the US administration by appointing General John K. Singlaub as its chairman in 1984.

Singlaub was a retired major general in the U.S. Army who had been commander from 1966-68 of what was called the Studies and Observations Group during the Vietnam War. After the war he became the dominant figure in a group of military personnel who insisted that the USA had not been defeated in Vietnam but betrayed by liberals and traitors in Congress. They believed that no lasting peace could be achieved until the Soviet Union had suffered a complete military defeat and so went under the sobriquet of the 'War Now Movement'. If open hostilities could not be brought about with the Communist superpower, then war must be pursued by other means on those sections of the front where the danger was greatest: South Africa, Afghanistan and, in particular, Central America.

The revolution on the West Indian island of Grenada was dead, but there was a brutal civil war going on in Nicaragua between the left-wing Sandinista government and the right-wing Contra guerrillas. And in countries such as Guatemala, El Salvador and Honduras, US-trained Central American troops were fighting guerrilla forces, while paramilitary guards and death squads were executing political activists and trade union leaders.

But in 1981 Congress halted military aid in the form of weapons to the much criticized Contra guerrillas in Nicaragua. Yet the veterans of the Special Operations Group continued their activities inside Nicaragua. Singlaub boasted that he had collected so much money from private donations that he could have sent $500,000 a month to the Contras.

The bitter harvest of the 1980s, according to Stieg, was to have an effect on Central America right up to our own day and it was made possible by the fact that right-wing extremists were allowed to pursue their activities unimpeded and under legal protection.

HÅKAN BLOMQVIST, today a historian at Södertörn College, south of Stockholm, was then editor-in-chief of *Internationalen* and remembers Stieg Larsson's unparalleled knowledge of the far Right: 'He was extremely productive. He might phone on a Thursday and say he wanted to write about the World Anti-Communist League, and on Monday an exceptionally well-informed and detailed five-page article would land on my desk. But I wouldn't go so far as to say that Stieg was our star reporter; he was one of many writing for us. I thought it was useful to have such articles, but they were not on the subjects that were a priority for me.'

Stieg's contributions to *Internationalen* were constructed in a similar way to most of his pieces on the far Right: they were surveys overflowing with individual names, the ideas they were disseminating, their contacts and the organizations they were working for. But they were rarely put in a broader socio-political or conceptual perspective. His analysis of fascism was expressed not in ideological expositions but in pointing out influences.

'We could of course see it as conspiracy theories, but I think it is more a way of thinking that played a significant role for the German Left of 1968, and to some extent for the French,' says

Håkan Blomqvist. 'A powerful impetus behind the Sixties Left in Germany was the enormous strength of their indignation that people who had perpetrated the most heinous crimes you can think of had never been made to pay for them. They had escaped punishment. To crown it all, they were still there, they still had a position in society. That was how it was in Germany, and also in De Gaulle's France, not to speak of Sweden, which had cooperated so very closely in various ways with Nazi Germany, and where the only official investigation was the extremely tentative findings of the Sandler Commission. Otherwise everything continued as before in Sweden.'

So the true anti-fascist must clear up once and for all what might have been started but never completed: seek out the fascists, expose them, call them to account.

The New Generation

SOMETHING HAPPENED TO YOUNG PEOPLE IN THE 1950s. It was as if a deep malaise permeated an entire generation. Teenagers overstepped boundaries and class barriers without any clear sense of direction. There was a restlessness in the air. One spark could suddenly ignite an outburst of violence. No one was sure why it was happening, but the authorities were worried. Then in the 1960s and on into the 1970s the young acquired a sense of direction, flags and banners were borne aloft and speeches declaimed. Now people knew what it was, it was called youth revolt, and the adult generation was divided in opinion. Some thought it good and healthy, others that it represented an acute danger to society. With the end of the 1970s and the beginning of the 1980s it all appeared to grind to a halt. The demonstrators had marched on into institutions and careers. Those who were left on the streets expressed neither disquiet nor hope. Only a dogged, gloomy bitterness that no one really seemed bothered by or even interested in.

Britain, the home of youth culture and the mecca of pop music, was a country in crisis, with factory closures and systematic welfare cuts for the worst off. The alienated young shaved their heads, got themselves tattooed and put on uniform jackets and military boots as if going to war.

These skinheads were the children of the 1980s. Their existence was a protest against the dissolution of everything: national borders, gender roles, the norms of cohabitation. But they were also children of the 1980s in their individualistic exhibitionism, in not hiding themselves away but saying: look at us, here we are, you are the ones who will have to adapt.

Wherever skinheads came on the scene the atmosphere felt menacing. Any little thing could trigger violence. Like all young people, they had their own music. Punk had arrived, harsh, noisy, vulgar, a kick in the teeth for respectability. It generally leaned to the Left, but not always. Going in the other direction might be even more rebellious. Either way it seemed to arouse dismay in the Establishment.

Ian Stuart Donaldson, a moderately successful singer in a punk band calling itself Skrewdriver, felt much more drawn to the Right. After a concert in London in 1978 which ended in racial skirmishes and the band being ejected, Stuart made a definitive choice of sides. Like most of those with similar views, he turned to the principal focus of the extreme Right, the National Front, where he became a youth leader and racist ideologist. He created the network Rock Against Communism, brought together the bands that played what had come to be known as 'white noise', organized concerts and recordings. This became an increasingly lucrative activity for the National Front, which annoyed Stuart, so he decided to leave the organization and set up the broadly Nazi and anti-Semitic organization Blood and Honour.

White Power music grew in strength, branched out and spread to other countries. New record companies came on the scene: Rock-O-Rama in Germany and Rebelles Européens in France. Stuart went to Sweden and helped found Rock Against Communism in Södertälje in the mid-1980s, and that was to have a decisive impact on the development of Swedish neo-Nazism. Some Swedish bands were already established and more were to come, forming rallying points for young skinheads with Nazi ideals.

This was undoubtedly something new: Nazism in association with modern popular culture, and an infrastructure producing records and concerts and magazines. The old men of the Swedish National Association could never have imagined anything like it.

Such Nazi-tinged rock music had a natural affinity with the cult-like features of some of the big commercial hard-rock bands. A new underground enclave was formed that borrowed many mystical symbols from historical Nazism or from early Nordic and Celtic mythology. It was a closed world and thus desirable. But outsiders could only look on open-mouthed. What was the meaning of a Swedish music group calling itself Dirlewanger? Probably just another weird name for a rock band. But initiates knew it was an allusion to the German Nazi Karl Dirlewanger, leader of a brigade in the Second World War that ravaged, murdered and burned in Poland and White Russia.

Neo-Nazi culture made its way into other spheres as well. Football hooligans in Britain, who in the 1980s generally called themselves 'firms' and set out deliberately to instigate fights at matches and beat up rival supporters, were also influenced by racist propaganda and provided yet another rallying point for the National Front and other fascist organizations. Soon racist chants were being heard in Sweden too, and so-called supporters took to mimicking ape noises when a black player on the opposing team (or sometimes even their own) got the ball.

Erik Blücher, who came to Sweden from Norway, was the first Scandinavian to see the potential of the skinheads for neo–Nazi organizations. 'We will not win respectability through collaboration with skinheads – but we will win respect,' he wrote in his English-language magazine *Nordic Order*. 'Our forces of young militant skinheads have saved the skins of many British patriots during demonstrations [. . .] The skinhead movement is changing into a pan-European army of national stormtroopers. Rough and unpolished, but also energetic and militant in their revolutionary nationalism, skinheads are the Vikings of the new dawn.'

The Nordic National Party (NRP) latched on to this, being a classic Nazi party and knowing what use could be made of stormtroopers of the SA type. In 1984 they created a number of what were called Riksaktionsgrupper (National Action Groups, RAG), mostly filled with skinheads. There was soon a marked escalation in right-wing extremist violence in Sweden. Those who came off worst were the sections of society the neo-Nazis really detested: Jews, immigrants and homosexuals. In Gothenburg in the mid-1980s two homosexuals were murdered by neo-Nazis. Vera Oredsson, the NRP leader, defended the murders by asserting, 'It was cleansing. We don't regard homosexuals as human beings.'

During the 1980s Nazi groups persecuted people with threatening phone calls and letters, surveillance, graffiti, unordered deliveries and the like. Threats were directed at politicians and celebrities who had expressed opinions against racism, like the actor and TV entertainer Hagge Geigert, but also against anti-racist activists and members of Jewish associations. Other favourite Nazi tricks were damaging or firebombing political buildings and left-wing bookshops, and vandalizing Jewish cemeteries. Some thirty skinheads from the NRP were prosecuted in 1985 for threatening behaviour and harassment. The NRP leadership backed off and refused to take responsibility for its stormtroopers.

The violence culminated on Midsummer's Eve 1986, when some skinheads beat twenty-year-old Ronny Landin to death on the coast in Nynäshamn as he tried to intervene in a fight between immigrants and neo-Nazis. Later that same year, at Halloween, a skinhead, Ronny Öhman, was murdered by four youths, most of them of immigrant origin, after an argument. Violence had become part of everyday life in Sweden. And it was obvious what subject would provide a unified focus for all the Swedish right-wing extremists.

IMMIGRATION HAD NOT BEEN a big issue for the far Right and neo-Nazis until then. Not even the Nordic National Party had really made any serious attempt to exploit it. Though there were traditions to fall back on. The slogan 'Sweden for the Swedish' had been heard as long ago as the 1880s during the protectionist campaigns of the era. But in the 1970s it was really only the grand old man of Swedish fascism, Per Engdahl, who saw advantages in reviving it. In a leading article in *Vägen framåt* (The Way Forward) in 1978 he wrote about immigration as being of momentous consequence for the country's future and demanded its immediate cessation.

In 1979 leaflets were distributed in the suburbs of Stockholm bearing the name of an organization calling itself Bevara Sverige Svenskt (Keep Sweden Swedish, BSS). It included the following: 'Swedes are becoming fewer and fewer every year. In four years' time there will no longer be a Sweden of the Swedes. We'll probably have a Turk as dictator and a black as foreign minister. The population will be a chocolate-brown mixed race who don't speak Swedish but a cacophony of different languages.' And quite soon the letters BSS started to appear everywhere as graffiti on walls and in public places. Yet there were not many people who knew what it actually stood for. It was a faceless organization in which those behind the scenes preferred to avoid public exposure. They wanted to let it appear as if BSS was some kind of spontaneous protest welling up from the people.

If the Nazi skinheads' attitude could be expressed as 'we are the outcasts, the ones ordinary Swedes hate and who hate in return', then the subtext in everything written by BSS was 'we are the ones who say straight out what all ordinary Swedes are thinking'.

The claim that immigrants were taking over from native Swedes was in any case not true. In the late 1960s Sweden had experienced quite a large labour force immigration, with a peak in 1970 of 77,000. But in the first half of the 1980s immigration was running at just over 30,000 a year. Net immigration in the years 1981–3, taking emigration into account, was no more than 2,000–3,000 a year. The Swedes were definitely not drowning under an influx of foreigners.

BSS WAS AN ATTEMPT TO PROVOKE public debate on a pressing issue. That is what the founder, Leif Zeilon, asserts in a book he wrote about the organization. All they did was put together a leaflet. Then came the reactions. But the truth was somewhat different.

Stieg Larsson and Anna-Lena Lodenius, in their book *Extremhögern* (The Far Right), described BSS as 'Sweden's first modern anti-immigration party'. It was a movement that 'formally distanced itself from racism while actively opposing political refugees and non-

Scandinavian immigration'. And the people behind it were by no means political fledglings but had considerable experience as activists in ultra-Right groups. Leif Zeilon, Niels Mandell, Christopher Jolin and Sven Davidsson were some of the principal figures, and the invisible Zeilon was the driving force. He had previously lived in Rhodesia and was a sympathizer with Ian Smith's regime, and had probably been a member or supporter of the Nordic National Party. Mandell had for a time been a leader of one of the party's RAG groups. Davidsson, who seemed not to have been in BSS from the outset but became its first official chairman, had been involved with Per Engdahl's New Swedish Movement. Jolin, as mentioned above, was the man who diagnosed the swing to the Left in Sweden and who subsequently revealed himself to be a fascist and anti-Semite.

When BSS set out a coherent programme in the early 1980s, the main points were that immigration should only be permitted for what they called 'serious persons from culturally and ethnically related countries', and that refugees should only be allowed in if they were from countries ethnically related to Sweden. Other refugees should be sent straight back home, or, in BSS terminology, 'repatriated'.

It was clear too from their attitude to international adoptions that BSS really was racist and not merely anti-immigration. Adoptive children from Third World countries, who often came to Sweden at the age of a few months, could scarcely be called bearers of a foreign culture. Yet such adoptions were to be totally banned and any such children sent back to their countries of origin.

The BSS strategy had manifest similarities to that of the British National Front. And in letters to the minister for immigration they wrote: 'So far 13,500 leaflets have been distributed in Stockholm, and there will be more if the present insane immigration policy is not halted. Keep Sweden Swedish is the embryo of a Swedish National

Front which will continue the battle for our people's survival.' And just as the National Front in Britain did, BSS started using intimidating gangs of skinheads as bodyguards when distributing leaflets.

When BSS was featured in a TV documentary, it led to Leif Zeilon being dismissed from his job at the construction firm BPA. The far Right had got a martyr, a development they exploited to its maximum.

BSS also had wide coverage through the local radio station Open Forum, where Rolf Petersson, a taxi driver, aired his uninhibitedly xenophobic views and drew in many members and sympathizers to BSS.

Keep Sweden Swedish was rather shambolic in the way it operated and it closed down in 1986. But that was not as significant as it sounds, since the organization was most of all a portent. The genie was out of the bottle. The far Right had got its big issue.

HOWEVER, RACISM MET WITH RESISTANCE. A demonstration was held in Stockholm on 30 October 1982 which attracted 5,500 people. Following this came the formation of Den gemensamma arbetsgruppen mot rasism (The Communal Working Group Against Racism), which was renamed in 1985 Riksförbundet Stoppa rasismen (The National Association to Stop Racism). 'The need to act against racism was of the utmost importance for us,' *Internationalen*'s editor Håkan Blomqvist remembers. 'Trotskyism was not just internationalist and cosmopolitan. We believed that national states had outlived their role. We were pursuing a campaign in the early 1970s that we called "Strangle Fascism at birth" [Krossa fascismen i ägget], based on our belief that fascism can begin to flourish in times of economic crisis if it presents itself as an instrument of order and stability. If you think there's a danger of that, you have to make sure the fascists don't appear orderly and unopposed. You have to go out and break up their demonstrations, which is what we did with the Narva Association and similar groups in the 1970s. There were fights, of course. First we threw their wreaths in the water at Nybroviken, then we got a beating from them on Östermalmstorg. But I became increasingly sceptical of it all: it didn't affect ordinary people, it was just a sort of sectarian theatre performance.'

But now in the 1980s the situation was different. The racists were more numerous and the anti-racists knew they had to launch a much broader counteroffensive. A crucial element in this was publishing *Stoppa rasismen* (Stop Racism), a journal providing information about 'actual cases of racism, discrimination and hostility towards immigrants', but also discussing the causes of racism. Stieg Larsson eventually worked on the paper, though not as a member of the editorial team. He was able to bring to it a depth of knowledge of the historical links and roots of post-war fascism that few people in Sweden possessed. It continued to appear until the beginning of 1995.

In two substantial articles in 1987 he reported on the neo-fascist equivalent of the far Left's notorious Jackal, Illich Ramirez Sanchez. This was an Italian almost entirely unknown in Sweden, Stefano Delle Chiaie, who had recently been arrested in Venezuela and extradited to his homeland, but was later acquitted of charges of helping organize the 1969 bombing of a Milan Bank.

It was a remarkable story of the birth of post-war fascism in Italy and of the secret connections between the Italian security police, the extreme right-wing Catholic lodge P2 and a fanatical elite force, Avanguardia Nazionale. Stefano Delle Chiaie was involved in all these organizations.

The closed groups in Italy had worked out their own theory of how fascism could regain power in the country. They called it 'the strategy of tension', and Stieg Larsson believed that Stefano Delle Chiaie was the real brains behind it. His contacts in the police and security services and with the ultra-conservative groups within the Church fitted him perfectly for the role.

According to Stieg, the "strategy of tension" was for the fascist organization to be divided into two elements, one public and respectable, consisting of conservative politicians, industrialists and civil servants, and the other underground and with elite soldiers who would use ruthless terror methods to fight for their aims. The tactics of violence would frighten ordinary people into submission and sow mistrust between the populace and their elected politicians. When this lack of confidence reached a suitable level, the official fascist organization would be ready to seize power.

From the late 1960s onwards through the next decade Italy was to suffer not only the terrorist actions of the left-wing Red Brigades but also a series of horrific bombings which were all anonymous but have been linked to neo-fascist groups, from the bombing of the National Agricultural Bank in Milan in 1969, which killed seventeen people, to the dreadful explosions in Bologna railway station in 1980, with eighty-five fatalities and more than 200 injured. Stefano Delle Chiaie was acquitted of charges stemming from both of these attacks.

When Stieg Larsson gave an account of this background in *Stoppa rasismen*, it was not just a general history lesson. He knew that BSS took much of its inspiration from the National Front, which in turn had secret contacts with the violent Italian neo-fascists. And that BSS had had the National Front ideologist Derek Holland's book *The Political Soldier* translated and was now selling it in Sweden.

Terrorist acts were a possibility even in Sweden, although there were very few who really believed it could ever happen. And terrorism could be used as part of a broader strategy for undermining democracy.

IN A SWEDEN WHICH WAS COMPLETELY caught off guard by BSS propaganda in the early 1980s, there was by the middle of the decade a plethora of organizations and activities directed against racism and xenophobia. Young anarchists set up a group called Bevara Sverige Blandat (Keep Sweden Mixed, BSB), going round changing BSS graffiti to BSB, and from France and its SOS Racisme came the badge showing an open palm with the slogan 'Hands off my pal'. The murder of Ronny Landin in 1986 was perhaps the most pivotal single event to mobilize Swedish anti-racists. The number of demonstrations rose steadily and as a symbolic gesture Stop Racism initiated a Ronny Landin Prize.

But the xenophobic organizations were active as well, and not only the mysterious, semi-covert BSS. Similar slogans could be heard from other sources, such as the motley crew of what were called the parties of discontent, who pursued single issues, regarded themselves as the mouthpieces of ordinary citizens and mostly advocated simplistic solutions. They wanted more freedom, but also less – for those who did not fit in, who could not look after themselves or were otherwise a burden on society, to which categories all too many immigrants belonged.

These parties of discontent included the Centre Democrats, the Skåne Party and the Sjöbo Party. Since they were for the individual and against the state, authorities, rules and regulations, they slotted well into the 1980s economy and some of them experienced a rapid, if short-lived, growth. Their leaders wanted to emulate their paragons in Denmark and Norway, Mogens Glistrup and Carl Hagen, which proved easier said than done.

The party of discontent which seemed to have the most potential was the Progress Party (Framstegspartiet), which had taken its name from successful Scandinavian sister parties and which attracted a number of well-known figures and quite a sizeable membership, before they went down the usual route of divisions and dissensions. It adopted a more aggressively xenophobic rhetoric in the early 1980s, especially in its local radio broadcasts. There may thus have been some logic to its merger with BSS in 1986 to form the Sweden Party (Sverigepartiet).

ACTIVITIES COMMENCED FOR THE NEW PARTY in the spring of 1987 with major leafleting campaigns in Stockholm. Kenneth Lewis, now a lawyer, was one of the prime motivators of Stop Racism in the mid-1980s. He recalls the increasingly dramatic confrontations between racists and anti-racists: 'In central Stockholm the racists occupied the pavements between the station and Sergels torg, in full military garb, with heavy boots and Swedish flags, handing out their propaganda. We were contacted by immigrants who found it unpleasant and intimidating, so we decided to go along and organize a counter-demonstration. This brought extensive press coverage and unfortunately also some scuffles. Then the police decided that no one would be allowed to cause an obstruction, so both racists and counter-demonstrators had to withdraw.'

In fact the Sweden Party adherents simply moved down the street to Drottninggatan and the anti-racists followed them, growing in number all the time. The long-drawn-out trial of strength continued until the racists gave up.

By this stage the anti-racists had also realized the hugely symbolic value of demonstrations around the statue of Charles XII. They mounted a big demonstration on 30 November 1987 against the march of the far Right to the statue, and this was to be repeated in succeeding years.

One problem for those trying to oppose the racists was the uncertainty about whom they were dealing with. It was a conscious tactic, not least on the part of the BSS, to go public only in exceptional circumstances. It attracted people with racist views and had probably had them on board for years, but did not really wish to be publicly associated with them. Some felt it was a good thing that the racists kept to the shadows, thus attracting less attention to their message. Others, like Kenneth Lewis, took an opposing view: 'I advocated, and may have been the originator of, the theory that we should not hush up the racists but rather turn the spotlight on them. A great many of them would rather not stand up and be counted. If the light were trained on them they would soon crawl back into their burrows. There were also some who would jump ship if they were shown up, which was also a result we were hoping for.'

To gather the necessary information, there were activists connected to Stop Racism who concentrated on investigating individuals and organizations on the far Right. Stieg Larsson was one of the most industrious, but there were also academic researchers, such as Heléne Lööw, who was preparing a PhD thesis on the history of Swedish Nazism – submitted in 1990 under the title *Hakkorset och vasakärven* (The Swastika and the Vasa Sheaf).

'Those of us in Stop Racism had the same objectives as those who were investigating the extremist groups, and we operated in a sort of symbiosis with them. For example, Graeme Atkinson of *Searchlight* paid us a visit, since that magazine was a paradigm for us,' says Kenneth Lewis. 'We often went into schools to talk about racism and found the material collated by Stieg and others very useful.'

It was now becoming clear that the racist and fascist groupings could be differentiated into two divergent tendencies: one hoping to emulate Le Pen in France by creating an acceptable brand of fascism, the other wanting to tackle society, immigrants and political opponents head on, by violent means.

'We concluded that there was a kind of tacit agreement between the two factions; they had decided on a division of roles, but in reality there were many strong ties between them, as was evident from the research Stieg and others had done.'

ON THE CUSP OF THE 1990S, more or less by chance, Stieg Larsson had the opportunity to consolidate in book form the vast amount of knowledge he had accumulated on the far Right.

The journalist Anna-Lena Lodenius had published a book in 1988 called *Operation högervridning* (Operation Right Turn), written with the philosopher Sven Ove Hansson, and they had planned to write a second book together which would take a more sweeping look at the ultra-Right, but Hansson happened to be offered another book commission and so suggested Stieg Larsson instead, knowing him to be an expert on the subject. The two authors met and decided on a comprehensive presentation of organizations on the far Right, their history and the development of their ideas. They would profile the leading personalities in the parties and include not only overtly fascist and Nazi organizations but parties of discontent, survivalist groups and other fringe phenomena too. It would also provide an outline of right-wing extremism in the most significant countries of Europe and in the USA.

'We became well acquainted over a period of several years and it was fascinating to get to know a person with such a focused commit-ment,' says Anna-Lena Lodenius.

Stieg had enormous stamina when it came to gaining insight into and unearthing information about the more elusive groups. He might, for instance, produce a convincing survivalist magazine himself – printed in three copies – simply to make contact with someone he wanted to pump for information on such a movement, and the stratagem would succeed.

However, his exceptionally powerful motivation meant that he found it hard to compromise. 'When we discussed the structure of the book there were hardly any problems, but when he gave me his finished text it would be something quite different from what we had decided. When I pointed that out, he could not see it as a difficulty.' In the end the two authors divided the book between them and worked independently on separate sections, Lodenius on the Swedish and Scandinavian chapters and Stieg Larsson on all aspects of the international scene.

The book, *Extremhögern* (The Far Right), received a lot of attention when it came out, with publicity for the authors themselves and invitations to TV chat shows and the like. 'But Stieg hated such appearances, so I had to take them all on,' Anna-Lena Lodenius remembers. 'He became a skilful public speaker later, but he never liked doing it without meticulous preparation.'

The book also meant that the authors came under fire even more from the increasingly militant neo-Nazis. A couple of years after the first edition appeared, the Nazi skinhead magazine Storm published a list of names, photographs, addresses and telephone numbers of about fifteen well-known Swedes, including the national chief of police and the chairman of the police union, with an exhortation that these people should be 'lined up against the wall'. Anna-Lena Lodenius and Stieg Larsson were among them. In her case the magazine urged its readers to 'cut short her career'. The editor was subsequently prosecuted and convicted of incitement to hatred, the first time in Sweden that anyone was convicted for a threat expressed in print.

But Anna-Lena Lodenius found the price of this sort of exposure too high: 'I had recently had a child, and for me the family had to come first. I was not prepared to sacrifice as much as Stieg was. I don't think he really understood my position. He just wanted to keep going further. The fascists had to be exposed and called to account. He wanted to show no mercy.'

Some years earlier, in an article on Harry Bidney, one of the organizers of anti-fascist networks in Britain, Stieg Larsson had written: 'There are a few who go the whole way and devote all their energies and their entire lives to active battle. They are the warriors who are all too aware of the extent of the far-Right threat to democracy, human rights and human dignity.'

STIEG LARSSON AND ANNA-LENA LODENIUS'S BOOK was published in 1991. It was a year when Sweden entered a new and dramatic phase. The liberalization of the economy was a matter that had been pushed by the Swedish Employers' Federation and the Moderates to start with, and had afterwards gained advocates in the Social Democratic Party as well. The credit market had been deregulated in 1985, introducing the period of so-called Santa Claus credit. Having big loans was seen as a good thing in itself, especially if you didn't need them. Finance companies like Nyckeln, Gamlestaden and Independent expanded their activities by lending large sums for extensive speculation, especially in property – not only in Sweden but in European cities such as London and Brussels. Property values shot up, to be succeeded by the inevitable crash. When Nyckeln went bankrupt in September 1990 the crisis was a fact: property companies and finance corporations collapsed and soon even the major commercial banks began to wobble. There now came frequent admonishments that people were living beyond their means, particularly if they had not earned a penny from the rise in share values. It was all stick and no carrot in the emergency programme introduced by the Social Democrat government in the spring of 1990, with a wage freeze, suspension of local taxation and a prohibition on strikes.

The crisis brought not only unemployment and fear in its wake, but also extremism and xenophobia. The press agency TT, where Stieg Larsson still had his full-time job, was sending out regular reports of arson attacks, Molotov cocktails thrown at refugee camps and assaults on individual immigrants, bombs hurled into immigrant-owned shops, crucifix-burning in immigrants' gardens and so on.

From 1989 to 1991 there were ninety such incidents. They were described as a series of deplorable offences without any real connection. Sweden did not want to admit that it had a wave of terror on its hands.

By the beginning of the 1990s Stieg Larsson was no longer active in the Socialist Party, concentrating all his energies instead on the struggle against right-wing extremism and racism. But the party still existed. In fact it had had its best days in the mid-1980s, unlike other left-wing groups. Håkan Blomqvist remembers how different things were in the summer of 1991, when the party tried to hold an election meeting outside Åhléns department store in Stockholm: 'This was a low point when everything went pear-shaped. Very few people wanted to turn out and campaign for us, and when we tried to sell Internationalen to young passers-by, they laughed scornfully. Then, as we were about to make our speeches, all we got was loudspeaker feedback, and at the very same moment a real blast from Sergels torg, from a sound system that actually worked: "All together now! Here we come! All against the nanny state!" And above us floated a cloud of yellow balloons bearing the face of a cheerful old man and I remember a girl next to me putting her head in her hands, and we all thought, "My God, how far away the 1970s seem." It really was a new era that had arrived, and we hadn't noticed, not until that moment.'

IN THE AUTUMN OF 1990 Sweden acquired a political party that was unlike any in its history. It was set up by a record company director from the town of Skara who had made millions from Swedish dance band music, and a buffoon from the nobility who had recently been a senior manager in business but had been sacked and now wanted to take his revenge by embarking on a political career. New Democracy (Ny demokrati), as the party was called, lacked organization but was helped on its way by an article in the national daily *Dagens Nyheter*, and was soon said to have the support of more than 20 per cent of the voters. If that were indeed the case, it was not just the economy that was in crisis in Sweden.

New Democracy was at least 50 per cent a true child of neo-liberalism. Ian Wachtmeister had been one of the motivating forces in the New Welfare Foundation, the think tank that advocated market solutions and the reduction of the public sector. He had wanted to turn the foundation into a political party, but his proposal had been rejected. He now had a further opportunity to play the politician. And with Bert Karlsson as his squire, the popular emphasis was guaranteed.

Meetings were held across the whole country, with a really catchy campaign song that helped draw the crowds. The media covered it all, for this party, with the cheerful old man as its symbol, was a sign of the times and quite unlike any of the others. With their demands for reduced taxation and cuts in public expenditure, and their scathing criticism of the political establishment, they were of course labelled a typical party of discontent; their response was that they were more a party of contentment, because they were so much more fun than all the other parties. Immigrants and refugees were less than reassured, however, since New Democracy flirted fairly openly with the growing xenophobia of public opinion.

In the autumn of 1991, when Sweden got a Conservative government under the leadership of Carl Bildt, the party entered parliament with a not unexpected 7 per cent of the vote, and with a considerable potential influence, since neither of the two main blocs had an overall majority. The 'Reality Party', as New Democracy styled itself, had arrived at the centre of power.

But it was still a party which, despite claiming a broad popular base, actually represented only a tiny sector of the electorate.

Stieg Larsson made the cynical observation that 'The interests New Democracy represents are obvious when you examine the composition of its parliamentary group: 22 of the total of 25 who were voted in are men, and over half of these New Democrat MPs call themselves directors. Every second New Democrat in parliament has his own business, and a third have at some juncture been declared bankrupt.'

IN AUGUST THAT YEAR, in the middle of the most intensive of election campaigns, an Eritrean student was shot and wounded in Stockholm. The victim thought he had seen a dancing red spot on his jacket before the bullet hit him. At first the police assumed it must be some irresponsible youths playing around with firearms. Then in October an Iranian student was shot in the head, but survived, and shortly after that there were two more such attacks. It seemed that there must be a madman on the loose, aiming a laser weapon at dark-skinned people and shooting to kill. The newspapers christened him Laser Man and printed column after column on this frightening figure lurking in the shadows and aiming his laser sights at anyone with the wrong skin colour who happened to pass by.

While this was going on, the press were also writing about a new Nazi group with a more vicious reputation than anything previously experienced. It called itself Vitt Ariskt Motstånd (White Aryan Resistance, VAM), borrowing the name from one of the most extremist groups in the USA. VAM recruited from among Nazi skinheads who had acted as bodyguards for the Nordic National Party, Keep Sweden

Swedish and the Sweden Democrats. The young skinheads had done what was asked of them on the streets but were barely even thanked for it. In fact, as soon as these organizations decided to clean up their grubby image, they were abandoned and kicked out.

Their idol was the White Power rocker Ian Stuart, who had had a similar experience with the National Front in Britain. Like Stuart, they decided to rely on their own resources. They already had their own music and had started publishing their own magazines, encouraged by and even given financial support by their British equivalent, *Blood & Honour*. And these magazines, like *Vit Rebell* and *Storm*, could now, without external pressure or censorship, be filled with endless diatribes against Jews, Communists and the mass media, tributes to former Nazi leader Rudolf Hess and conspiracy theories about the Zionist Occupation Government.

VAM went furthest of all. Some of its adherents were in direct communication with the much-feared American terror group The Order and, following their example, saw themselves as an armed underground resistance movement that would liberate Sweden with an out-and-out race war. Burglaries of military stores and bank robberies would bring in weapons and money. But the police located VAM's headquarters, in a house on Drottningholm, only a stone's throw from the royal palace. They went in and discovered enough equipment for a small army; the two leaders, however, Klas Lund and Christoffer Rangne, managed to get away. A countrywide manhunt was launched and they were eventually run to ground in Funäsdalen, in the county of Härjedalen, up near the Norwegian border, and brought to court in the main town there, Sveg, on a charge of bank robbery.

On the day the trial opened, a number of sympathizers who had come to lend support stood to attention in the visitors' gallery and gave a Nazi salute to the accused, who returned the greeting, without the stunned court being able to do anything to prevent them.

The trial of Lund and Rangne began on 8 November 1991. That very day a thirty-four-year-old Iranian was shot dead in Stockholm. Laser Man's attacks had notched up their first fatality.

In early 1992 Laser Man more or less ran amok, using a revolver to shoot six people in the course of one month, two of them on the same day. All the victims survived. But the public mood was growing tense and immigrants no longer felt safe on the streets.

People all over the country, immigrants as well as Swedes, now felt they had to act. One proposal for a protest, from Kurdo Baksi, a columnist and newspaper editor, was for a one-hour immigrant strike under the slogan 'Without immigrants Sweden would grind to a halt'. Baksi was contacted by Stieg Larsson, who wanted to know why Swedes could not also show their solidarity with those now under threat. Baksi and the strike committee made the necessary adjustment and included Swedes in the call to the strikes and demonstrations beginning on 21 February 1992. Production lines stopped at ten o'clock in many of the major industries in Sweden – Saab in Trollhättan, Scania in Södertälje, Volvo's Torslanda factory near Gothenburg – and all was quiet for an hour, or in some cases just ten minutes. There were demonstrations in the evening in Stockholm, Gothenburg and elsewhere, and extensive media coverage.

All this increased pressure on the government, who now updated themselves daily on the ongoing police hunt. As the atmosphere became more tense, the feeling grew that some proactive measures were required. But making exhortatory anti-racist speeches was not exactly Carl Bildt's style. So when Bildt and immigration minister Birgit Friggebo found themselves at a heated meeting in the immigrant suburb of Rinkeby in early February, they didn't really know how to handle it;

in a desperate attempt to pour oil on troubled waters, Friggebo called on the gathering to sing 'We Shall Overcome'. As might have been expected, it brought neither communal singing nor calm. Needing to do something, Bildt was finally forced to address the nation on TV about the attacks, while the police were working flat out on what was the biggest police investigation since the murder of Olof Palme.

But attitudes towards Laser Man were ambivalent and would remain so for years to come. Jan Lindström, a journalist on Expressen newspaper, made an apposite comment when he wrote that he was 'the personification of the prevailing mood in Sweden'. But for many he was a lone madman, a confused individual who might have pointed his gun at absolutely anyone.

Stieg Larsson was emphatically not of that opinion. He had read the American writer William Pierce, author of the novels *The Turner Diaries* and *Hunter*, the latter a homage to the solitary man of violence who, without revealing his ideology, fights for a racially pure society. So Laser Man could be seen as a role model and was also praised as such in neo-Nazi papers. He was a man for his time, although Sweden did not want to acknowledge that.

Stieg Larsson subsequently wondered about writing a book on him, but it was a project which never came to fruition. It was written instead by the journalist Gellert Tamas, and published in 2002, cogently describing how the perpetrator might have been affected by the xenophobic attacks, the growth of New Democracy and reports in the media of a deepening conflict between Swedes and immigrants.

THE YEAR 1992 WAS WHEN the world became aware of the horrors of the war in Yugoslavia. The cause was considered to be the mutual enmity of different ethnic groups, and so they had to be separated. The expression 'ethnic cleansing' began to appear in the media. It stood for exactly what the nationalist and xenophobic parties in Europe were advocating. Now, when it was seen in practice, it became clear what it meant.

The siege of Sarajevo began that year and a thousand refugees a week were arriving in Sweden, exacerbating a crisis situation. The value of the Swedish krona seemed to be entirely in the hands of international and domestic currency speculators. Bengt Dennis, head of the Bank of Sweden, flexed his muscles and raised the marginal interest rate to a sensational 75 per cent in September. It had no impact, and a week later the pale but determined Dennis announced that the rate was now to be 500 per cent. In the end the pointless defence of the krona was abandoned and it was allowed to float free against other currencies, which led to a 10 per cent devaluation but also solved the acute currency crisis. It was a crisis the outcome of which no one dared to predict. The budget deficit reached record levels, several hundred thousand people lost their jobs and the banks were getting their credit losses underwritten by the state – that is, by the taxpayers. What else could have been done? The system could not have been allowed to collapse.

Yet it was also a gratifying period for those who wanted new economic policies with more stringent budgetary reviews – and for those who demanded tougher measures against immigrants. The council leader in the Stockholm suburb of Solna, who had been lauded for making savings that had brought the lowest council tax in the country, followed up with stiffer measures on immigrants too. After an alleged spate of thefts in the area, he argued without batting an eyelid that all the Kosovo Albanians in a refugee camp in the borough should be extradited. Something really had changed in both the economic and the political climate. The question of the 1980s had been whether the Swedish model should be ditched. Now there was no longer any need to ask.

Even the new Left that was beginning to take shape among young anti-racists around then was a typical child of its times. It was individualistic, militant, extremely decentralized, frequently calling itself autonomous. The movement did not form organizations with committees and programmes. Activists often came from Syndicalist or anarchist roots and preferred direct democracy and direct action. Others saw themselves more as socialists or Marxists. And they wanted open physical confrontation with the Nazis for ownership of the streets.

In the summer of 1992 the anti-racists were able to celebrate the fact that the hunt for Laser Man was finally over. John Ausonius was apprehended during a bank raid and the police were certain he was the frightening serial attacker, a charge to which he eventually confessed.

And New Democracy, despite its influential position in parliament, had already started on a downward spiral of self-destruction with internal conflicts, exclusions, resignations and ever more overt xenophobia. Once again it seemed impossible for a party of discontent on the far Right to gain a real foothold in the Swedish political system.

A Very Little Magazine

IT WAS A PRETTY MIXED BUNCH OF YOUNG PEOPLE with journalistic ambitions and anti-racist commitment who met in Stockholm in the spring of 1995 to discuss the possibility of launching a new magazine. Most of them knew one another already and had some kind of background in journalism, and most had been active in anti-racist campaigns. One person was older and considerably more experienced than the rest: Stieg Larsson, who worked for the TT Press Agency and had established himself as one of the greatest experts on right-wing extremism both in Sweden and internationally.

In the late 1980s and early 1990s there were quite a few journalists interested in the ultra-Right. And a lot of nasty things were being attributed to the extremists, so there was good reason to keep an eye on them. Stieg Larsson used to meet up with professional colleagues at the Press Club on Vasagatan in Stockholm to share experiences. Apart from that, there was hardly any other journalistic investigation of neo-Nazism at all.

Stieg had also noticed that there tended to be a dichotomy within anti-racism, towards either increasingly militant activism or a more political and theoretical approach. And there were those who belonged to neither camp: young people who wanted to work systematically against right-wing extremism and racism and were worried generally about developments in Sweden. The individuals who started *Expo* came into the latter category. Stieg described his own role in this context as 'a sort of consultant', which was most definitely an understatement.

Setting up a magazine is a dream that nearly all journalists harbour at some stage or other in their youth. Actually doing it requires great determination, but it was obvious that the young editorial staff had this. They had also concluded that enough was enough, that it was time to take active steps to halt the advance of the neo-Nazi and racist groups.

However, it was not a particularly well-planned project, according to Andreas Rosenlund, who was one of those establishing the tenor of what was to be the first editorial team. The venture owed more to the energy and dedication of those involved than to any clear concept of how the editorial work should be performed. He himself had come up to Stockholm from the province of Småland, where he had worked on *Smålandstidningen* in Mariannelund. He had been involved in the Stop Racism movement and saw the new magazine as a natural continuation of what he had already been fighting for.

Another member of the group, Tobias Hübinette, had used the name *Expo* for a stencilled information leaflet on Nazis and right-wing extremists that he had published. The others thought it sounded good and so the magazine's name was decided upon. It was going to concentrate on monitoring, fact-finding and exposing, rather than publishing opinion and argument.

Expo had affinities with the journal *Stoppa rasismen*, for which Stieg Larsson had worked as a writer, but the remit of detailed research on far-Right and fascist organizations would be much stronger. This was to be proper investigative journalism.

Expo had a team of idealistic writers and plenty of topics to write about. What it lacked was financial backing. But the editorial team nevertheless managed to scrape together enough money from various sources to enable them to rent a little office in Zinkensdamm on Söder-malm, so they were sure they could publish at least the first issue.

They sent out order forms to everyone they knew and since a surprising number took up the subscription offer it looked as if they might even be in a position to continue for a while.

THE PREPARATORY WORK LEADING UP TO PUBLICATION OF *Expo* was done in the summer and early autumn of 1995. Some might have thought it was actually several years too late to take this initiative, because the majority of the hard-line VAM activists were safely under lock and key in various prisons and VAM itself had been disbanded, though replaced by something more like a political party, the National Socialist Front. New Democracy had received only 1.4 per cent of the votes in the 1994 elections and thus lost all their seats in parliament at one fell swoop. The most recent opinion poll showed them to be down to a record low 0.5 per cent. The Sweden Democrats, the party that had succeeded the Sweden Party, were spending most of their time on internal squabbles and continually threatening one another with court proceedings, and seemed generally exhausted.

But those like Stieg Larsson with experience of the way the far Right functioned did not hold out much hope that they would disappear so easily from the scene. He used to say such things went in waves – a suspicion that was to be confirmed in a terrifying fashion even before the first issue of *Expo* came out.

IN THE MIDDLE OF AUGUST THAT YEAR a fourteen-year-old schoolboy, John Hron, from the little village of Kode near Kungälv in western Sweden, had gone camping by a lake with a friend. They had made a fire in the evening and were sitting chatting. Not far away a gang of Nazi youths were drinking beer when they saw the fire and decided to go and see who their neighbours were. The youngest of the boys recognized John as someone he had quarrelled with at school. This would be a good moment to make him pay for it. The whole Nazi gang set upon John, beating and kicking him about the body and head. They threatened to kill him, forced him to praise Nazism and finally threw him in the lake. But they regretted doing that as soon as they saw that he was swimming away and would escape from them. So they threatened to kill John's friend unless he called John back, which he did – and John turned and swam ashore, straight into the hands of his tormentors, who resumed the beating even more savagely, a long-drawn-out hour of torture ending with John lying unconscious on the ground. They then flung him in the water again. This time he sank like a stone, while the perpetrators calmly lit up cigarettes.

Only a few weeks after this a young refugee from the Ivory Coast, Gerard Gbeyo, was found dead in a park in the small town of Klippan in northern Skåne. He had been lying there some hours before anyone reacted. He was just visiting, having arrived by bus on the Friday evening, and had been spotted by some drunken skinheads with Nazi sympathies. One of them pointed at him and suggested that they should 'stick him'. Before the sixteen-year-old murderer stabbed his victim he put on a swastika armband.

A few days after this a black-painted turnip was found in the bushes where Gbeyo had lain dead, with a handwritten note on a piece of paper attached: 'In memory of a man who brought us nothing, except great expense. Residents of Klippan'.

In this as well as in the Kode case, the police were able to identify and arrest the assailant and his accomplice quite quickly.

WHEN *EXPO* PUBLISHED ITS FIRST ISSUE IN EARLY OCTOBER 1995, Sweden was still reeling from these barbaric murders. But while many people, including the police, saw the events as unrelated, the new magazine was able to demonstrate that they were part of a broader pattern, and that a further six murders had been carried out by, or with links to, the extreme Right that very same year.

With its rather dreary A4 format, its lack of colour printing and its cheap paper, the magazine didn't look much. The name, typographically rendered as *eXpo*, was also its logo and identifying device. The editorial box gave an impression of semi-secrecy with its abbreviated form of names (M. Karlsson, J. Larsson), but on the back cover they were able to list a number of well-known politicians, religious leaders, writers, musicians and sports stars who publicly endorsed the new project and indicated the breadth of coverage it was aiming at.

Expo was a little magazine which had sprouted from left-of-centre activism. It comprised a small circle of people who had taken it upon themselves to monitor groups which were fiercely secretive and also potentially violent. There was an obvious risk that the anti-fascist group would begin to resemble its antagonists in introverted and conspiratorial thinking, regarding with suspicion or contempt those who might profess opposition to racism without the same degree of awareness and determination as themselves.

Stieg Larsson had certainly seen all too much division and infighting on the Left. He still remembered the bitter experience of Grenada, where friends and party colleagues had murdered one another. He was no stranger to the need for a certain measure of secrecy, but at the same time realized that *Expo* had to open itself up to society at large if it were to survive. He pointed out that opposition to Nazism and racism was the only factor that united all the democratic parties and organizations. So it was important to keep up contacts with every established party, and especially the individuals and associations who shared the magazine's objectives: 'To defend democracy and freedom of expression in the battle against racist, right-wing extremist and totalitarian ideologies'. It sounded like the old united-front thinking from the glory days of the Left. But the difference was that there was now no hidden agenda.

So even before starting they had made contact with the political youth groups and received support from all except the Moderates – although the latter came on board after the first few issues. Some other firms, organizations and journals backed the project, such as the Swedish Committee Against Anti-Semitism, the Workers' Educational Association, the investment firm Proventus and the record company MNW. The editor-in-chief initially was Mikael Karlsson. Andreas Rosenlund took over from the beginning of 1996 until his resignation from the magazine in 1997.

Managing *Expo* was a full-time job, but everything had to be run on a shoestring. 'Basically, everyone was paid a salary if there was any money,' Andreas Rosenlund says. The magazine did not have any capitalist owner behind it. Nor were there enough funds to form a limited company, so instead they created a non-profit trust, the Hill Foundation, named after Ray Hill, *Searchlight*'s mole within British fascism.

As well as the compilation of neo-Nazi murders, the first issue of the magazine included an article describing the arrival in Sweden of the neo-Nazi international intelligence service, which had been set up by the violent British fascist organization Combat 18. Its aim was to monitor in turn all the anti-fascist activists in order to threaten and harass them whenever the opportunity arose. This was a far-sighted article, as events would show a few years later.

Expo also wrote about the wave of desecrations of Jewish cemeteries in Sweden. And they introduced what they called their calendar, which was the magazine's central feature. It was not, as might have been assumed, a list of events they wanted to publicize, but a much more depressing review of right-wing extremist acts of violence, campaigns, meetings, concerts, etc. which had taken place since the previous issue. The material was submitted by a network of reporters or garnered from various provincial newspapers. They also ordered copious trial proceedings from courts around the country. Collating the material was a laborious task, but the effect of the compilation was striking. When it was all brought together like that, the picture that emerged was very much more dramatic than anything else that had reached the public domain.

The first issue of the magazine aroused a good deal of media attention. *Dagens Nyheter*, one of the two leading national dailies, commented: 'When the Laser Man shot a dozen immigrants in 1991 there were widespread protests and revulsion. According to *Expo*, racist organizations were responsible for seven murders in 1995. But the protests are less vociferous. That is why we need *Expo*.'

The Stockholm daily, *Aftonbladet*, said: 'It's a crap job, but somebody has to do it. So the rest of us can get on with ours.'

THE IDEA OF A BROAD POLITICAL COALITION was not shared by everyone fighting the far Right. Antifascistisk Aktion (Anti-Fascist Action, AFA), for example, rather like the Trotskyists in the 1970s, thought the fascist groups should not be allowed public space to show their growing strength and unity, but must be confronted directly on the streets and prevented from holding their rallies. The lack of interest in the far Right displayed by society in general in the years around 1990 strengthened AFA's conviction that they themselves were the only ones standing up to the dangers of fascism.

When it became apparent that Stop Racism did not intend to organize any counter-demonstration against the fascist march on 30 November 1991, a group of anarchists and Syndicalists formed an anti-fascist working party with the aim of halting the demonstration. The young left-wingers blocked off Karl XII torg and forced the Nazis to retreat. That was the first occasion the name Antifascistisk Aktion was used.

Hostilities were even more extreme in Lund, where the so-called BZ-ers from Copenhagen turned up, in full gear with masked faces and wearing crash helmets, and joined with Swedish activists in building barricades and closing off the whole of Stora Södergatan, the main street in the town, stopping the right-wing extremists' Charles XII march completely.

In September 1993 a score of different anti-fascist groups from all over Sweden met at Bona folk high school (near Motala) and decided to formalize Anti-Fascist Action as a countrywide network. AFA's methods became more and more aggressive and went beyond mobilizing activists against neo-Nazi demonstrations to include threats and assaults on individuals.

'We had a huge debate within Stop Racism about the use of violence,' Kenneth Lewis remembers. 'The view of the majority, which I shared, was that violence could only be justified in self-defence. The groups which had combined to form AFA were of quite a different opinion. They wanted to hunt out and attack their opponents, and there was an inevitable split even though we tried to avoid it for as long as possible. This unfortunately meant that much of the broad-based support the anti-racist movement had gained in the 1980s, from trade unions for example, evaporated, and there's no doubt that the bellicose groups with their covered faces and their glorification of violence damaged the anti-racist cause.'

A seething hatred arose between the militant youth at the far extremes of Left and Right. *Expo* was in the thick of it and yet detached from it.

The original *Expo* group included people who had belonged to AFA, but, according to Andreas Rosenlund, all of them left when the magazine started: '*Expo*'s task was not to do what AFA was doing, taking to the streets and confronting the Nazis with their own methods. Rather, it was opinion-forming, persuading society to accept its responsibility for fighting xenophobic propaganda and neo-Nazi brutality.'

STIEG LARSSON'S FIRST ARTICLE IN *EXPO* concerned an event he was to return to on several occasions and to which he clearly attached a great deal of significance – the bomb attack on the federal building in Oklahoma City in the USA which took place in April 1995 and in which 168 people lost their lives. The perpetrator, Timothy McVeigh, was not a Nazi, as far as was known, but rather an extreme libertarian, an opponent of all state control, and the outrage was, by his own account, revenge for the authorities' assault on the apocalyptic Davidian sect in Waco in 1993.

Yet the Oklahoma massacre had obvious links with the far Right, since McVeigh's inspiration was an obscure novel by a writer who called himself Andrew McDonald but whose real name was William Pierce. He was far from unknown in American neo-Nazi circles. As a young man he had studied physics and had set his sights on an academic career, but he became obsessed with the Jewish question and taught himself political history, turning in a very short time from the promising Dr Jekyll of the natural sciences to a bloodthirsty Mr Hyde of racist ideology.

Pierce soon rejected the traditional right-wing extremists in the John Birch Society, of which he had been a member. They may have had the correct views, but they did not understand the importance of total devotion to the white cause. What Pierce dreamed of was an elite white force, all-out battles and unadulterated violence, and he injected these fantasies into a fictional narrative, a sort of science-fiction novel published under the title *The Turner Diaries*.

The book is set in a future where the USA is governed by a mixed-race administration, a decline without parallel of course, and in the chaos that ensues a few determined men form a guerrilla movement and take up the struggle against state authority. They are ruled by a mysterious group of ideologists called The Order, who have realized the battle has to be waged without any restraint or moral scruples. The white guerrillas blow up FBI headquarters and many hundreds of people die. The conflict intensifies, the multicultural mixed-race society collapses and the resolute white forces take control and set about hanging racial traitors and exterminating all the Jews. Other countries of the world go through the same process, and in the grand finale all non-white peoples are eradicated from the earth and the

Aryans' descendants start to build the higher civilization they were originally intended to create.

The Turner Diaries became a cult book unlike any other in US extremist circles. It was said to have sold half a million copies, and one of these evidently found its way to McVeigh, who put it to practical use: the bomb that he planted in Oklahoma, an explosive charge of artificial fertilizer and engine oil, is described in exact detail in the book.

IN A LITTLE TOWN IN THE CRISIS-STRICKEN agricultural Midwest a kind of white Free State for 'Christian autonomy' had been set up in the early 1980s. It soon became a haven for the most extremist of the militia groups, anti-federalists and White Power adherents. An organization called Aryan Nations took shape, and under its auspices the tenets of American neo-Nazism were formulated, above all the notorious ZOG concept, the Zionist Occupation Government, which was an umbrella term for everything the neo-Nazi groups were fighting against – Jews, Negroes, advocates of mixed races, the liberal media and politicians.

The whole mish-mash of ideas seems so bizarre, so far removed from any recognizable reality, that it is difficult to see how it could gain popularity at all. But when in the early 1990s the Swedish neo-Nazi skinheads affiliated to *Storm* magazine first read about and then made contact with Aryan Nations, it was not long before the ZOG term came to Sweden. It was a sort of password, a doctrine of salvation and a key to understanding that the world was completely different from the way the politicians and media defined it and people in general believed it to be. It was rather like the science-fiction film *Matrix*, where the secure everyday environment that humans are living in is found to be technologically simulated by evil machines that have subjugated the planet.

Only those who have attained higher enlightenment can see through the illusion and take up arms against the system that enslaves them.

In *The Turner Diaries* the secret society The Order plays exactly that role. And fiction became fact when a guerrilla group of that name, originating from Aryan Nations and a few other extremist associations, declared war on ZOG. It carried out a number of barbaric acts before it was broken up by the police. One of the leaders was shot dead in a siege and other individuals were given lengthy prison sentences.

This was the complex of ideas that Stieg Larsson drew attention to, and indeed to the propensity to violence and the expertise in terrorism that had built up around it. Moreover, precisely the same ideas about ZOG and the same cult of violence were now to be found in Sweden, principally in an organization centred on the discontinued magazine *Storm* which had taken the name Storm Network and whose members had been convicted of numerous serious crimes of violence.

One reason why groups of this nature could establish themselves relatively undisturbed in the USA was that the country lacked laws prohibiting extremist groups and hate propaganda. The ringleaders behind The Order could not be prosecuted, for instance, only the foot soldiers.

But Sweden was no different. In fact, if anything it was even more liberal than the USA, Stieg Larsson thought: 'A Swedish racist who throws a bomb at a refugee facility, an outrage which would bring an automatic ten-year prison sentence in Italy, might get a few months in jail or a fine for arson. The crime of political terrorism in Sweden is reserved exclusively for foreigners, and only Kurds have ever been imprisoned for it.'

STIEG LARSSON WANTED TO CREATE A SWEDISH *SEARCHLIGHT* or something like it – not simply to publish a magazine, but also to build up a solid archive of information on the far Right. Only meticulous documentation would enable extremist groups to be exposed and not escape justice.

Stieg had collected a large amount of material himself before the arrival of *Expo*. But now the opportunity had arisen to assemble a comprehensive archive consisting of printed matter, press cuttings, books and other information on the ultra-Right, not least their own newspapers, magazines, leaflets, records, catalogues, stickers and so on. In due course, as *Expo* acquired more and more contacts within the groups through people who had defected or who were on the point of leaving, it had access to internal minutes too.

But Stieg actually had higher aims than that. He wanted *Expo* to cooperate with the world of research, and the knowledge and documentation the magazine possessed to have a broader application. It would be via contacts and recognition in the academic world that *Expo* would throw off its reputation of being a journal for political activists and achieve recognized expert status in its field.

While still a young student, Ulla Ekström von Essen, lecturer in the history of ideas at Södertörn College, had wanted to write an essay on the doctrines of the Swedish White Aryan Resistance (VAM), but in those days, the early 1990s, it was not so simple. Their beliefs were perceived as too eccentric and extremist to be assimilated into the history of ideas and scarcely any academic work had been done on the modern far Right then. She got in touch with Stieg Larsson instead and received immediate encouragement and advice, including a lot of material from him that was not easy to obtain.

'I visited him at TT and remember him copying the whole of *The Turner Diaries* for me, because he thought I absolutely must read it. We continued to work together later on, when I was giving a course on the history of racist ideas.'

For Stieg himself *Expo* provided the opportunity to write almost without limitations on the subject that was the great commitment of his life and that he knew better than anyone else in Sweden. He kept rather in the background, however, and did not aspire to any of the editorial posts on the magazine. Yet he influenced it in various ways, especially in the direction he wished it to take.

Its international focus, for instance, was fundamental. Without that, it was impossible to see how personal alliances were forged across borders and how ideas were further disseminated in extremist circles and networks on the far Right. From the outset, therefore, regular cooperation was established with sister journals in Europe – as well as *Searchlight* in Britain, there was *AntiFaInfoblatt* in Germany, Reflex in France and *Monitor* in Norway.

Through his international grapevine Stieg was also able to involve writers from other countries in *Expo*. He got Andrew Vachss to contribute as a columnist; he was a prominent crime writer, lawyer and public voice against the ill-treatment and sexual abuse of children. Likewise on board from the very first issue was the film-maker Michael Schmidt, well known for his shocking and challenging film on German neo-Nazism, *Wahrheit macht frei* (Truth is Liberating – a title alluding to the notorious concentration camp slogan '*Arbeit macht frei*').

In Germany, overtly Nazi organizations were and still are illegal, the swastika and Nazi salute forbidden. So the German Nazism that evolved in the 1980s was very much a covert activity, difficult to get to grips with and also full of rancour, loathing and thuggery. But Schmidt nevertheless resolved to infiltrate it and make a documentary film to lift the veil, succeeding beyond all expectations. He made contact with the best-known neo-Nazi of the day, Michael Kühnen, leader of the umbrella organization GdNF (Gesinnungsgemeinschaft der Neuen Front), or Die Bewegung (The Movement) as it was usually called. Kühnen was very positive about the film proposal: he thought it would be useful for Nazi propaganda.

Michael Schmidt was secretly in close communication with *Searchlight* and Graeme Atkinson during his preparations for the project, and he also met Stieg Larsson. Stieg put him in touch with Swedish Television and producer Birgitta Karlström, whose support facilitated the editing. The film had its premiere on Swedish TV, attracted a lot of attention and was subsequently shown in many European countries.

At about the same time that the film was on TV in Sweden, the autumn of 1991, Germany was celebrating the first anniversary of reunification. But a deep shadow was cast over the festivities by serious outbreaks of systematic Nazi attacks on refugees and refugee facilities, starting that year and continuing into the next. The culmination was in Rostock, the East German Baltic port, where racist youths terrorized a transit camp for Vietnamese refugees for several days with firebombs, while the local police were unable to control the situation. It all ended in rioting after the Ministry of the Interior sent in special police reinforcements to put a stop to the attacks.

Schmidt's film dealt with the root causes of these events. Reading about neo-Nazis in newspapers and books was one thing, but seeing their hatred erupting, hearing their anti-Semitic diatribes and witnessing their delight in violence and their secret weapons training in vivid, close-up, moving images was even more shocking.

In the book he went on to publish, Michael Schmidt recounted his experience of the unreal reality of neo-Nazism, describing a meeting addressed by the Dutch Nazi veteran Et Wolsink:

Wolsink gives the Nazi salute, a genuine one. Again all the skinheads roar their bellicose *Sieg Heil*, repeatedly. This is not a show, Wolsink's arm movements are pure reflex. How naturally this veteran passes on the rituals of the Third Reich! I suddenly have a feeling of being in another world whose existence I knew nothing of just a year ago. Hitler is worshipped here, in all seriousness. In circles sworn to secrecy people are working towards a single goal: to destroy democracy and reinstate a dictatorship.

THE FIRST NUMBER OF *EXPO* and articles in subsequent issues took up what was perhaps the most remarkable element of Sweden's right-wing extremism: White Power music. Racist hard rock had been born in Britain and one of its biggest names, Ian Stuart, performed in Sweden when Rock Against Communism was created in 1988. The music became a shared culture for the independent skinhead groups, giving vent to their aggression and also creating a sense of commu-nity. It developed into something of a speciality for Swedish neo-Nazi youth. In the early 1990s Sweden had as many White Power bands as the whole of the USA put together. Swedish record companies and distributors were sending it out all over the Western world.

Music meant money for the neo-Nazis, proving more profitable than the old criminal methods of financing their activities. To paraphrase Bertolt Brecht, they must have thought robbing a bank was nothing compared to founding a record company.

But the new musical vogue had a variety of nuances, at least as far as the lyrics were concerned. Crude Nazi expression à la Ian Stuart and his Swedish disciples was not the only option. In Nyköping, for instance, a town known for its resistance to taking in refugees, there was Ultima Thule, a band with a more vaguely Old Norse flavour. They sang about Thor and Odin, sacrifice and Valhalla, but above all about something that never existed in the Viking era: Sweden. In the late 1980s they were playing to the xenophobic supporters of Keep Sweden Swedish, and in 1990 released a record with a Nazi-linked record company in Germany under the jaunty title *Hurra för Nordens länder!* (Hurrah for the Nordic Countries!). They made hard-rock versions of the Swedish national anthem, *'Du gamla du fria'* (Thou ancient, thou free), and of Ulf Peder Olrog's *'Schottis på Valhall'* (Schottische in Valhalla) and seemed to be gaining in universal popularity. Bert Karlsson, always highly sensitive to potential trends, suspected that this was tapping some emotion deep in the collective unconscious and was quick to sign them up to his label Mariann Records. That was the commercial breakthrough for Viking Rock, and the band, now said to be distancing themselves from racism and Nazism, even achieved two gold discs before Bert Karlsson terminated their contract in view of all the vehement criticism he had to endure because of his abusive protégés.

Even though it was a big step from Mariann Records, with its old-fashioned dance bands, to 88 Music AB and Ragnarock Records, with their clamorous death-metal bands like Dirlewanger and White Aggression, the breakthrough of Ultima Thule into the mainstream mass market was a huge inspiration to new bands in Sweden. A rather grey area arose midway between the general homage to Swedishness, Swedish history, Vikings and the like, and the crystal-clear ideology of racist patriotism. This of course was easy for the people and producers behind White Power music to exploit. And it led – by no means least – to neo-Nazism getting its first well-produced propaganda publication, *Nordland* magazine. In external appearance, with its four-colour printing on the cover and fairly professional layout, it looked like any other magazine, but in terms of content it was mainly an advertising medium and mail-order catalogue for White Power music. The actual journal was financed from record sales and so quite a high proportion of each print run could be distributed free, to schools for example.

The adult generation did not notice much of all this. But the younger generation certainly did. Green Party politician and journalist Gustav

Fridolin, born in 1983 and raised in a little village in northern Skåne, wrote a book, *Blåsta: Nedskärningsåren som formade en generation* (Conned: Recession Years that Formed a Generation), in which he describes Viking rock being

> as obligatory at teenage parties as witches' brew and cheap booze. When I think back to memories of shaven skulls headbanging to cover versions of *Kostervalsen* [a traditional waltz named after a type of Swedish west coast boat], it's difficult not to burst out laughing. But then, in the rush of hormones and fury at feeling excluded, that seemed a perfectly normal thing to do. New versions of Sven-Bertil Taube, Ulf Lundell and the national anthem were the obvious accompaniment to our resentment.

THERE WERE SEVERAL FACTORS THAT LED to Sweden becoming a centre for White Power music, but one, as *Expo* and other journalists pointed out, was that Sweden, unlike many other European countries, had no laws expressly prohibiting neo-Nazi organizations or businesses. The lyrics of the neo-Nazi music might be prosecuted as incitement to hatred of ethnic minorities, but that charge rarely secured a conviction. The record producers also learned the trick of altering the printed lyrics, so that, for instance, the word *Jew* would be written as *you*, and anyone trying to check for indictable transgressions would find it almost impossible to catch what was actually being sung against the cacophonous instrumental background.

Ultima Thule had been able to rehearse their Viking songs with support from their local council and in Stockholm the young skinheads had been allocated their own sanctum that was both approved and financed by the municipal authorities. Fryshuset (The Icehouse) was and still is a respected activity centre for young people situated in Norra Hammarbyhamnen in Stockholm. It was set up in the 1980s by Anders Carlberg in cooperation with the Swedish YMCA (KFUM).

Carlberg was one of the more legendary leaders of the 1968 generation, to which Stieg Larsson also belonged, but he went on to become a Social Democrat politician and a passionate advocate of the need for society to do much more to help socially excluded youth.

At the time, Stockholmers felt frightened by young skinheads of intimidating appearance with Nazi symbols adorning their clothes and few people wanted to have anything to do with them. But Carlberg thought that was precisely what was required. They should be listened to, given a sense of direction, activities of their own, and thus inspired with a more positive view of society to pull them back from racist sectarianism. It was an admirable strategy, of course, but Fryshuset's provision for skinheads actually turned out to be far more problematical.

Expo expressed criticism of what had been going on for some eight years or so among the skinheads on the Fryshuset premises. The magazine conducted a detailed examination of all the activities and concluded that the skinheads had been allowed to cultivate their subculture and their alienation from society, and even their beer drinking, undisturbed and unhindered. And that the notorious VAM had been using the premises as a recruitment base, that Nazi magazines had been openly sold there, that White Power bands had held gigs there and that they had used public money to teach themselves desk-top publishing, with visible results in the typographical improvements to the White Power magazine *Nordland*.

But Anders Carlberg thought that bands such as Ultima Thule were not so much racist as actively nationalistic. He felt that these dysfunctional youths could be brought round to a more positive masculinity by taking part in survival courses, having a taste of tough commando training, along the lines of the American poet Robert Bly's book *Iron John*, a typical cult philosophy of the 1990s.

Skinhead culture really flourished after Ultima Thule's success, and even the king came to Fryshuset and played darts with the shaven-headed young men beneath the VAM symbol of the wolf's hook. But on New Year's Day 1995 a sixteen-year-old boy was found murdered outside the premises, with one hand severed, and the media began to publish articles critical of the activities there, which in turn led to cutbacks and the introduction of tighter controls.

STIEG LARSSON HAD IMBIBED FROM *SEARCHLIGHT* a highly developed awareness of the need for security which had already been applied in the editorial offices. Many of the paper's writers were anonymous. The address was just a postbox number. Outsiders were not admitted without checks. As well as protecting themselves, this must also have contributed to the air of mystery surrounding the magazine. Andreas Rosenlund thinks in retrospect that it was rather too paranoid in some ways. But in Britain people were used to even more stringent measures than in Sweden.

And it was not long before the potential threat turned into grim reality. In the first issue of 1996 Stieg Larsson wrote an article on the formation of the National Alliance which he called 'the big political event of the winter for the far Right'. The man who had taken the initiative was Christoffer Rangne, the VAM member who had ended up in prison for armed robbery and become a martyr in the eyes of neo-Nazi youth. He had now been released and was able with some authority to try to revive what seemed a dead project – gathering the various neo-Nazi groups under one umbrella organization.

There were very good reasons to take the National Alliance seriously, Stieg argued. The sanitized far-Right party, the Sweden Democrats, was in decline, while White Power music was in the ascendant, which created a situation that radicalized the young towards the Right.

The unambiguous singling out of the National Alliance caused *Expo*, which had only published three issues, to be seen as a thorn in the flesh of the neo-Nazis, and they began a consolidated campaign against the magazine in the spring of 1996, including attacks, harassment and menaces against individuals and firms that had dealings with it.

The first such sabotage was aimed at a tobacconist who sold the magazine in his shop. The windows were smashed and the owner received death threats. Then it was the turn of a number of political youth groups which gave financial or moral support to *Expo*, as well as other political associations, like the Syndicalists, the Red Room bookshop, the Workers' Educational Association and the kibbutz association Svekiv. The gravest incident was the firebombing of Green Youth in Stockholm. After further threats directed at retail outlets, Guiden Tryck, the printing house in Bromma which produced the magazine, was targeted. The culprits smashed windows and sprayed swastikas on the walls with warnings not to print *Expo*. The printers admitted they were no longer willing to risk printing it, many retailers refused to stock it and *Expo*'s position soon became precarious.

Andreas Rosenlund remembers that it was all very oppressive. The Nazis didn't know where *Expo*'s editorial office was located, which was why outsiders were bearing the brunt.

The media had not reported what had been happening because the police thought that publicity might impede their investigations. The staff at *Expo* were frustrated. Stieg Larsson and his editorial colleagues tried in vain to make the police listen to their view that these were not isolated acts but a centrally organized campaign.

The situation soon became untenable for them and they decided to go public. First of all a summary of events was published in the liberal magazine *Nu* (Now), then *Dagens Nyheter* picked it up and other media followed, one after another. The *Expo* affair suddenly sparked a national media frenzy. The well-known historian Peter Englund, now secretary of the Swedish Academy, appeared on television with harsh criticism of police passivity.

The indignation was understandable. It was unprecedented in Sweden for a publication to risk closure because of threats from those of different convictions. The evening newspapers *Aftonbladet* and *Expressen* agreed they would both publish *Expo's* latest issue on the same day, 10 June, as a supplement to their papers. *Expo*, with an average distribution of a couple of thousand copies, suddenly jumped to over 800,000.

The police also invested more resources in the hunt for the perpetrators. Even before the joint publication by the evening papers, they had raided the National Alliance in the middle of a party on their premises. The leader of the organization was taken in for questioning. But there was no definitive evidence that they had been behind the series of attacks, so there was no prosecution.

The campaign against *Expo* nevertheless represented a real own goal by the neo-Nazis. The magazine they had wanted to silence continued to be published and was actually much more widely known than before. The National Alliance was dissolved shortly afterwards, early in 1997, though the young activists soon found new groups to join. Expansion, splitting, disappearance and re-emergence in alternative guises were the habitual pattern of neo-Nazi activity.

Expo's problems continued, however. Despite the free publicity in the media, it was hard to balance the books financially. The print run had to be reduced rather than increased and, as with all non-profit journals with almost non-existent income, holding on to staff proved difficult. Nor did any significant financial contributions flow in, as might have been expected after the threats. *Expo* had applied for 700,000 kronor from the Swedish Arts Council to pay for an editorial post and cover the rent. They were awarded 20,000, which they returned as a gesture of anger and disappointment. By the end of 1997 it was fairly evident that they were on the verge of bankruptcy, and at the beginning of the following year it was decided to close down.

Most of those working on *Expo* were reconciled to there being no possibility of continuing, at least as an independent magazine. But all were agreed that the unique archive must be saved.

In the spring of 1998 Stieg Larsson turned to Kurdo Baksi with a proposal. He wanted *Expo* to be included as a separate and clearly defined section of Baksi's multi-cultural magazine *Svartvitt* (Black and White). Baksi's periodical would be responsible for printing and distribution and Baksi himself would be editor-in-chief and publisher for the merged magazines. Baksi agreed and the plan was implemented in the autumn of 1998.

Stieg remained convinced that *Expo* had to continue publication. The threat from neo-Nazi groups would not diminish. Events over the ensuing year would prove him right.

The Last Year of the Millennium

STIEG LARSSON HAD PRESUMABLY UNDERSTOOD what was going on. He had seen the extreme Right regrouping. He saw the ideological Nazis, in organizations such as the Swedish Resistance Movement, National Youth, National Socialist Front, National Front, Blood and Honour Scandinavia and the Aryan Brotherhood, heading yet deeper into their gory fantasies of hatred and violence, while the sanitized extremists in the Sweden Democrats, now with eight seats in the local council elections of 1998, had been confirmed in their conviction that they could produce a party that was both acceptable and xenophobic.

In 1997 he had witnessed something that had not been seen since the 1930s: neo-Nazis holding an anti-Jewish demonstration in commemoration of the anti-Semitic terror of *Kristallnacht*. And there had been almost no outcry at all from society at large.

And then in January 1999 Nordland, Blood and Honour, and the National Socialist Front had held a joint meeting with the aim of bringing together all the various neo-Nazi groups in Scandinavia. They prophesied that the summer of 1999 would go down in history as the 'summer of blood'.

AS THE CENTURY DREW TO A CLOSE much was said about fundamental changes and the start of a new era. It was a typically turn-of-the-century outlook. But whereas in the closing years of the nineteenth century there had been a general mood of gloom and despondency which acquired the name fin-de-siècle, now it was the opposite: society was on its way into an unprecedented phase of human history. The economy was throwing off its dependence on heavy industry and gliding into the virtual world. Knowledge and creativity would flourish while muscles atrophied and machines were sent to the scrapheap. Perhaps it was a second 1968, a youth revolution – though with quite different lodestars, of course: not politics, not ideology, but the economy and, above all, information technology.

The new heroes, young men, and more or less only men, flocked in their jeans and trainers into the new IT firms' trendy cell-like offices. These were firms hitherto unknown, but already prominent names in all the newspapers and on all the radio and TV channels: Framtidsfabriken (Future Factory), Icon Medialab, Spray, Adcore.

Journalists and politicians thought they could hear the engines of Sweden's future economy throbbing. This was a different society in the making, with new working conditions and new relationships between employers and employees. Trade unions, negotiations and agreements were things of the past. They were no longer needed now that the employees were the company and the company was a family or at least a clan. A clan that worked hard together all day and then went out for a beer together in the evening, before going back to the office and resuming work.

It somewhat resembled *Expo*, but with a different motivation: people had to fulfil the enormous expectations of financial success imposed on them by the media, investors and politicians.

Investment capital was sucked into the gaping hoppers of these new firms, but considerably less came out at the other end in the form of dividends. This was not thought important, since everything was predicated on expectations and share values. It was rather like a conjuring trick.

So stocks and shares soared upwards. The Swedish parliament had voted in a revised pension system in 1998, linking pensions to the performance of the economy and the stock market in particular, since the basic idea was that the bulk of pension fund money should be in stocks and shares. And it was not even very difficult to get broad support for such a measure. The crisis of 1990 had been forgotten and the stock market was guaranteed to go on rising for ever, at least in the long term.

Everyone seemed obsessed by the economy; saving through shares was the new Swedish popular movement and ordinary people suddenly began referring to the Nasdaq Exchange. Financial reporting was the new journalism, expanding in a growing abundance of share and investment magazines, like *Finanstidningen*, *Kapital*, *Vision*, *Smart*, but also in the increasing coverage of the major daily papers. Financial reports would be the only news people needed in the future. Though what was happening in politics and out in the wider world would continue to have its place in journalism because of its impact on the rise and fall of the stock market.

Of course there were a few who reacted against all this, who talked about another stock-market bubble and an impending crash. Stieg Larsson made no secret of his distaste for the uncritical financial journalism that had begun emerging in the 1980s and was now celebrating even greater triumphs, and he would probably have liked to write a revelatory book on the whole genre, as his fictional hero Mikael Blomkvist did.

BUT EVERYONE KNEW THERE WERE WINNERS and losers in this game. And the losers, as might have been expected, were immigrants in the big city suburbs, female care-workers, low-wage-earners in general and the unemployed.

There were many intellectuals who felt a deep unease about such developments. Many identified more with the losers than with the winners. One such was the playwright Lars Norén, a man constantly drawn to those furthest down the social scale: drug addicts, prostitutes, criminals. In the spring of 1998 he received an unexpected letter from Tidaholm prison beginning 'Dear Mr Norén'. The sender was Carl Thunberg, leader of the notorious gang known as Militärligan (The Military Mob). He wrote that a number of maximum-security prisoners had expressed an interest in taking part in a theatre project, and he wondered whether Norén might possibly help them, whether he had a play that might be appropriate for such a group; but in any case he was welcome to pay them a visit at the 'institution'.

Norén went to the jail and decided to try to create a play with the prisoners that would be about themselves and their lives, about problematic childhoods, humiliations and male aggression, and imprisonment, in both a physical and a psychological sense. Besides

Thunberg, there would be two other people on stage with avowed Nazi sympathies. Norén felt that Nazism must be included, as representing the lowest level of perdition. The convicts themselves were not keen on expressing their ideology quite so openly to an audience, but for Norén it was integral to his concept.

The play was actually finished, against all the odds, and entitled *Seven Three*, after a clause in prison regulations which restricted freedom of movement for the most refractory prisoners. It had its premiere on 6 February 1999, with the northern city of Umeå as the chosen venue.

There was total silence during the first performance. The actors thought the audience disliked what they were watching, but when the play ended the applause was deafening and there were six curtain calls. The critics were mostly positive. Swedish theatre had never before come so close to the underside of real life. But questions were immediately asked and there was even a complaint to the police about incitement to hatred of ethnic minorities. Was this theatre, fiction, or were the Nazi views expressed genuine ones? And if they were, how could audiences enjoy it as an artistic experience and applaud the performance?

Hundreds of newspaper articles were written about the production, an exhaustive book was published on the subject and a satirical play performed in Uppsala Stadsteater. Everything has been analysed and yet is still inexplicable. It seems like two parallel worlds moving alongside each other, colliding momentarily and separating again. It was a dramatist's dream of digging right down into the depths of rejection and loathing, portraying the unbearable, putting it on stage in such a form that no one could avoid confronting it. And there for all to see was the world of Nazi racial ideology, itself full of fictional notions and fantasies, yet a very real and present threat.

Some of those who observed all this at close quarters were alarmed by what they saw and detected the acrid odour of approaching catastrophe. Because even though the two prisoners were outwardly in agreement with Norén's project, they also had a hidden agenda. And that was not about taking the opportunity provided by the world of theatre to return to democratic society and a law-abiding life. The two actor-prisoners were ideologically motivated warriors in the race war and one of them, Tony Olsson, had previously been a member and district leader of the neo-Nazi organization the National Front (Riksfronten).

The final performance of *Seven Three* was at a theatre in Hallunda, south of Stockholm, on 27 May. Tony Olsson went back to Österåker prison just as he should. But he had requested and been granted parole for the following day. He was met that morning by two of his friends, Jackie Arklöv and Andreas Axelsson, who were also blatant Nazis and with whom he had had frequent contact throughout the rehearsals. They had a complete arsenal of weapons in their car.

What happened next is well known in Sweden and was endlessly discussed in the media. Having robbed a bank in Kisa in Östergötland and made off with a haul of two and a half million kronor, the trio were first pursued by one police car, which they stopped by shooting at it, and then by another. Coming to a halt by a lake just outside the village of Malexander, the robbers and the policemen in the second car opened fire on one another. The two policemen, Olov Borén and Robert Karlström, were subsequently found dead, shot at close range.

Were the events in Malexander a bank robbery that went wrong or something entirely different? The Swedish branch of the international network Blood and Honour had its explanation ready: 'The shoot-out between the National Socialists who liberated bank funds and ZOG troops is due revenge for the murder by the police of our fellow patriot Martin Krusell in Malmö in 1991.'

Later in the autumn of the same year, when the National Socialist Front were holding a meeting in a community centre near Nybro, the participants chanted, 'Up with Malexander! Two–nil to Tony Olsson!' before the police threw them off the premises.

A MONTH AFTER THOSE MURDERS, on 28 June, a journalist called Peter Karlsson was taking his eight-year-old son to his car, which was parked outside his block of flats. As he opened the car door, explosives fixed under the chassis detonated with such force that they blew out the windows in the adjacent building. Father and son were both injured, the father seriously, and the mother, who witnessed the atrocity, was in a state of severe shock.

Peter Karlsson and his partner, Katarina Larsson, were well known for investigating and publishing articles on right-wing extremist groups. They had both previously been frequent contributors to *Expo* and also wrote about political extremism for the Stockholm *Aftonbladet*. They had exposed secret producers of White Power music in Italy, which must have created resentment in far-Right networks. They knew they were a target for the neo-Nazis, lived under false identities and had been given what was called a security package, but despite all that the neo-Nazis had managed to track them down.

The official investigation of the car bombing was fruitless and the police were criticized for not finding the culprits despite the limited circles in which they must have moved.

Stieg Larsson felt increasingly indignant that society's reactions were still so muted. Could people not see that this was also an assault on the freedom of the press and freedom of expression, the cornerstones of democracy? Could they not see that these were very deliberate acts by politically motivated individuals? He wrote about the car bomb later in *Expo*:

The attack on the two journalists was not the work of an isolated psychopath. It was a carefully planned and callously implemented terrorist outrage which was intended to kill two journalists who had damaged the White Power industry with their exposés. The bomb was an attack on the very fundament of our democracy: freedom of expression and freedom of the press.

So it is all the more remarkable that the bomb in Nacka has not set off any corresponding political debate. One demonstration has been held – on Sergels torg in Stockholm the week the bomb exploded [. . .] The authorities continue to treat neo-Nazism as a youth phenomenon of drunken skinheads making trouble on Saturday nights: a social rather than a criminal problem. That may be a convenient description – but it is not true. If nothing else, the Nacka bomb ought to have put an end to that sort of naïve interpretation once and for all.

IN VIEW OF WHAT HAD ALREADY HAPPENED THAT YEAR and the extreme threat represented by the neo-Nazis, it seemed only a matter of time before there would be a purely political murder in Sweden – and indeed it became brutal reality only a few months later. On 12 October 1999, just before nine o'clock in the evening, several shots were heard from the stairwell of a block of flats on Lövsätravägen in the Stockholm suburb of Sätra. The police were on the scene within ten minutes and found a man lying dead outside the door of his flat, shot ten times with a .22-calibre pistol. He was identified as Björn Söderberg, a trade union official politically active in the Syndicalist movement, an avowed anti-Nazi and a keen sportsman.

The police were quick to apprehend three suspects. According to court proceedings, a young man by the name of Hampus Hellekant had been seen keeping watch on the journalist couple Peter Karlsson and Katarina Larsson before the attack on them. The security police had had him under surveillance since September and they knew that he had made at least one phone call to Björn Söderberg in early October and that on the day of the murder he had been with two other young Nazi sympathizers, Björn Lindberg Hernlund and Jimmy Niklasson.

The surveillance team had followed them assiduously all day, right up to the moment Niklasson had parked his car at about eight o'clock on Kristallvägen in Solberga, and then went off duty just after eight thirty. Only minutes later the three men drove away again, heading for Sätra. Two of them, Hellekant and Hernlund, went up to Björn Söderberg's flat on the third floor and rang the bell. Söderberg, who apparently knew them, yelled at them to go away.

The three went back downstairs but stopped at the outer door. For some reason Söderberg followed them down, barefoot and wearing only shorts, and began arguing with them. During the row one of the Nazis, or possibly both, drew guns. Söderberg ran upstairs but they pursued him and he never made it back into his flat. He was struck by bullets to the head and abdomen on the landing outside his door. The perpetrators fled and rejoined Jimmy Niklasson, who had stayed in the car.

The motive was plain enough. Björn Söderberg had been working at the warehouse of the office supplies company Esselte Svanström in Stockholm. When he realized that a member of the committee of the local branch of the Swedish Commercial Employees' Union (Handels) was an active Nazi, he tipped off the newspaper *Arbetaren*, which had then published an article. The man in question, Robert Vesterlund, was no ordinary neo-Nazi. He had begun his political career as chair of Sverigedemokratisk ungdom (Swedish Democratic Youth) but gone over to more unambiguously Nazi groups and become editor of the leading neo-Nazi journal, *Info-14*. He was one of the men behind the Salem March, the biggest neo-Nazi rally in Sweden since the Second World War, held annually to commemorate the stabbing of a young

Nazi in a fight between two groups of youths in the Swedish town of Salem in December 2000.

The article led to Vesterlund's dismissal from the committee and he left his job shortly thereafter.

Both the Stockholm district court and the court of appeal decided that even though it could not be established which of the two men had shot Söderberg, they were jointly guilty and each was sentenced to six years' imprisonment by the lower court, nearly doubled by the higher court to eleven years each, while Niklasson, as the driver, was convicted of being an accessory to murder. Vesterlund was cleared of the charge of inciting the murder, but convicted for illegal possession of firearms and possession of anabolic steroids.

When the police searched the three men's homes, they found material indicating that they were active distributors of Nazi propaganda and also engaged in compiling a register of political opponents.

The previous neo-Nazi outrages of 1999 had stimulated some reaction, though not as much as might have been expected. But after this murder the media and democratic organizations woke up in rather the same way they eventually had in response to the wave of attacks on *Expo* four years earlier. There were demonstrations in various parts of the country against neo-Nazi violence and as many as 20,000 people gathered on Medborgarplatsen in Stockholm to honour the memory of Björn Söderberg.

And just as after the *Expo* incident, these 1999 events brought about cooperation between some of the country's leading newspapers. This time it was the four Stockholm-based national dailies, *Dagens Nyheter*, *Svenska Dagbladet*, *Aftonbladet* and *Expressen*, who all published the same article on the Charles XII anniversary day about the menace represented by neo-Nazism. The extensive report identified sixty-two people from a variety of neo-Nazi organizations and motorcycle gangs by name and photograph. It was by no means uncontroversial: critics saw it as indefensible in terms of press ethics, and were concerned that the list included some young and simply imprudent individuals who were now likely to suffer complete social ostracism.

Stieg Larsson's opinion was that even though the article stretched the boundaries of press ethics, it was a necessary countermeasure. Swedish journalists had to call a halt at some point, had to say that enough is enough of murder threats, car bombs and shootings.

> To claim that neo-Nazism is just a transitory fashion is a myth that has been allowed to take root for too many years. The effect is that the authorities – for lack of any better alternative – call in social workers in the mistaken belief that neo-Nazis are youths with alcohol problems or dysfunctional backgrounds. Nazism is a political movement. Nazis become Nazis for exactly the same reasons that others become Liberals or Social Democrats – from belief and conviction. A political movement has to be fought by political opposition.

For Stieg it was only natural to see the attack in a broader perspective. This was not violence or murder in the normal sense, it was political terrorism exported across borders. The authorities, the police and the security services seemed to have trouble recognizing the fact. The usual picture of right-wing extremists was that they might be full of hatred and aggression, but that they were not particularly clever or well organized. However, these groups had been honing their methods for years, had learned to use new technology and had developed quite a sophisticated intelligence network. The car bomb in Nacka had been preceded by reconnaissance activities and the neo-Nazis had managed to track down the two journalists even though their identities had been disguised and they had a secret address.

It was the same with Björn Söderberg. A few weeks before the murder someone calling himself Peter Karlsson had taken copies of his and a score of other passport photographs from the police passport files. Stieg Larsson's was among them.

This was nothing new for Stieg. He was probably the person most under threat in the whole of Sweden. His name appeared on neo-Nazi websites all over Europe. He was constantly receiving threats in the form of anonymous letters and telephone messages. He coped so well because he had learned to be careful and adopted strict safety procedures. When he knew he was being watched, he would deliberately arrive late for meetings. When he went to a café he preferred to sit with his back to the wall.

On one occasion during his time at TT, when the press agency had its offices on Kungsholm torg, a group of neo-Nazis were waiting for him in the park across the street, armed with baseball bats. But since Stieg took his usual rear exit from the office as a security measure, he spotted them in time and was able to slip back into the building.

This safety consciousness was also the reason he and his partner Eva Gabrielsson never married, so that they could avoid being traced through official registers. Even so, Stieg usually wrote under his own name in *Expo*, and in the autumn of 1999 the journal announced that in future the editorial staff would include their photograph with their byline to demonstrate that they would not be intimidated by perpetrators of violence.

When Stieg heard the details of the Björn Söderberg case, he was appalled that the police had failed to give the man some basic advice, such as not opening his door to strangers (even though, admittedly, that would not have helped in these particular circumstances).

STIEG LARSSON BROUGHT TOGETHER HIS EXPERIENCE and knowledge in a brochure for the Swedish Journalists Association entitled *Överleva deadline: Handbok för hotade journalister* (Surviving the Deadline: A Handbook for Journalists under Threat), in which he discussed various scenarios and gave sound practical advice to journalists at risk.

A journalist in such a position should first and foremost evaluate the nature of the threat and try to ascertain its source: whether it comes from a lunatic, an individual of serious intent or an organization; whether it is personally or politically motivated; and not least whether it is simply an expression of anger at an article, or comes into the category of unlawful intimidation – in other words, makes specific threats and might thus be an indictable offence.

Threats that are ignored tend to fade away. So at *Expo* they made it a point of principle never to comment on them or publish details unless they were of a serious nature. Stieg cites as an instance of the latter the occasion in 1999 when Kurdo Baksi, editor-in-chief of *Svartvitt*, had a bullet fired through his living-room window. But anyone who is subject to numerous threats should take appropriate safety measures, of which Stieg gives several examples, like never answering a telephone directly, keeping a record of all threatening calls and letters, checking whether anyone has requested a photo from your passport record, removing any name plate from the door of your flat and installing a security door, changing all your locks, putting in a spyhole and never opening the door to strangers, making sure that people outside cannot see in, relocating mirrors that might provide a view inside, and fixing fire alarms in the hall in case of an arson attempt through the letter box.

Stieg also used his knowledge of security procedures when depicting the firm of Milton Security in the Millennium Trilogy, especially the sophisticated alarm system and protective measures that Milton install in Erika Berger's house when she is a victim of what she takes to be a stalker in *The Girl Who Kicked the Hornets' Nest*.

TOTAL PROTECTION AGAINST those who are determined to harm you is quite difficult, however. Most of the active Swedish anti-Nazis were on the neo-Nazis' own register of enemies and other objectionable persons. They called this operation 'Anti-AFA' and sometimes also 'Redwatch'.

As increasing numbers of younger people joined the far-Right network, computer expertise was swiftly improving and IT played a larger part in their campaign, spreading propaganda through websites, collecting and recording information and maintaining contact between individuals and groups.

The three men arrested for the murder of Björn Söderberg all had links with Anti-AFA. Hampus Hellekant in particular was very interested in computers and owned several himself. In their search of his house the police came across a comprehensive list of names of political opponents – in fact, surveillance and information-gathering seemed to have been his great passion. During the 'Reclaim the City' festival in Stockholm in September 1999 he had spent the entire time listening to police radio and noting down the names of left-wing activists.

He also had close links with people who had even more expert knowledge, especially three who went under the code names Ivalde, Paint and Strape. They communicated with one another on the Internet via anonymous email addresses and encrypted files. They obtained details of selected individuals, such as names, National Insurance numbers, addresses, phone numbers and places of work. They could even find out about people with disguised identities. They had a lot of help from the mother of one of the three, who was a case manager at the National Insurance office. In May 1999, a few weeks before the attack, she extracted the secret address of the two Nacka journalists from the files, together with the addresses of journalists at *Expo*. She was later convicted and fined for infringing the Official Secrets Act, and her son was convicted of incitement to do so.

Another member of the group was fined for breaking data protection laws, but the fourth was released without charge. A police search of their two homes in the spring of 2000 uncovered a register of 1,247 people, arranged by ethnic origin, political views and sexual orientation.

WHEN MIKAEL EKMAN WAS SIXTEEN and still a schoolboy in Karlskrona, he saw a classmate one day in Nazi uniform. He found it totally incomprehensible, felt an indescribable rage welling up in him and went over to the boy and asked him how the hell he could be a Nazi. His classmate responded by asking if he had heard of the National Movement. It was not a subject Mikael would have bothered with normally, but since he was a bit of a know-all, he had to look into it, and he borrowed four hefty volumes from the library: Alan Bullock's biography *Hitler: A Study in Tyranny, Mein Kampf,* Heléne Lööw's study of Nazism in Sweden *Hakkorset och Vasakärven* (The Swastika and the Wasa Sheaf) and *Extremhögern* (The Far Right) by Stieg Larsson and Anna-Lena Lodenius. He ploughed through all four in rapid succession and discovered exactly what Nazism stood for. The last book became something of a bible for him, containing everything anyone needed to know about neo-Nazi and neo-fascist groups, where they came from and who their leaders were.

He then joined Youth Against Racism. At one of their congresses he happened to speak to David Lagerlöf from the recently launched journal *Expo* and realized that what they were doing was just what he himself wanted to get into. He rang *Expo* and Stieg Larsson answered. He suggested that Mikael should submit some reports about what was happening in Karlskrona, which was a town with considerable neo-Nazi activity. It was here that the new organization the National Socialist

STIEG LARSSON AT WORK as a news graphic illustrator at the Swedish TT Press Agency feature and photo desk in Stockholm, Sweden, 1984.

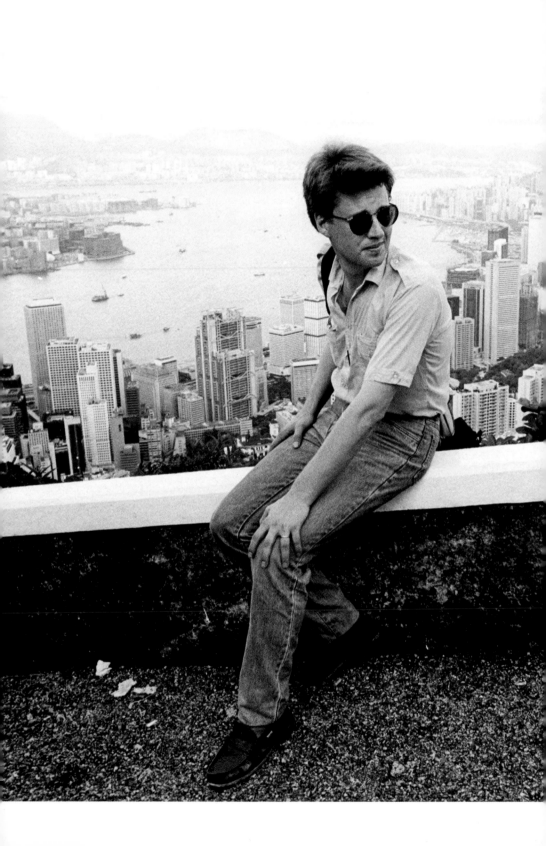

From July to August 1987, Stieg went on assignment for TT and *Vagabond* magazine, traveling the Trans-Siberian Railway from Moscow to Hong Kong and on to Beijing. **Left**, he sits atop Hong Kong's Victoria Peak. **Above**, Stieg in a rail dining car with unidentified passengers.

Above: STIEG AND EVA GABRI-
ELSSON, his lifelong partner, at
a café in the city of Strängnäs,
Sweden, in the 1990s.

Right: STIEG IN HIS OFFICE at
TT, January 1994.

GUESTS WAIT IN LINE to enter the Sergel cinema in Stockholm, Sweden, September 14, 2009, for the gala premiere of *The Girl Who Played with Fire*, the second film of the Millennium trilogy. In November 2004, Stieg knew that all three books would be published in Sweden and then in a number of other countries and that they would in all probability be filmed. Less than a year after this movie premiere, Stieg Larsson's books had been sold to 44 countries and achieved sales of 26 million copies.

Left: ERLAND LARSSON AND JOAKIM LARSSON, Stieg's father and younger brother, in Stockholm.

Below: EVA GABRIELSSON poses on January 27, 2011, at a hotel in Paris, during a publicity tour for her recently published memoir.

Front had been formed in 1994 by people who had previously been active in White Aryan Resistance.

So Mikael began collecting newspaper cuttings, attending local courts and meetings, and accumulated a mass of material to send to *Expo*.

In February 1996 he went up to Stockholm to see Stieg Larsson for the first time. They met outside TT and Mikael was invited to Stieg and Eva Gabrielsson's flat for cheese and wine. They sat talking far into the night. For a sixteen-year-old from the province of Blekinge this was a major event. Back home among his schoolmates the *Expo* crowd were 'shit hot'.

So he became one of *Expo*'s correspondents, sending in notes of Nazi and racist activities for the journal's calendar. In 1998 he actually joined the National Socialist Front himself to be able to report on it from the inside. They knew he was not a true Nazi, but they thought he was young and easily influenced and hoped to win him over. What they did not know, of course, was that everything he heard and all the material he acquired ended up with *Expo* in Stockholm.

On one occasion when Mikael was at the home of a National Socialist Front leader, one of the most notorious neo-Nazis in the country arrived with a bag in his hand. It turned out to contain a pump-action shotgun, which the man proceeded to assemble. 'This is what we should use to go in and clear out parliament,' he said.

Given the man's history of violence, it was a horrifying thought, but nothing came of it. Mikael stayed on in the NSF for a while longer but resigned in 1999. He left school that year and moved to Stockholm, with the aim of working for *Expo*.

IN THOSE DAYS *EXPO* WAS STILL FIGHTING for survival in its little offices on Kungsholmen and was being published as part of the magazine *Svartvitt*. That was also the year, 1999, when TT, Stieg

Larsson's employer, began cutting posts and Stieg was one of those offered redundancy with eighteen months' severance pay. He decided to seize the opportunity and devote himself fully to *Expo*.

Mikael Ekman remembers there being enormous pressure on the *Expo* editorial team when he arrived there in the autumn of that year. The Malexander murders and the bomb attack on the Nacka journalists had taken place only a few months earlier, and the murder of Björn Söderberg occurred just after Mikael came to Stockholm. The neo-Nazis were campaigning against *Expo*, but demand for its services had increased among public institutions. *Expo* staff could give lectures and get paid for them, with the money being immediately ploughed back into the journal. The finances were still in dire straits, however, and Mikael Ekman could not count on receiving an editorial staff salary. He got by with work for the post office and as a waiter at Globen restaurant.

Stieg Larsson was, of course, under stress from the multiple threats and the poor state of *Expo*'s finances, but he was pleased that more and more predominantly young people were making contact. And he was freed from trying to combine two jobs, at TT and *Expo*, even though he did not slacken his pace. His capacity for work was legendary.

'Many people say that Stieg was very industrious and worked all day and night. Which is true. He often carried on all day and night, but he didn't need to,' says Mikael Ekman. 'It was just that he always made time. He devoted an enormous amount of time to everything and everyone. No matter whether it was little old Mikael with no grasp of anything and needing support, or a member of the Sweden Democrats writing angry letters. Everyone had to be dealt with, even if it meant he had to stay up half the night. No one has that kind of patience nowadays.'

Many also describe Stieg as reserved, as keeping himself in the background and only taking part in discussions when he had something of importance to contribute. But to the *Expo* team he was the constant raconteur, always making them roar with laughter; they even sometimes referred to him as Anecdote-Stieg.

'Some of the stories he told at the beginning made me wonder if he was a pathological liar, but I came to see there was always a basic element of truth in them even if they were a little exaggerated,' says Mikael Ekman.

Stieg was also happy to expatiate on how he wanted *Expo* to function.

'He could come across as a real chatterbox. But the structures he was advocating in 1999 are the ones we have in place now. It has taken ten years. But we've got there in the end. He turned out to be right, both in his anecdotes and in his vision. Even on matters that are no cause for rejoicing, like the successes of the Sweden Democrats, for instance. Stieg predicted that ten years ago. And he was right on that too.'

The Sweden Democrats

ONE DAY AROUND THE END OF MAY or beginning of June 2001 I had a phone call from Stieg Larsson at Ordfront Förlag, where I was publisher. He proposed a joint project on a book about the Sweden Democrats. *Expo* was planning a campaign against the party, which had now been actively disseminating its xenophobic rhetoric on the political scene for a decade or more. They intended to gather together all the documentation they had on the party, its history and ideology, and bring it out in book form. *Expo* could have produced it under their own imprint, of course, but if it were published by Ordfront it would ensure bookshop distribution and perhaps also fit into Ord-front's own socio-political book-club list.

It sounded interesting, so we swiftly arranged a meeting between Stieg Larsson and Mikael Ekman from *Expo* and myself and Ordfront's managing director Leif Ericsson.

Stieg was not one to start immediately singing the praises of his own project. In fact, he was restrained, not to say reticent, but as soon as the conversation turned to points he deemed essential or crucial, his knowledge and opinions came pouring out.

It was a long meeting that had very little to do with book production but a lot to do with politics. Especially about the Sweden Democrats posing a real threat to democracy in Sweden. I was rather sceptical myself. Not on the question of whether the Sweden Democrats were a xenophobic and racist organization. On that I was in complete agreement. My scepticism applied more to their capabilities. I felt the party had already blown its chances of becoming the major unifying xenophobic party in Sweden. As the situation stood in 2001, it did not seem very likely that they could win more than the odd per cent or two in the parliamentary and local elections due in 2002.

But Stieg argued forcefully that they should be taken very seriously indeed. One reason was their international contacts, especially with Jean-Marie Le Pen's National Front in France.

'Remember,' Stieg said, 'that Le Pen endured exactly the same sort of hopeless existence on the margins year after year. Then in 1995 he thoroughly shocked the country by winning a majority in three French cities. Suddenly everyone had to consider the National Front and take Le Pen seriously.' He cautioned: 'If a person with that background can come across as at least semi-respectable, it's equally likely that a party such as the Sweden Democrats can do the same.'

As Stieg observed, the Sweden Democrats had already digested the most important lesson the National Front had to give – that a party of that kind has to be built up from the ground with intensive work at grass-roots level.

'But Le Pen doesn't like close inspection, and nor do the Sweden Democrats.'

That was precisely what Larsson and Ekman intended to subject them to now in their book: take their words and their analysis of society seriously. They claimed to be the party for all who believed in law and order.

'But if we vote in the Sweden Democrats to restore law and order, we really will be turning poacher into gamekeeper, since they are by far Sweden's most lawless party.'

Expo had collated figures showing that 20 per cent of the party leadership of the 1990s had been convicted of a crime and even more had well-documented connections with neo-Nazi groups or parties. That was the sort of information Stieg Larsson and Mikael Ekman wanted to make the public aware of.

'We need to get the book out fast. It has to be this year, and in time for the Charles XII anniversary, 30 November, when *Expo* will be launching its campaign.'

That sounded fine in itself, but I had to point out that it was not feasible. It was already summer and the book had not even been started. To have any chance of getting it printed for publication by the end of November and also include it in the book club, it would need to be ready for press by 1 October at the latest. That was only four months away. It was impossible to produce a book to such a timescale.

'I'm sure you're right,' said Stieg. 'In normal circumstances it can't be done. But you've never worked with us before. If we say we can do the book, then we'll do it, if you're prepared to publish it.'

We agreed to publication on the spot. Projects were usually discussed internally before a decision was taken, but in this case there was not time even for that. Stieg Larsson's powers of persuasion had triumphed.

The year 2001 was a dramatic one. In mid-July, just as they were starting work on the book, the EU summit meeting in Gothenburg was disrupted by violent protests and more than 500 people were arrested. We called on *Expo* in their anonymous, secret and well-protected editorial offices at the top of an unprepossessing residential building on Kungsholmen.

'There's no doubt that *Expo* is under threat,' said Stieg, sounding quite matter-of-fact about it. He went on to explain that *Expo* was actually rather more than just a magazine about fascism and the far Right. It was also a centre for the assemblage of information and documentation about these movements. They had built up the biggest archive in the country on right-wing extremism. Without that collection they would never, of course, have been able to write a book about such a multifarious organization as the Sweden Democrats in such a short space of time. They had not only the official publications of the neo-Nazis and the fascists going back for a very long time – leaflets and stickers, discs and mail-order catalogues – but also internal papers, minutes, letters, material sent in by informants and defectors or which *Expo* staff had acquired in other ways. Research reports, press cuttings from every available newspaper in the country, photographs, many taken by *Expo*'s own staff or contributors, police reports and court proceedings – all had been kept and archived.

'We don't simply assert that the ideology of the far Right is repugnant. First of all we examine how things actually are, what the various organizations really stand for, what their propaganda consists of, what they say for external consumption and what they say within their own four walls, what mutual contradictions there are, what they are planning. Everything they want to keep out of the public domain. That's what has made *Expo* so reviled among neo-Nazi groups.'

It was precisely because these groups were so expert at concealing themselves that the media coverage was so limited. There was no access to the overall picture and therefore no recognition of how strong the international links were.

All the far-Right groups, the uniformed Nazis as well as the Sweden Democrats in their jackets and ties, called themselves nationalists, and they presented themselves as if they were active only at the domestic level; but in fact there was extensive cooperation across borders. They held meetings and maintained contact and inspired one another. But preferably in secret. The ordinary established parties boasted of their international connections, but the Sweden Democrats denied them for as long as they could. Stieg Larsson drew attention to the fact that they were at that very moment collaborating with a network called Euro-Nat, which was more or less autocratically controlled by Jean-Marie Le Pen and his National Front.

The Sweden Democrats had good reasons other than the purely ideological for keeping up these contacts. A substantial part of their budget for the 1998 elections was paid by Le Pen's movement via the international network.

IT WAS ONLY THREE MONTHS LATER that the terrorist attack on the World Trade Center in New York took place. The whole world held its breath, but Stieg Larsson and Mikael Ekman were entirely focused on the Sweden Democrats. Stieg declared, when I spoke to him, that the work was going well and that the finished book would be a major exposé. The party's façade would come crashing down when readers became aware of their roots in the nationalist movement of the 1920s and 1930s, and when they saw who the founder members were and who had held leading positions.

Mikael Ekman remembered afterwards that he really had little idea what to expect when he sat down to start writing. Stieg knew, but his attitude was that they just had to stick with it.

In June he and Eva went sailing in the boat they owned, *Josephine*, while Mikael continued researching for the book. From July onwards they more or less lived in the editorial offices. 'It was tremendously enjoyable, and we learned an incredible amount, even if the conditions were pretty appalling.'

As publisher I was somewhat concerned about the end result. There was barely time for any of the usual editing process; it would just be a matter of one revision of the text at a proofreading level. But *Expo*'s competence on the subject had already been well demonstrated. No other fact-checker in the country could beat them. That said, when I saw samples of the text that Stieg sent over, I was not particularly impressed. They were dry and too full of facts, and not exactly inviting for the general reader.

That aspect would be sorted out in the final stage, Stieg assured me. Though there had been a development that autumn which would affect the content of the book and complicate their task still further, he added.

In the spring of 2001, immediately before work on the book began, it had become clear that there was a serious rift within the leadership of the Sweden Democrats. Two prominent members, Anders Steen and Tor Paulsson, who had been responsible for the party's almost sensational success in the Stockholm suburb of Haninge at the last elections, had left the committee at the party congress in April. Shortly after that they were expelled. The inference was that their views were far too extreme for a party which was now fighting hard to make itself acceptable before the following year's elections.

But it turned out that the two men had greater support among fellow members than the inner circle had bargained for. There were rumours that a breakaway party was to be formed under the name National Democrats, and that soon proved to be the case. For *Expo*'s sake, and to make the book as up to date and well documented as possible, it was essential to include the new split, the outcome of which was still unknown. So Stieg and his team decided that the only way to ascertain the facts quickly was to send in a mole.

A young journalist from Uddevalla, Daniel Poohl, whom Mikael Ekman knew from the days when they were colleagues at *Värnplikts-nytt* (National Service News), volunteered to take on the assignment on *Expo*'s behalf.

Before getting in touch with the National Democrats he was given precise instructions as to the limits of his involvement. 'Stieg was very insistent that I was not to help advance their party, take the initiative in any actions or do anything that might be illegal. I should also not contemplate trying to "rescue" anyone from the organization. I could distribute leaflets and I wrote for their web page as well,' Daniel Poohl remembers.

In August Poohl rang Tor Paulsson, who became very enthusiastic when he found that a nationalistically inclined youth from the provinces had already heard of the National Democrats and was making contact. He suggested that Daniel come to an important convention soon to be held in Stockholm.

When the National Democrats held their inaugural meeting at Brygghuset in Stockholm a few journalists tried to get in, including *Expo*'s reporter, but they were brusquely sent packing and called 'bloody terrorists' by the leaders, Tor Paulsson and Anders Steen. Whereas the young sympathizer Daniel Poohl was able to take his seat as a pre-registered participant and listen to the rousing speeches about the national campaign being resurrected after some years of lying fallow. He was also able to note that there was quite a selection of the usual revisionist histories for sale on their book table. Anders Steen was not entirely happy about that and ordered some of the most flagrant Nazi literature to be removed.

Daniel managed to win the confidence of the leadership quite easily. When he was asked to write a text for the party's website, Stieg dug out and re-edited an old article for him about nationalism by the ideologist of the Sweden Democrats, Johan Rinderheim, one of the people most detested by the National Democrats. They were delighted with it, believing they had found a sympathizer who was both intellectual and a good writer, and ironically enough it was placed next to a vituperative attack on *Expo* magazine.

The question of his safety had been discussed before Daniel got involved with the National Democrats. 'Going about in Stockholm, there were always people from *Expo* relatively near at hand. It felt a bit more insecure when I had to go abroad to the Czech Republic or Germany to meet representatives of various other nationalist parties, but at least I had the name of a contact I could phone if problems arose.'

Daniel was provided with a video camera to document the visits on the party's behalf, something which they were to regret bitterly later on, when clips from the film eventually turned up in a TV documentary on the far Right in Sweden.

Stieg Larsson and Mikael Ekman finished their book at about the time the trip ended, and so Daniel had to stop his undercover reporting. And indeed he was very soon unmasked, by pure chance.

'I was travelling on the tube in Stockholm with Mikael Ekman, and there was one of the National Democrats that I had had most to do with sitting directly opposite us. Our eyes met and I could see that he grasped the situation immediately. It was not long before I was exposed on their website. From then on I was quite nervous about what might happen, but nothing ever did.'

IN THE FINAL PHASE STIEG LARSSON and Mikael Ekman worked on the book every hour of the day, and more. The night before the deadline Mikael went home at about three or four o'clock in the morning and was back in the office at nine. When he came in he found Stieg fast asleep in his chair with his feet on the table and the disk of the finished book in his hand. The cigarette stubs in the ashtray were still warm. Stieg wanted to take public transport to the publisher, as they would normally do, but Mikael thought that for once they should take a taxi.

The book was not just ready in time: it was fine. It might have benefited from one more revision, but it was factually accurate and well written. How it could have been done under those conditions was difficult to imagine.

One central argument in this book about the Sweden Democrats was that the party was never a spontaneous expression of people's disapproval of immigration, but an organization which incorporated a significant history. That was why it was subtitled *The Nationalist Movement*. More specifically, its historical roots were in the party which was called the New Swedish Movement, led by the legendary fascist ideologist Per Engdahl. Engdahl lived to a ripe old age: he was born in 1909 and died in 1994, remaining politically active to the end. And he never apologized. He published his far-Right newspaper, *Vägen framåt*, for sixty years, almost without a break. He saw himself first and foremost as a Mussolini-inspired fascist campaigning for a society on the corporate model, meaning that the leadership principle should supersede the majority principle, abolishing political parties and trade unions and replacing them with professional associations to which both employers and employees would belong. Engdahl kept his distance from German Nazism, but his anti-Semitism in the 1930s and 1940s was as virulent as that of the worst Nazi leaders. He would express in print such comments as, 'We've seen enough of repulsive, curly-haired, hook-nosed sons of Jacob on our streets arm-in-arm with blonde Nordic Swedish women.'

Engdahl was the eternal loser among Swedish right-wing extremists. Only after the war, when by any humane judgement fascism should have been buried for ever, did he play for a short while the glittering role he had always dreamed of. It was when Mussolini's Fascist party was recreated in Italy less than two years after the end of the war under the name Movimento Sociale Italiano. Then it changed its garb and became the Alleanza Nationale, which has now merged with Berlusconi's Forza Italia in the new party Il Popolo della Libertà. The Movimento Sociale Italiano immediately began trying to rebuild a European network of nationalist parties, in which Engdahl somewhat surprisingly had the position of theorist and principal author of European fascism's post-war programme. He also hosted the second Fascist Congress after the war, held in Malmö in 1951, and one other congress after that, in 1958.

Engdahl's days in the limelight were brief, however. His New Swedish Movement lost its direction in renewed bickering and soon began to wither away, like most of the other extremist sects on the far Right. But the indefatigable old man, by now completely blind, carried on as before, and in the 1970s it was he who mapped out the path the ultra-Right was to take – to redefine itself as anti-immigration. A few months after this Keep Sweden Swedish (BSS) was formed, as a leafleting campaign.

Mikael Ekman and Stieg Larsson were certain that many of the founder members of BSS were in contact with Engdahl and inspired by him, at least at the beginning. When BSS later tried to turn itself into a normal political party, as the Sweden Party, it had a short period of positive progress and a rather longer one of constant internal strife before it finally split. The old BSS nucleus was back to square one. But they had the embryo of a new organization to hand: the magazine-publishing historical society Gjallarhornet (The Bugle, named after the warning horn of the god Heimdal). In 1988 they were able to transform this into the new party called the Sweden Democrats. And just like the BSS and the Sweden Party, it was set up as a single-issue party focusing on immigration. Their argument was that mass immigration threatened Swedish identity and led to unemployment, social tensions and crime waves. Above all it was the immigration of people from completely different cultures which constituted the greatest threat. But they insisted they were not a racist party. Nevertheless, one of the demands in their first manifesto was a total ban on adoptions from non-European countries, just like the BSS.

Another recurring theme from the BSS period was that a mafia of politicians and media people were colluding to conceal the truth and that they themselves were subject to constant discrimination.

If the party was aspiring to acceptability, the choice of Anders Klarström as its first chairman was hardly a wise one. He had a past record in the campaign group of the Nordic National Party, the Rik-saktionsgrupp (National Action Group), and had also been accused of making death threats to the TV entertainer and anti-Nazi Hagge Gei-gert. Klarström and Ola Sundberg were nominated official spokesmen for the party, and the latter missed no occasion to air his opinions. One of his notorious remarks was, 'I don't want to use the word race, but it disgusts me to see two [Swedish] parents with an Indian child.' And with Klarström as party leader, the Sweden Democrats not surprisingly turned out to be a mix of old BSS members, general opponents of immigration and, not least in the case of the younger members, Nazis pure and simple. BSS had in its time made menacing references to the British National Front. The Sweden Democrats kept that tradition alive by adopting as their party symbol an almost exact copy of the National Front emblem: a burning torch with the flame emerging in the shape of a flag, for them of course in the Swedish colours of blue and yellow.

The Sweden Democrats now shifted their emphasis towards more public appearances and externally orientated activities and demonstrations. They established the Engelbrekt March (named after the fifteenth-century rebel leader and proto-nationalist Engelbrekt Engelbrektsson) as the far Right's own alternative to the May Day celebrations of the Labour movement. And symbolically they took over the arrangements for the 30 November Charles XII demonstrations, which had become less easy to run than before in view of the increasingly large counter-demonstrations. In the mid-1990, disagreements between the old BSS nucleus and the younger members developed into a real civil war, resulting in Klarström vacating his position, and many of the old BSS crowd, including the pioneer Leif Zeilon, were thrown out amid insults and verbal abuse.

Into the post of leader came instead the Centre Party defector Mikael Jansson, a more colourless person, difficult to place ideologically, who modelled himself on his favourite politician of the disaffected, Austria's charismatic Jörg Haider. He emulated Haider in trying to smarten up the party's image. He introduced a ban on uniforms at meetings, somewhat to the annoyance of the younger members who belonged to both the Sweden Democrats and the neo-Nazi Nationell Ungdom (National Youth).

In the 1998 elections the party won 20,000 votes and eight local council seats. The biggest surprise was the Stockholm suburb of Haninge, where it gained two seats after an aggressive campaign in the Le Pen mould. Though the rejoicing was rather short-lived, since it was the organizers of this successful campaign who were thrown out in 2001 and set up the new National Democrats party.

The book on the Sweden Democrats sold well and was also widely read in organizations and study groups, so it went on influencing public discussion for some time. It did not, however, prevent the party's comfortable success in the 2002 elections, with 76,000 votes and about 1.5 per cent of the total vote, and forty-nine seats overall in some thirty local councils across the country.

IN 2003 STIEG LARSSON BECAME EDITOR-IN-CHIEF OF EXPO. In practice he had had that role for quite a while, but it was only when *Expo* reverted to publication in its own right, after Kurdo Baksi's magazine *Svartvitt* folded, that the arrangement was formalized. Once again, the financial situation was precarious. Some of the staff doubted the ability of *Expo* to continue independently at all, or thought it might be an opportune moment to take a break to consolidate and perhaps publish only on the Internet. But that was never an option for Stieg. *Expo* had to appear in print to play an authoritative part in public debate.

Finding new writers was not a problem. More and more young freelancers gathered around the magazine. *Expo* had become really well known over the years. Its persistence had had an effect. And from 2003 it was able to stand on its own two feet.

Stieg Larsson was the oldest of those involved. But he was never one to hold others in check or advise caution. Daniel Olsson, a young freelancer who had now begun writing for them, remembers that it was quite the opposite.

'I think he threw himself into things, occasionally against his better judgement. He had the will and he would never say we had to prioritize. He always wanted the truth to come out. And he excelled at encouraging new writers. When you came up with an idea, he used to say, that'll make a long feature article. If it was really good, he would say, that's a book. He was very much in favour of writing books. He used to say it wasn't difficult. One piece of reportage is a chapter. Ten pieces and you have a book.'

It was no secret that Stieg Larsson wrote novels in his spare time and that the plots revolved round a journal called *Millennium*. Maybe it was wish fulfilment through fiction. *Millennium* had a circulation of 20,000, sheer heaven for *Expo* with barely a tenth of that. It had a modern magazine layout, professional management and the resources to undertake proper investigative journalism. Politically it was difficult to categorize, but it was always an irritant to those in positions of power of any kind. Or, as it says in *The Girl with the Dragon Tattoo*: '*Millennium* is generally viewed as critical of society, but I'm guessing that the anarchists think it's a wimpy bourgeois crap magazine along the lines of *Arena* or *Ordfront*, while the Moderate Students Association probably thinks that the editors are all Bolsheviks.'

Daniel Olsson thinks *Millennium* resembles what Stieg wanted *Expo* to be, but what of course it was not. Perhaps could never be, since its coverage was so specialized and limited. 'But Stieg must have yearned to play a role like Mikael Blomkvist's for *Millennium*. The fact that it is a powerful financier who is under investigation in the first book speaks for itself. As soon as my own ideas pointed in that direction, to investigate extremist right-wing companies, for example, they were very well received.'

But that was still something for the future.

'To be honest,' says Daniel Poohl, who was the editorial secretary from 2003 and is now editor-in-chief, 'I have to say that *Expo* wasn't very professionally run at that stage. Stieg was no expert at managing a magazine. He made up most of it as he went along. It was always a struggle putting copy together and making people stick to deadlines. We were often late getting it to the printers.'

BUT *EXPO* CAME OUT ANYWAY, as it always had done, despite physical threats and chronic financial difficulties. The main theme in the first issue of the relaunched *Expo* of 2003 was hatred of homosexuals among far-Right groups. Of course that was nothing new. In *Expo*'s very first year, 1995, an exceptionally brutal and homophobically motivated murder took place, when Peter Karlsson, a successful ice hockey player, died of more than sixty knife wounds inflicted by a nineteen-year-old skinhead. The editor-in-chief of *QX* magazine, Jon Voss, wrote in the inaugural number of *Expo*:

> Horror of gays is not so much fear of gays as fear that one might oneself have sexual feelings for a person of the same sex.
>
> That is one of the similarities to xenophobia and racism. Not contempt for the 'weakness' of others, but a paranoid and alarming fear that the culture, appearance, political convictions, religion or sexuality of others are stronger.
>
> Contempt for the weak is mainly contempt for one's own weakness.

There had always been an element of self-torment in Nazism's attitude to homosexuality. Paradoxically enough, quite a few leading Nazis were homosexual. The SA leader Ernst Röhm, who was murdered on Hitler's orders on the Night of the Long Knives, was openly so, while one of the best-known figures of German neo-Nazism, Michael Kühnen, who was responsible for many homophobic attacks, kept his own orientation secret for as long as he could.

Nazi art idolizes the powerful male body with an aesthetic in which the erotic overtones are palpable. But for that very reason homosexual tendencies have to be resisted all the more vigorously and the distinction between acceptable and unacceptable sexuality maintained at any price. Hatred then becomes even more irrational.

The extreme right-wing hate-propaganda had also been constructed on the basis of conspiracy theories about an influential gay lobby deliberately trying to break down the nuclear family and thus destroy the foundations of a healthy, racially pure nation. Homosexuals were always described as sickly, defective and perverted.

The number of crimes with homosexual motives has remained consistently high in Sweden since the mid-1990s. It was between 150 and 200 a year in the period 1997–2001. That covered everything from serious crimes like murder, grievous bodily harm and arson, to various types of harassment and nuisance like insults, graffiti, defacement of posters, T-shirt slogans, attacks on premises or meetings.

In his leader in that issue Stieg Larsson likened hatred of homosexuals to 'terrorism of the kind that military strategists in the Pentagon call low-intensity warfare', expressing itself in a constant stream of abuse in articles and pamphlets, Internet campaigns, rabble-rousing speeches:

One thing is clear. Society is not much bothered about this form of low-intensity terrorism. Inciting homophobia is fairly risk-free.

If this hate campaign had been waged against any other representative group in Sweden the reaction would have been radically different. If the targets of the attacks had been Telecom employees, bus drivers or provincial politicians, much stronger countermeasures would have been implemented.

If five employees of the Ministry of Justice, for example, had been murdered and the rest of the staff subjected to daily systematic violence or harassment simply for being civil servants, there would by now be a state of emergency declared in Sweden.

A New Era, a New Magazine

NOW THE TWENTY-FIRST CENTURY HAD ARRIVED and it was obvious that lots of things were changing. The 1990s had been the decade of freedom of choice, at least for people in the West. Choices in every field imaginable: merchandise of all kinds, brands, never-ending streams of consumer goods, even choice in areas where previously there had been little or none, such as savings, pension funds, schools, doctors, utilities like electricity and telephones, and more TV channels.

Choice was not only a right, it was almost a civic duty.

But in one sphere there was no freedom of choice – economic policy. Margaret Thatcher had already laid it down in one of her best-known political slogans: 'There is no alternative.' A decade on and the Swedish prime minister, Carl Bildt, was talking of the politics of the 'one way'.

After the fall of the Soviet Union the big ideological battles were over, liberalism and the free-market economy had won the final victory – so maintained the American academic Francis Fukuyama in his book *The End of History and the Last Man*. The advent of information technology and the remarkable proliferation of new IT-based companies only served to confirm it.

At the turn of the millennium the bull market for dot-com companies had reached its peak. A year or so later it was clear that the IT boom was just another financial bubble. New firms were going under on all sides. In Sweden businessmen often sold in time and got out with considerable fortunes, while small investors usually lost their savings. And in the aftermath of the IT crash came a change of scene on the political front, with astonishing speed.

From having been none, there were now any number of alternatives. 'Another world is possible' was the current slogan. That was also the theme of the mass demonstrations against the prevailing world economic order and of the on-going discussions between social scientists and political activists in the West and in the Third World under the title World Social Forum.

A highly intellectual French association called Attac (Association pour la taxation des transactions pour l'aide aux citoyens) acquired a Swedish offshoot in early 2001 and gained several thousand members almost immediately.

A young Canadian journalist, Naomi Klein, wrote a political book, *No Logo*, that became a universal bestseller and essential reading for anyone interested in the structure of society; it was virtually a manifesto for opponents of globalization. She dismissed all claims about the coming of a new humanistic society free from restraints and able to network in infinite measure, painting instead a picture of a society where people were being transformed from citizens into consumers. A world in which the primary task of companies was no longer to produce useful things but to build up brands. Enormous sums were being invested in sophisticated marketing, while the actual production of goods was to be a low-cost operation transposed to vast industrial ghettos in Asia or Latin America. But Klein also described the growth of resistance to this brave new branded world, manifesting itself in huge protests against meetings of the financial and political elites in cities such as Seattle, Genoa and Nice.

Gothenburg now joined the ranks of these cities: the EU summit which took place there in the summer of 2001, while Stieg Larsson and Mikael Ekman were writing their book, included a cursory attendance by the president of the USA, George Bush. The mood was nervy and febrile. More than 50,000 people marched in three enormous peaceful demonstrations. And large numbers of activists attended seminars and discussion groups on globalization issues and the development of the EU. But what Swedish TV audiences predominantly saw, in sharp close-up, was masked demonstrators shattering bank windows and smashing and setting fire to café chairs along Gothenburg's main boulevard, Kungsportsavenyn. A little further north in the city, on Vasagatan, live bullets were fired at demonstrators, something that had not happened since the 1930s, and one activist who had thrown stones was so badly wounded that he hovered for quite a while between life and death.

Behind the masks in the activist groups that went under the name of the Black Block were many anti-fascists and anti-racists from Antifascistisk Aktion, the movement which had come about with the intention of confronting the Nazis on the streets and which was now trying to attack capitalism in all its forms.

The media drew the conclusion that the riots were carefully orchestrated and that the peaceful demonstrations gave the groups in the Black Block a convenient excuse for their violent excesses. The young activists did little to deny this. For them the commercial media were by definition the enemy, and they themselves were not particularly interested in public opinion. Throughout its history AFA had not bothered to explain itself or fit into any ideological fold. Nor did it have any membership register, executive committee or party programme, preferring to define itself primarily through its actions. The AFA's view was that socialist demands caused inexorable conflicts with the police. But it seemed a circular argument, since the definition of 'socialist demands' frequently necessitated police intervention, as, for instance, when they involved breaking the windows of porn shops or organizing street festivals without a permit.

It was the children of anti-fascism who were fighting on Gothenburg's main boulevard. There was no escaping the fact. AFA was a kind of shadow following in *Expo*'s footsteps. And there was a similarity between AFA's actions and the militancy of the radical anti-fascists of the old days, like the British who stopped Oswald Mosley's fascists marching in the East End of London. But times were different now and AFA had no base in the working class, nor were they making much effort to build one.

The militant anti-fascists, with their violence and rejection of parliamentary democracy, were diametrically opposed to *Expo*'s fundamental principles. But the magazine did not mount any serious campaign against them.

'When I wrote about right-wing and left-wing extremists spurring one another on in the battle for the streets, Stieg was fully in agreement,' Daniel Olsson remembers. 'But even so he preferred to avoid the subject. He had been there and didn't want to get into it again, he said. It required too much time and energy.'

Stieg expressed his opinions to the journal *Humanisten* in 2002, 'I participated in a public discussion with one of the leaders of AFA and it seemed quite clear that I don't have the same view of the world as they do. AFA is a tiny organization, but they get about 90 per cent of the media attention. They have almost become synonymous with anti-racism. Yet the big anti-racist movement is in the schools, among teachers, in trade unions, in business and among politicians.'

Stieg thought that what was happening in Gothenburg was a passing storm which would soon blow over. He saw other dangers, new battles looming.

THE WORLD BEFORE 1989 was divided in two. Two superpowers, two ideologies had been striving for supremacy. Then the Soviet Union collapsed and the world was unified: one superpower, one system, one way. And then, around the turn of the millennium, a thousand possibilities seemed to be opening up. But that feeling was to last only until 11 September 2001. After the terrorist attack on New York the world was again polarized. Fukuyama was replaced on the throne of conservative philosophy by Professor Samuel P. Huntington. He had already published *The Clash of Civilizations* in 1996. Now its thesis that the decisive conflicts of the future would be fought out not between national states or ideologies but between cultures, civilizations, was moved to the top of the agenda in the West. But of the seven great civilizations that Huntington describes as competitors on the world stage, the logic of events seemed to indicate only two, the Western and the Muslim.

In the shadow of the hunt for terrorists and the Iraq War, Taliban rule and fundamentalism, the parties on the extreme Right also developed a new way of reading the world. 'Scientific' racial theories were phased out and replaced by the concept of culture or civilization. The argument was more attractive to a wider public when attention was drawn to the spread of a hostile culture in religious garb, infiltrating, invading Sweden, Denmark, Switzerland, the Netherlands or whichever country it might be.

UNSURPRISINGLY, IT WAS THE SWEDEN DEMOCRATS who picked up on this trend in Swedish politics and ran with it. Stieg Larsson warned that they might become the main unifying xenophobic party in Sweden. Most of what has happened has proved him right, although it took a while, at least until halfway through the first decade of our new millennium, before it really became clear, and by then Stieg had passed away.

In 2005 the chairman of the party's youth wing, Jimmie Åkesson, came in as party leader and gathered round him a circle of young men with academic backgrounds who continued the process of change within a party whose symbol was no longer the National Front torch but a gentle blue anemone.

If they were to stand any chance of getting into parliament, the bonds to the party's brown past had to be severed. Racism must be held in check, anti-Semitic actions banned. Some of the leading members now described themselves as 'proud friends of Israel'.

Propaganda was directed less and less against immigrants in general, but more specifically at the one group who were regarded as the pre-eminent threat to the Swedishness that the party was so keen to safeguard: Muslims.

In a much-discussed article in *Aftonbladet* in the autumn of 2009, Jimmie Åkesson argued that Muslims were the biggest foreign menace to Sweden since the Second World War. He maintained that Swedes had already begun to capitulate to the onward march of Muslim culture. Male circumcision, separate hours for men and women in swimming pools, ritually slaughtered meat in the shops – all were seen as danger signs. He asked rhetorically how the situation would look in a few decades when many European cities, including Malmö, had a Muslim majority. The BSS leaflets of the 1980s, which had predicted the end of the 'Sweden of the Swedes' within four years, perhaps with 'a Turk as dictator and a black as foreign minister', may have had a cruder tone, but the alarmism was unaltered.

The Sweden Democrats got the breakthrough in public opinion they wanted when they achieved 6 per cent in a poll of voting intentions in the autumn of 2009. This presaged something that Stieg Larsson had been warning of and seen as a real likelihood as early as 2001: the presence in parliament of an overtly xenophobic party.

Sweden has the highest percentage of foreign-born inhabitants in Scandinavia, yet it is the only Scandinavian country not to have a significant xenophobic party represented in parliament. The Sweden

Democrats may be on their way to changing that, though it will not be an easy path. With their obvious roots in right-wing extremism, the Sweden Democrats have had a steeper hill to climb than the two successful models in Norway and Denmark: Fremskrittspartiet (Progress Party) and Dansk Folkeparti (Danish People's Party) respectively, both founded very much as parties of discontent. Dislike of taxation and distrust of all forms of authority were the core of their message, presented with glaring examples and effective populism by both leaders, Carl Hagen and Mogens Glistrup. The latter in particular knew how to make headlines, such as by proposing that the Danish military should be scrapped and replaced by the recorded phone message 'We surrender' in Russian.

The Danish People's Party, formed in 1995 as a breakaway from Glistrup's Fremskridtsparti, quite unexpectedly became a decisive factor in Danish politics at the start of the new millennium. A liberal-conservative coalition under Anders Fogh Rasmussen won a landslide victory in 2001 and the Danish People's Party entered government in a supporting role to the two which were more established, Venstre (The Left) and Konservative Folkeparti (Conservative People's Party). But it soon turned out that the Danish People's Party, with scarcely any opposition at all, was able to get its principal demand for a stricter immigration policy accepted, and from then on its policies had an influence on the entire political and cultural climate in Denmark.

The Norwegian Progress Party, now led by the economist Siv Jensen, has not had any similar influence, despite being larger than its Danish counterpart, with more than 20 per cent of the vote (compared with the Danish party's 13.8 per cent at the last election). The most dramatic change (which applies to the latter as well) is the Norwegian party's penetration of the traditional working-class vote, where they now predominate.

Norway is the most decentralized country in Scandinavia. The rural areas have always been more important than the cities and even Arbeiderpartiet (the Labour Party) was seen in its best days as the movement that provided opposition to the big-city elites. That role has been taken over by the Progress Party (FrP), according to the journalist Magnus Marsdal in his book *FrP-koden*. Those who turn to the Progress Party are to a great extent ordinary people who feel that politicians and the media are continually looking over their shoulders. FrP is for those who feel they have never been given any handouts and are annoyed that others, especially immigrants and Muslims, are receiving them. But Marsdal also points out that the gap between the elite and ordinary people is real and has widened over recent years. And the FrP is building up its organization with traditional Norwegian popular-movement methods in a period when all the other parties are turning away from them, creating a political base that no one else can hope to emulate. Yet the Progress Party is very much neo-liberal right-wing, with policies which, if introduced, would hardly favour the industrial workers and ordinary people of Norway's remote communities.

And Siv Jensen has warned, exactly like the Sweden Democrats, about society's Islamicization by stealth, citing the example of Malmö as a dire warning.

The Sweden Democrats, who similarly pursued a neo-liberal line very critical of trade union influence on the labour market, have swung to the left in recent years. In a Sweden hit by financial crisis and unemployment, they present themselves as the defenders of the welfare state. They have made Per Albin Hansson, the father of the Social Democratic 'people's home', their ideological archetype. And, they say, it was the ethnic and cultural uniformity of Sweden that was the basis of the entire welfare structure.

The Sweden Democrats have reinvented 'the people's home' as a Utopia, not of the egalitarian society but of the ethnically homogeneous nation: a dream of an age when Swedes were Swedes, when Africans and Asians were colonial subjects, when economic migration and refugees were unknown concepts and when reference to Swedishness was the daily fare of political debate.

The myth of the Swedes as an unusually pure, 'unmixed' people, of Sweden as the original home of the Germanic tribes, has been widespread among historians, anthropologists, linguists, writers and politicians, and well anchored in the popular consciousness through schoolbooks and encyclopedias. It was created in the nineteenth century, as author and science writer Maja Hagerman has demonstrated in her book *Det rena landet: Om konsten att uppfinna sina förfäder* (The Pure Land: On the Art of Inventing One's Ancestors), and was kept alive until the end of the Second World War, when it was quietly swept under the carpet in embarrassment.

Per Albin Hansson actually borrowed the term 'people's home' for the welfare state from the extreme conservative and nationalist political scientist Rudolf Kjellén, a fact some Swedish Democrat ideologists see as further proof that the original welfare state is an entirely Swedish product. Their passion for Kjellén also indicates the ideological continuity within the Sweden Democrats. Fundamentally they have still not shifted very far from the point where they began and where they were placed by Stieg Larsson and Mikael Ekman – firmly in the nationalistic tradition represented by Per Engdahl.

THE MORE EXTREME NEO-NAZI GROUPS have been struggling to find a survival strategy in the new millennium, and it looked for a while as if they had found it in the Stockholm suburb of Salem. In December 2000 a seventeen-year-old lad with some connection to the nationalist movement was viciously murdered by a gang that included immigrants. A week after the crime there was a march of thousands, mainly from various neo-Nazi groups, in memory of the boy, who was soon raised to the position of national martyr and was even called 'the Horst Wessel of our day' by the British racist magazine *Blood & Honour*.

By 2003 this annual demonstration had become the far Right's biggest propaganda action in the post-war period. All the significant right-wing extremist organizations were represented: the leading neo-Nazi magazine *Info-14*, the Swedish Resistance Movement, the Nordic Association, Blood and Honour, the National Democrats, the Sweden Democrats and others. The two last-named were later to withdraw.

The Salem March was organized by the Salem Foundation, whose driving force was Robert Vesterlund, editor of *Info-14*, by then one of the main frontmen of Swedish neo-Nazism. In the years 2001–3 the march drew some 2,000 supporters and was thus one of the biggest neo-Nazi demonstrations in post-war Europe. But not unexpectedly it met with resistance from left-wing anti-fascist groups. AFA as usual tried stopping the march by physical confrontation, and the police involvement increased from year to year.

In 2003 the content of the speeches turned more radical. One of the leaders of the Swedish Resistance Movement declared, 'I have not come here to mourn . . . I have come here to state that the time for mourning is past and the time for total resistance has arrived.'

The splits and quarrels between the various participating groups were not helped by the unwillingness of the more extremist Nazis to continue subordinating themselves to the whole, and from 2004 the number of participants in the march began to decrease. Over the years that followed, as the Sweden Democrats strengthened their position as the unifying and largest force on the xenophobic fringe, the Salem March continued to wane. In 2009 the demonstrators were down to a total of about 500.

But Daniel Poohl, *Expo*'s editor-in-chief from 2006, was not so sure that this should be interpreted as a definitive decline of Nazism in Sweden: 'What is happening instead is that groups within the White Power movement are increasing. It is easier to form a new group now than it was, and the neo-Nazis are getting better at using the Web, so propaganda is making a faster and greater impact nowadays.'

EXPO'S FINANCIAL PROBLEMS WERE STILL HANGING over them in 2003 and 2004, and Stieg Larsson bore a heavy burden with applications for grants and approaches to potential sponsors, often of course resulting in disappointment.

Daniel Olsson says, 'He would return from a meeting to report that so-and-so was now with us and we're going to mount a campaign together. And then nothing would come of it. I don't know how he managed to keep it up year after year. But you could see he was wearying of it.'

Otherwise things carried on as usual. Stieg sat writing with his feet up on his desk and his white Apple Mac on his lap. It was taken for granted that he was the hub of the editorial process, the one who embodied the history not only of *Expo* but also of modern Swedish anti-racism. He had become the accepted authority who was consulted by well-known politicians and who gave lectures on violent right-wing extremists to the police, even to Britain's Scotland Yard.

'When we discussed the future and what the magazine should cover, Stieg would often be diplomatic and a bit reticent, as if he were intrigued by what was happening to the *Expo* he had helped create,' Daniel Poohl remembers.

And all this while he was untiringly writing away at his thrillers. His colleagues found it slightly puzzling that he made no secret of it.

'Stieg talked about his books the way others talk about their hobbies,' says Daniel Poohl. 'I've never been all that interested in crime fiction myself, but we listened politely. I remember asking once how it was going, and he said that the characters had now taken on lives of their own; they were doing things he hadn't thought they were capable of – it was fantastic. It made me realize how serious it was, that he really had become a novelist, because he was even expressing himself differently from normal. Otherwise he had never been very keen on anything aspiring to culture.'

Stieg was convinced from an early stage that his novels would be successful, that they would sell. If they did, it would solve many problems, including *Expo*'s perpetual financial troubles. It would also mean that Stieg could gradually reduce his own involvement. For there was now a new generation able to continue the work.

'There was one occasion in particular when this became apparent in an almost symbolic way,' says Daniel Poohl. 'It was when we were bringing in a graphic redesign and meeting the people from the bureau that was doing it for us. I remember Stieg, unprompted, introducing all the *Expo* staff round the table in a very encouraging manner, as if to say: this is the team who are taking over; now I can take a back seat. There was a lot that needed to be developed at *Expo*, not least computer skills.'

Daniel Olsson says, 'Stieg had a great interest in computers. He had long held the dream of having someone really technically competent at *Expo*. He was not all that good on the technical side himself. But he sat at his computer every night and answered all the emails that arrived, however unpleasant they were. He once spent an entire night replying to spam mail, writing in perfect English to Viagra sellers and the like to tell them that we were not interested in their wares and to remove us from their list. The rest of us were really pissed off when we heard what he'd done, because the result of course was an increase in spam.'

But it was obvious that Stieg had acquired a considerable amount of expertise in computer technology by the time he wrote the novels.

When Lisbeth Salander hacks into others' computers and uses the Asphyxia program to download information from their hard disks and view everything on her own screen, when she talks to Mikael Blomkvist through an ICQ chat room in real time on screen, or when she connects to the Internet via a Palm hand-held and a mobile phone, the description is on the whole realistic and expert – that is the opinion of the journal *Ny Teknik* (New Technology), which consulted a number of security specialists in the autumn of 2007. 'Stieg Larsson is more credible than Dan Brown,' was one verdict.

THE AMBIENCE AT *EXPO* HAD BEEN rather nerdy and laddish, and that was something else Stieg Larsson thought it important to change. They ought to get some women on the team and modify the tone and direction of their reporting. He also devoted considerable thought to the connection between feminism and the topics *Expo* dealt with.

'I especially remember one occasion when Stieg had been at a conference and came back more than ever convinced that feminism and anti-racism were linked, and, as I recall, it had to do with the question of honour killings,' says Daniel Poohl.

The murder of a young Swedish-Kurdish woman, Fadime Sahindal, in 2002, by her own father, had sparked off a fierce debate. She had appeared on TV and talked openly of her father and brother, who disapproved of her independent lifestyle, keeping watch on her, threatening her and ill-treating her. She had even spoken in parliament about her situation in a seminar in 2001 on violence towards women. Then when she went to visit her family in Uppsala, her father killed her.

There was a tremendous outcry right across Sweden about the concept of honour killings and honour-related violence, often giving rise to crude generalizations about foreign cultures and about Kurdish and Muslim men's attitudes to women. An association was formed to spread information about honour-related crimes, under the name 'Never forget Pela and Fadime'.

Feminism and anti-racism were connected, Stieg Larsson had declared, but in fact the public debate that followed Fadime's murder seemed to suggest the opposite. Young women, many from immigrant backgrounds, came forward to express strong criticism of the attitudes and moral codes of certain immigrant groups. Social anthropologists wrote articles on the cultural background of the honour concept.

Stieg Larsson was both indignant and worried as public discussion revealed some feminists as racists, and anti-racists were accused of being reluctant to oppose violence against women. Together with his *Expo* colleague Cecilia Englund, he immediately commissioned an anthology in which nine writers analysed the whole honour-killings issue. The premise in the foreword was that

> men from the Middle East in general and Kurdish men in particular have been the focus of debate [. . .] They have been the target of accusations of representing a 'barbaric culture' and an 'outmoded attitude to women'. This has been the broad-brush reaction in a climate of opinion where no accusation seemed too absurd and where even respectable newspapers expressed almost preposterous racist assertions apparently without any proper consideration.

All nine contributors more or less shared the view that the entire public debate was based on racist, cultural and ethnocentric preconceptions. Cecilia Englund in her own essay called it 'the debate that ran off the rails'.

Stieg Larsson's piece contrasted the case of Fadime Sahindal with the brutal murder of twenty-two-year-old Melissa Nordell from Åkersberga, who was ill-treated, tortured with a stun gun, subjected to sexual abuse and finally suffocated by her former boyfriend. 'There was no attempt to explain this murder in cultural terms,' Stieg Larsson wrote. 'Such reasoning is exclusively reserved for "immigrants", "Kurds" or "Muslims".'

But in actual fact, Stieg continued, some fifteen to twenty Melissa-murders were committed every year in Sweden and many women had to seek protection in the country's 200 overcrowded women's refuges. There really were men who hate women (the title of the first volume of his trilogy in its original Swedish), far more than we think.

The anthology was typical of Stieg's way of reacting to social issues. His urge was to dive straight into the discussion, pulling no punches, taking a firm stand and identifying the opposition. The anthology as a whole did little to clarify matters. Did honour killing and honour violence actually exist, or was this a construct to cast a slur on immigrants and cover up the truth about how widespread violence against women in Sweden actually was?

Stieg Larsson is not exactly clear on this point. But his meaning was unambiguous enough: the debate on honour killing gave a free hand to Swedish men. He rejected entirely the attempts to explain the murder of Fadime in terms of cultural anthropology. The explanation was much simpler: 'The problem is that in male-dominated societies women are killed by men.'

9 November 2004

THE YEAR 2004 WAS A HECTIC ONE FOR STIEG LARSSON, to put it mildly. The book on honour killings came out in January; he was contributing to another anthology, *Sverigedemokraterna från insidan* (The Sweden Democrats from Within), edited by a colleague at *Expo*, Richard Slätt; and he had to produce his *Handbok för demokrater* (Handbook for Democrats), written with Daniel Poohl, for Malmö Museum by the end of the year. In the summer he had attended the European Security Conference on behalf of the Swedish Foreign Ministry.

Poohl remembers Stieg as being unusually stressed that autumn. He was being pestered on every side. Various institutions and schools had been phoning to ask him to come and give a lecture or a classroom talk. Stieg had always regarded lecturing as an important part of his activities, but now he was beginning to tire of it and was looking forward to scaling down.

But he also had reason to be cheerful. By this juncture he knew his novels would be published and that he could go on writing crime fiction. All he had to do was submit new manuscripts and they would be accepted.

In October he was interviewed by Lasse Winkler, editor-in-chief of the book trade journal *Svensk bokhandel*. The article began: 'Make a note of the name Stieg Larsson. He's not like other authors.'

It must have occurred to Stieg by now that the anonymous way of life he had chosen was coming to an end, that he would henceforth be under the spotlight, not so much as an anti-racist but as a writer of thrillers. He might even have to be interviewed on the TV chat shows he so detested.

He guessed too that he would earn money from the books. The publishers gave every indication of having scented a bestseller in the making. He was by no means averse to that: it would ensure not only his own financial security but also the future of *Expo*, and enable him to give money to other causes he regarded as vital, like women's refuges.

Taking a taxi one day that autumn, he found it was being driven by an old colleague from TT. Stieg told him elatedly about the novels and the publisher's belief in them. 'Can you imagine, it looks as if I'm going to be bigger than Mankell!'

FOR THE STAFF OF AN ANTI-RACIST MAGAZINE LIKE *EXPO*, 9 November was a significant date, with sombre associations.

The events of the night of 9–10 November 1938 came to be known as *Kristallnacht*. In cities throughout Germany people heard the sound of breaking glass and saw flames from burning synagogues. What was happening out of sight was even worse: beatings, lynchings, the transportation of thousands of Jews to concentration camps. *Kristallnacht* was a ratcheting up of the persecution of Jews: 9 November was a harbinger of the Holocaust.

It was a day when *Expo* staff would often be out at meetings around the country, and that was the case on this day, 9 November 2004. Stieg himself was booked to appear that evening at the Workers' Educational Association hall (ABF-huset) in Stockholm with Kurdo Baksi. During the day he would be working in the editorial office. His partner, Eva Gabrielsson, had gone up to Falun in Dalarna on a job, and Stieg took the bus from home to the editorial offices on Kungsholmen. When he arrived he found the lift out of order, so he had no option but to climb the seven flights of stairs to the office. He greeted his colleagues and all seemed normal. But then they noticed that something was not quite right. Stieg looked incredibly pale, and he suddenly slumped across his desk and fell to the floor. His colleagues rushed over, could not make him respond and realized it was serious.

They immediately phoned for an ambulance, which arrived within minutes and rushed him off to the nearby St Göran's hospital.

Mikael Ekman was on his way to Umeå, Stieg's home town, that day to give a lecture on Swedish neo-Nazism and take part in a rally to commemorate *Kristallnacht*. He was also going to call on Stieg's father, Erland, as Stieg had asked him to.

At the airport Mikael received a phone call from Ulrika Svensson at *Expo* to tell him that Stieg had collapsed and been rushed to hospital. He rang Eva Gabrielsson and his *Expo* colleague David Lagerlöf. Then he switched off his phone and got on the plane. When he arrived in

Umeå he didn't switch it back on. He knew things looked bad for Stieg, but he was determined to carry out his commitments.

'When I'd given the lecture and was on my way to the rally I turned on my phone and found a number of messages, all with the same news: Stieg had died.'

Eva Gabrielsson took a plane back to Stockholm as soon as she got the call on her mobile phone, despite the sketchy information. Arriving at the hospital that evening, she was given the devastating news.

Erland Larsson was on his way home from doing some family history research in the local library when his partner, Gun, came to meet him and tell him that Stieg had collapsed. He managed to get a phone number for the hospital, but it was a mobile and the doctor he spoke to 'just rambled on and knew nothing'. Erland also caught the first available flight to Stockholm to sit by his son's sickbed. 'But when I got there they told me he was dead. It just makes you want to die yourself.'

In the evening Mikael Ekman went out for a drink with Fredrik Malm, chairman of the Liberal People's Party Youth League, and Alexander Bengtsson of the Left Party of Sweden Youth League and others. These two had met in a debate earlier in the day and both had done work for *Expo*. It was a strange, mournful atmosphere, more like a wake. 'We sat talking about what had happened and reflected that we were actually a damned odd bunch,' says Mikael Ekman. 'There was me working for Strix Television, owned by the MTG Group, a bastion of capitalism, in company with liberals and leftists. All of us sitting there together. It says a lot about Stieg.'

MIKAEL FLEW DOWN BY THE FIRST PLANE IN THE MORNING. He met Eva and Erland in the lift up to *Expo*. He says he had kept a stiff upper lip after the news the day before, but as soon as he crossed the threshold into the office he 'started to cry like a baby', because it was so empty.

The future also seemed uncertain. What would happen to *Expo* now?

At that point hardly anyone was giving a thought to Stieg's as yet unpublished novels. The notion that everything was going to change, be turned upside down, because of those books was not even a glimmer on the horizon.

CRIME WRITER

IT'S THE DARKNESS THAT'S SO ALLURING. People's lives are overshadowed by past injustice and misdeeds, the fabric of society is torn to shreds, everything that once was good is in the process of being destroyed. Hope has more or less vanished.

That is one image of Sweden in 2010, as conveyed to the world by countless numbers of Swedish crime thrillers.

Yet to many Swedes it feels strange and unfamiliar. More than anything else, Sweden has always been the land of light, the land of equality and belief in the future, the land of eternal prosperity far up in the north.

Nevertheless in real life the Swedes seem quite content with their newly acquired darkness. Because it means that the country attracts attention and tourists come to see for themselves what things are actually like in a country so fraught with menace. It brings export income too. Swedish crime fiction has become an unrivalled sales success, an international brand.

To the list of universally known Swedes like Olof Palme, Astrid Lindgren, Ingmar Bergman, Ingvar Kamprad (of Ikea fame), Abba and Björn Borg can now be added a number of crime fiction authors: Henning Mankell, Håkan Nesser, Camilla Läckberg, Liza Marklund, Åke Edwardson. And then along comes Stieg Larsson, the unique phenomenon who both completes and breaks with the Swedish crime fiction tradition.

Writing Thrillers is Easy

IT WAS SOME TIME AT THE BEGINNING of the new millennium. Stieg Larsson was at home drinking whisky with his colleague Mikael Ekman: 'It was one of the rare occasions we sat and got drunk; you didn't often get drunk with Stieg.'

They were talking about the future and what they might do after retirement. Stieg declared that he wasn't a bit interested in saving for a pension and all that crap. 'I'm going to write a few thrillers instead and become a multi-millionaire.'

'It was like so much else with him: he just went ahead and did it, and it was as simple as that.'

In the one and only interview Stieg gave about his crime novels, for *Svensk Bokhandel*, he said, 'Writing thrillers is easy. It's much harder to write a 500-word article where everything has to be 100 per cent correct.'

Stieg would often sit up late into the night writing his books. This was not because he was trying to keep the project secret. Indeed, Eva has said that she played an active part in the writing process and contributed ideas on both content and style. And he was only too pleased to tell colleagues and friends what he was doing.

Stieg wanted other people's opinions, so as soon as the manuscript of the first book was ready he handed it out to those whose views he valued. Reactions, however, were somewhat mixed.

'I was a nerd who would rather plough through dissertations on Nazism than read novels,' says Mikael Ekman, 'so it was quite a while before I took the manuscript home, and to be honest I did it more out of politeness, because I knew he'd put his heart and soul into it. But when I read it, even with my vague notions about fiction, I could tell it was good.'

Robert Aschberg, well-known TV personality and chairman of the Expo Foundation, remembers learning of the manuscript's existence and recollects, 'The first things I read by Stieg which were not to do with *Expo* were short stories, or mini-novellas, based on facts he had researched, that he sent out to some of his acquaintances. I don't know why he wrote them. It might have been because he was overflowing with excess energy, but they were so well written that you just wanted more. I heard about the crime novels and he said himself that they were meant to be a modern Pippi Longstocking, so I thought, "What is he up to now?" I borrowed the manuscript of the first volume and began reading it one evening, and I didn't switch off my bedside light till four in the morning. So I borrowed the next volume. I realized then, if not before, that this was really big.'

From Maria Lang to Henning Mankell

WHEN STIEG LARSSON WAS WRITING HIS NOVELS in the early years of the new millennium, the vogue for crime fiction in Sweden had spawned a sequence of previously unknown writers who had begun selling sensationally well. A female thriller wave, initiated mainly by Liza Marklund, had started to replace the male line. Swedish crime fiction was already becoming a concept in Europe, especially in Germany, where it was somehow linked in the popular imagination to the faintly exotic picture of Sweden conveyed by Astrid Lindgren's children's books, with red cottages, dense silent forests and little lakes.

Yet the crime novel ought really never to have become a Swedish speciality, because Sweden seems to lack the fundamental requirements. In modern times there is no tradition of violence to speak of. The country lies somewhere in the middle of the European average for crime, except in one category where it is significantly above: cycle thefts.

The accepted view of Swedish literature is that it is serious and substantial, but slow, with no great entertainment value. Sweden has produced many fine authors over the years but they have seldom – with some notable exceptions – developed into international bestsellers. At least not until the 1990s.

EVEN THRILLERS HAVE NOT BEEN VERY THRILLING IN SWEDEN. In the first half of the twentieth century, if Swedes wanted anything really hair-raising to read, they had to turn to translations, mostly from English, because the crime novel was an Anglo-American genre.

But after the Second World War a number of thriller writers who were very popular on the domestic front came to prominence: Maria Lang, Stieg Trenter, Vic Suneson and H. K. Rönblom. These four dominated Swedish crime fiction for at least several decades. They kept on writing, book after book, and the publishers were happy to continue publishing them, because there was a steady market among solid conservative readers schooled in the genre by Agatha Christie and Dorothy L. Sayers. The new Swedish crime novel was a transplant of the English crime mystery to a Swedish environment, which might be Stockholm in the case of Trenter or the little town of Nora for Lang. The exception in this company was Suneson, who actually introduced the police procedural in the 1950s with his own methodical team of detectives.

Stieg Trenter is the only one of the four who is still read, for his lovingly detailed descriptions of Stockholm. H. K. Rönblom was the best stylist, but Maria Lang's books about the mystery-solving duo Puck Bure and Inspector Christer Wijk were the favourites by far in their day. She was also the most productive, writing a book a year with mechanical precision, more to the delight of her publisher and faithful readership than the critics. And she was much translated into other languages, a fact few people remember nowadays.

So there was a market for Swedish crime fiction, even though it was nowhere near the size it is now. Maria Lang achieved sales of some 40,000 copies per title. But even adding all editions of her books together, they do not come close to Stieg Larsson's total, and in his case there are only three titles to her forty.

THRILLERS ARE ESSENTIALLY about the disruption and restoration of order. The classic crime novel ensures that decent, well-behaved citizens prevail over the malefactors, preferably doing so by virtue of their intelligence and powers of logical deduction rather than by physical force. Stolen goods and diamond necklaces are returned to their rightful owners. It was a dangerous world, but not *that* dangerous.

The Swedish crime story of the 1950s depicted middle-class society with irony and wry humour. But there was usually no sign of the deep mistrust that was to characterize later Swedish crime fiction, with injustice and abuse of power in the midst of the idyll. Where that existed it was in genres other than crime fiction.

The 1950s equivalent of Stieg Larsson, in terms of sales figures and media attention, was Vilhelm Moberg. His series of novels about the emigration of the peasant farmers Kristina and Karl Oskar Nilsson from the village of Ljuder in Småland to Minnesota in the United States was published in four volumes from 1949 to 1959. They sold over a million copies and were almost instantly regarded as modern classics.

Moberg himself was not at all pleased with his success. He was angered and aggrieved by the lies and corruption he discerned everywhere in Swedish society. In pamphlets and lectures and in articles in the Syndicalist newspaper *Arbetaren* he raged against what he called the putrefaction of Swedish justice. The senior ranks of the civil service, the judiciary and the royal court were able, he maintained, to commit injustices and crimes without being called to account, because they were protected by other highly placed individuals.

So it was Moberg, the renowned chronicler of the peasant classes, who provided the uncompromising and revelatory portrait of society. Crime fiction was not a suitable vehicle for social criticism, neither from the Right nor, most definitely, from the Left.

IN A SWEDEN OF EXPANDING welfare provision, book reading was rapidly gaining ground among the working classes, lower-paid white-collar workers and the less well educated generally. Since detective fiction was easy to read and often published in cheap series sold beyond what for some was the refined world of the bookshop, its sales ought to have increased for those reasons alone. But they didn't, and the cause was largely political. In 1907 the Social Democratic Youth League had campaigned against what they called 'dirty books'. They were trying to shame the anonymously authored stories of Master Detective Nick Carter in particular. Such books, 'dealing with the excesses and orgies of morally degenerate individuals in one vice after another', were in their opinion simply exploitative and should not be on public sale.

Over the next few decades the Labour movement evolved an unsurpassed educational idealism and set up its own educational arm, ABF (the Workers' Educational Association), its own publishing house and various cultural institutions: Konstfrämjandet (Society for the

Promotion of Art), Litteraturfrämjandet (Society for the Promotion of Literature) and the National Theatre.

The literary sphere benefited from a brilliant innovation: in 1941, right in the middle of the Second World War, the magazine *Folket i Bild* launched the series FiB Folkböcker (Popular Books). Most were realistically narrated novels by well-known writers, often with a connection to the Labour movement, that were sold at a low price by a corps of several thousand agents in the workplace and door-to-door in residential areas.

Against all the odds the FiB books were an unqualified success. Three million copies of the first forty-four titles were printed. Their popularity was so manifest that the major publishing house of Bonniers imitated the concept exactly, even down to the sales force of agents, starting Bonniers Folkbibliotek (Bonniers Popular Library), which, with the publisher's huge backlist behind it, became a powerful competitor to the FiB books.

Crime fiction was more or less excluded from these series because it was too speculative, violent and lacked serious purpose. This was a view shared by other educationalists, such as Johan Hansson, the liberal idealist who established the publishing house of Natur & Kultur. When he converted the company into a foundation he had a special clause inserted to prevent it publishing crime fiction – a restriction successfully circumvented in recent years, when they produced detective fiction by Karin Alvtegen and Mons Kallentoft.

IN THE 1950S EVERYTHING SEEMED SO SIMPLE and small scale. There were always solutions to problems if rational thought was brought to bear. Sweden was Sweden and the world was the world. The middle class and the working class were patently different from one another. And they both thought they were the ones making the decisions in society.

But the 1950s idyll was not entirely what it seemed. It was a time of security against a background of angst. Everyone knew there would soon be a third world war. And the newspapers reported that the enemy was already in our midst, in the form of traitors and saboteurs. In 1952 the Communist Enbom Gang was exposed. Numerous people were arrested, all with links to the Communist Party, and seven were given exemplary sentences. Only later were doubts raised about the fantasy nature of Fritjof Enbom's confessions. But by then the sentences had been passed.

The Swedish thriller of the 1950s was a mirror of society, or rather of part of society, just as much as crime fiction is today. In an article in 1955, H. K. Rönblom defined the crime novel as light entertainment for people who live in democratic countries; for those who were convinced the law would be applied and justice prevail. It was a genre not for the critical but for the contented, 'a diversion for the optimistic'.

So it remained until the mid-1960s. Then everything changed in Sweden within just a few years, both in society and in crime fiction.

ABOUT A WEEK AFTER THE FIRST Swedish anti-Vietnam War demonstration and the same year the Swedish police were nationalized, the detective story *Roseanna* by Maj Sjöwall and Per Wahlöö was published. This was the book which was to introduce the revolution in Swedish detective fiction and without which Jan Guillou's Hamilton books, Henning Mankell's Wallander series and Stieg Larsson's Millennium Trilogy could probably never have been written.

Sjöwall and Wahlöö threw out the old props of the ingenious sleuth assembling the suspects in the manor house library and instead placed the real, unromantic, crime-solving police centre stage.

Roseanna was just the start of a carefully devised plan. The man-

and-wife team had decided they would produce exactly ten novels over ten years, published under the collective rubric of *The Story of a Crime*. The books would use the detective story format to reflect and analyse contemporary Sweden. More than that: they would, in Per Wahlöö's words, 'rip open the belly of an ideologically impoverished society'.

Per Wahlöö had already had some novels published, mostly political thrillers, but Maj Sjöwall, who worked for the weekly press, was new to fiction. Both were politically committed and way to the left of the ruling Social Democrats.

Their views were not entirely surprising, even though several years ahead of their time. But the literary venture was a bold one. Crime fiction was middle class. In the circles they moved in they certainly got no brownie points for writing in that medium. Even from a commercial perspective, thrillers were no guarantee of success. The publishing director at Norstedts, Lasse Bergström, wrote in his memoirs, *Bokmärken* (Bookmarks), that he was rather disappointed when Wahlöö, whom he already knew well, came to the office with Maj Sjöwall to propose their project.

'But my disappointment was in total ignorance of what was to come,' was his later terse comment on his reaction at the time.

Sjöwall and Wahlöö wanted to try something new, something daring and unexpected. To hell with traditions, even those of the Labour movement. They would write for a broad public and make it so easy and exciting that the bitter pill of the authors' social critique would slide down without meeting any resistance.

And weren't class divisions in society a crime in themselves, anyway? And shouldn't they be depicted as such?

From Sjöwall–Wahlöö onwards, the Swedish crime novel – oddly enough given its context – has been a genre with a strong tendency to the Left.

Fortunately for the authors, it was as if the era itself was crying out for a fresh sort of literature. The expansive, realistic, elaborate epic felt played out. What was needed now was something more in keeping with the pulse of the new decade – edgy, nerve-tingling, straight to the point.

At that period, the documentary form predominated in all the arts. Truth carried more weight than fiction. Within the space of a few years the book market was flooded with current affairs and reportage. Sjöwall–Wahlöö, despite opting for the novel, were in perfect accord with the trend. Their blow-by-blow accounts of meetings in police headquarters, interrogations of witnesses and suspects, post-mortem reports and so forth convinced the reader that these procedures were completely true to life.

Such devices would go on to become the staple for all Swedish crime writers.

Sjöwall and Wahlöö were aware too of crime fiction traditions other than the Swedish, just as Stieg Larsson was thirty years on. In the USA Dashiell Hammett had introduced the hard-boiled school of crime fiction with his novels about the private detective Sam Spade. Hammett was an anti-fascist and member of the American Communist Party, and wrote about a society that seldom showed any mercy to anyone born on the wrong side of the tracks. And in France Georges Simenon had created his Chief Superintendent Jules Maigret, who not only solved crimes but also sought to analyse their cause and was able to feel sympathy for the perpetrators.

Sjöwall and Wahlöö had found a useful model in the American crime writer Ed McBain and his novels about the 87th Police Precinct in the fictional town of Isola. McBain depicts the cops Steve Carella, Meyer Meyer, Bert Kling and their laborious daily grind confronting a criminality of steadily increasing ruthlessness. These books were fine examples of the police procedural, detective stories where the efforts of the team are much more important than an individual detective hero's flashes of insight. Maj Sjöwall and Per Wahlöö decided to learn from McBain and even translated some of his books into Swedish.

Roseanna introduces a Swedish police team at the Homicide Bureau in Stockholm. They are Detective Inspector Martin Beck (later superintendent and head of the National Homicide Bureau of the Central Bureau of Investigation) and his assistants Lennart Kollberg and Fredrik Melander. The cast is gradually augmented: Gunvald Larsson, Einar Rönn, Åke Stenström (who is murdered in the fourth book and succeeded by Benny Skacke), and also Stenström's former girlfriend Åsa Torell.

This is the team that battles to solve various crimes and more often than not succeeds. Yet in the final analysis they always lose. In contrast to the crime stories of the 1950s, no equilibrium is restored in the police procedurals of the 1960s and 1970s. Society itself is constantly producing new and more serious, more audacious and better-organized types of crime. The Sjöwall–Wahlöö books are not reading matter for the optimistic.

These novels are about the triumphs and impotence of the collective. Young individualists and careerists who are too self-important are bullied and cut down to size, not least by Lennart Kollberg.

But the biggest difference of all in comparison with earlier crime novels lies in something more elusive: in the language, the style, the atmosphere:

The little black car hurtled forward through the darkness precisely and implacably, as if it were a weightless craft in space.

The buildings tightened along the road and the city rose up beneath its dome of light, huge and cold and desolate, stripped of everything but hard naked surfaces of metal, glass and concrete.

Not even in the city centre was there any street life at this hour of the night. With the exception of an occasional taxi, two ambulances and a squad car, everything was dead. The police car was black with white fenders and rushed quickly past on its own bawling carpet of sound.

The traffic lights changed from red to yellow to green to yellow to red with a meaningless mechanical monotony.

Here, at the beginning of *The Abominable Man*, the authors manage to get everything into one short sequence – the forward movement, the suspense of the thriller, the doom-laden feeling of imminent calamity, together with an evocation of the new Swedish capitalist society as they see it – cold, desolate, inhuman.

Something really had happened to Swedish crime fiction.

THE SJÖWALL–WAHLÖÖ BOOKS were written from the outset in a restrained objective style, but by degrees the text became more interspersed with ironical and critical comments on everything from beer prices and fashions to government foreign policy and the incompetence of the police force and its top management.

What the authors diagnosed in the mid-1960s was a welfare state degenerating, no longer class-equalizing but class-dividing, where people were oppressed by assembly lines and rationalizations, where original residential town centres were being demolished and the urban populace pushed out to so-called dormitory towns.

And the social drama was escalating as the volumes were being written. Vietnam demonstrations were attracting thousands of participants, police and demonstrators clashed, a tennis tournament in Båstad between Sweden and Rhodesia was disrupted by riots, a students' union building in Stockholm was occupied, a wave of wildcat strikes hit the whole country, the Establishment was rocked by the IB Affair of secret service malpractice, and a hostage drama on Norrmalmstorg and a terrorist attack on the West German embassy brought Stockholm to the attention of the world.

Politics had moved out on to the streets. Violence was making itself felt. The authorial voice became more explicit as *The Story of a Crime* progressed. At the very end of the last volume, as some of the main characters are sitting playing party games, it becomes over-explicit:

> They all turned their papers over and drew more squares. When Kollberg was ready, he looked at Martin Beck and said, 'The trouble with you, Martin, is just that you're in the wrong job. At the wrong time. In the wrong part of the world. In the wrong system.'
>
> 'Is that all?'
>
> 'More or less,' said Kollberg. 'My turn to start? Then I say X. X as in Marx.'

This final scene in *The Terrorists* is dated 10 January 1975. Four months later NLF troops marched into Saigon and the USA left Vietnam. The war that had brought the youth of the West to their feet was over. In Cambodia the Khmer Rouge took power and ushered in a period of unimaginable terror.

The Left to which Sjöwall and Wahlöö felt they belonged was about to experience disillusionment and factionalism. Nothing was straightforward any more. The unique combination of anger and hope that had swept the emotions along during the dramatic years when *The Story* of a Crime was being written was gone, never to return.

Maj Sjöwall and Per Wahlöö had wanted to write for the people and not for the Swedish Academy or the broadsheet newspaper critics. As a result they became the critics' favourites, which was to have a decisive impact on the Swedish crime novel. Because it was this interplay of effective popular storytelling, widespread media attention and positive reactions on the arts pages that brought the Swedish crime fiction vogue into being and allowed it to flourish.

With the praise came honours and prizes. In 1968 the authors received the Edgar Allan Poe Award, the highest accolade for a crime novel, for *The Laughing Policeman*. Now even the most dismissive of readers could bury themselves in a Martin Beck police thriller with a clear conscience.

It was not long before the Sjöwall–Wahlöö police team progressed into the film world. Martin Beck has been played by such stars as Keve Hjelm, Gösta Ekman, Carl Gustaf Lindstedt and Peter Haber. A German version of *The Man Who Went up in Smoke* featured Derek Jacobi in the role of Beck. Walter Matthau was given the part in the Hollywood version of *The Laughing Policeman* and Jan Decleir in a Dutch film of *The Locked Room*.

Ironically, it has only been in later years, with the industrial production of Martin Beck films on standardized thriller lines (twenty-six so far) that the protagonist has become well known to a really wide audience. Yet the Martin Beck and Gunvald Larsson we meet there have almost nothing in common with the classic detective story characters that Sjöwall and Wahlöö created.

THE SJÖWALL–WAHLÖÖ NOVELS arrived suddenly, like a bolt from the blue, illuminating the sky of Swedish crime fiction and vanishing just as fast. The authors had fulfilled their plan and that was it. During the writing of *The Story of a Crime* sequence Per Wahlöö had succumbed to cancer, and he died before the final volume reached the bookshops.

The tide of crime fiction seemed to be ebbing as rapidly as it had surged.

In 1986, some ten years after *The Terrorists* was published, the Stockholm newspaper *Expressen* discontinued its prestigious Sherlock Prize for lack of worthy candidates. A standard history of Swedish literature published in 1990 has this to say about the Swedish crime novel: 'Scintillating individual contributions from several writers not named in this survey cannot refute the picture of general decline in the period from about 1975 onwards. In fact this decline probably denotes a return to normal after the hectic years of 1945–75, which must in retrospect be seen as the golden age of Swedish crime fiction.'

One has to smile at such a monumental error of judgement. But seen in relation to the situation prevailing at the end of the 1980s it was probably a logical conclusion. For readers at the time, the Sjöwall–Wahlöö series appeared to mark an end rather than a beginning.

IT COULD INDEED HAVE BEEN SO. For even if the crime fiction boom that burst on the scene in the new millennium was anchored in the specific Sjöwall–Wahlöö form of police procedural realism, contemporary setting and social criticism, it was actually prompted by a series of events in Swedish society in the 1970s and 1980s.

It seemed as if reality had to be allowed to take its course for a few years, the vagaries of fate be allowed to spin their threads before fiction could pick them up again.

One chain of events centred on the magazine *Folket i Bild/Kulturfront*. It began publication in 1972 as a sort of revival in Maoist popular-front form of Karl Kilbom's classic popular-movement journal *Folket i Bild*. After a tentative start it had a breakthrough in May 1973 with one of the biggest journalistic exposés of the century: a covert Swedish spy organization, quite separate from the official intelligence services, with direct links to the government and employing methods that would not normally be acceptable.

This was the IB Affair, the Information Bureau scandal. IB was actually a merger between the C-Bureau within the Ministry of Defence, charged with the surveillance of Communists, and SÄPO (the Security Police), a network of informers which the Social Democratic Party had built up in major workplaces to counteract the influence of Communists on the trade unions.

The FiB report, which was illustrated by rather dramatically fuzzy clandestine photographs of the undercover spies, was signed by their staff reporter Jan Guillou and the then inexperienced freelancer Peter Bratt. But Bratt was the one who had brought the material to the magazine, having made contact with a whistle-blowing IB defector, Håkan Isacson.

The IB Affair had far-reaching consequences. First and foremost there was the question of trust. Good democratic Swedish politicians had evidently lied. If even they were not speaking the truth, who could be believed?

It was generally known that SÄPO kept a register of left-wing activists, but at least it was done under some sort of parliamentary supervision. Yet here obviously were secret groups within the apparatus of the state carrying out political espionage that the elected representatives had never even heard of.

Both journalists, Guillou and Bratt, were arrested and sentenced to three years' imprisonment for espionage, reduced to ten months by the Court of Appeal.

In the peace of solitary confinement Jan Guillou read the Sjöwall–Wahlöö books, which he had not done before, despite the fact that the Martin Beck novels were almost compulsory reading in left-wing circles. He had regarded crime fiction as a worthless and parasitical form of literature.

But as he writes in his memoirs, *Ordets makt och vanmakt* (The Power and Impotence of Words), this reading was 'one of the most important "aha" experiences' in his life. If the hard-boiled detective story, a literary genre normally leaning to the Right, could be given a bold twist and a radical left-wing message, the same might be done with the even more reactionary genre of the spy thriller, a field in which Guillou had now gained considerable insight the hard way.

Thus was born the concept of his *Coq Rouge* novels featuring the erstwhile count, former left-wing activist and now gentleman spy, Carl Hamilton.

The relatively youthful Hamilton was given an older boss and mentor, called the Old Man in the books. He too had a prototype in real life – no less than the head of IB, Birger Elmér, who had been so pitilessly exposed. Jan Guillou bumped into him by chance in a bank some years after the IB Affair, and both men burst out laughing when they recognized each other and went on to become good friends. Elmér not only provided the template for Hamilton's superior but contributed tips on modern intelligence work as well.

The Hamilton books are not crime novels as such, but they have influenced the Swedish boom in crime fiction in several ways. First, because they broke down a barrier. Swedish book production in the mid-1980s was divided into quality literature, dominated by the major Swedish authors, and the entertainment sector, which was unashamedly commercial and consisted almost exclusively of translated fiction from Britain and America. Authors such as Jackie Collins, Shirley Conran, Sidney Sheldon, Jean Auel, Judith Krantz and others were the big sellers in a book market wholly liberalized after 1970 and increasingly focused on bestsellers.

Now along came Guillou and his gun-toting Hamilton, equally unashamedly commercial but undeniably Swedish and with dissenting political opinions, and soon challenging and overtaking the sales of English-language novels.

The *Coq Rouge* series exemplified what could happen if Swedish authors began to write what might be called popular fiction – though they were showing little inclination to go in that direction.

The first book about Carl Hamilton came out in 1986. That was the year when a real-life murder not only grabbed the headlines but took over completely and changed the image of Sweden for ever.

In Sjöwall–Wahlöö's final Martin Beck novel, *The Terrorists*, Sweden's prime minister is murdered on Riddarholmen in the centre of Stockholm. He is not given a name but the description certainly called to mind the real prime minister, Olof Palme. And now, a mere ten years on, the murder of the prime minister occurred in real life. Olof Palme was shot dead on 28 February, at the corner of Sveavägen and Tunnelgatan in the city centre. All over the country the media reporting grew into one great big detective story, with the head of the investigation, Hans Holmér, as the classic police hero. There were clues, false trails, spent bullets, speculations, timetables, mystical observations, police in Palme's office, dramatic arrests, more speculations, and ever more police in the prime minister's office.

And all and sundry wanted to solve the murder. Private detectives, common protagonists in American crime novels, scarcely existed in Sweden, but now they were everywhere, authorized by everyone and no one. Even a publisher from Bonniers investigated, with official permission from the government and the national chief of police, and with financial backing from a well-known financier.

If a policeman is murdered, the felon is 100 per cent certain to be arrested. 'There are plenty of unsolved murders in Swedish criminal history, but not one of them is the murder of a policeman,' Sjöwall and Wahlöö claim in *The Abominable Man*. So how can a prime minister be murdered without the culprit being arrested?

That question still awaits an answer.

The Palme murder and its investigation began to take on increasingly postmodern characteristics over the course of time, and the distinction between real life and fiction seemed increasingly blurred.

There was nothing but a maze full of clues and signs that might or might not have some connection with reality.

As the author P. O. Enquist wrote in his collection of essays *Kartritarna* (The Cartographers):

This never-ending detective story was writing itself, becoming ever more complex and unfortunately not following any of the rules of the genre: there was no final gathering of the suspects in the dining room, no tying up of all the loose ends, no guilty party breaking down and confessing.

It was the never-ending great Swedish detective story.

And the nation loved it – until eventually everyone became desperate for a final chapter where we were not all detectives but where there was just one omniscient narrator to summarize and collate everything, one penetrating intellect to give us the solution.

Finally, the case was resolved. A lone murderer, demonstrably insane and already notorious, brought the story to its innocuous conclusion. No conspiracies, thank goodness. It was the alcoholic who did it, in line with all the statistics. Yet not even this ending was conclusive. The lone madman could not be convicted, so everything was back at square one, and still is.

What remains is the crime. And in this Sweden, with its completely unsensational crime statistics, undeniably has something that no other country in Europe has: a major iconic murder mystery right at the heart of the nation.

After that the Palme investigation definitively crossed over into fiction, when both the chief of police, Hans Holmér, and the publisher, Ebbe Carlsson, produced their own crime novels. But that too turned out to be a blind alley. It was not the policeman and the private detective who would lead the Swedish crime novel into a new era. On the other hand, there is no doubt that the Palme murder itself was to play a part in the crime novels that were yet to come. For underlying everything was a shift in the way people saw the world around them: solidarity and trust had been lost, the concept of justice had been distorted. Something had broken in Sweden. And it happened at that moment in February 1986.

In 1990, four years after the Palme murder, the new era for the Swedish crime thriller began. The Berlin Wall had recently been opened up and then totally demolished. The Soviet Union was about to dissolve itself. Almost everyone was happy at the course of events. Conservatives felt the winds of freedom in their sails. There would be a clean sweep and everything that smacked of socialism would go: public systems of support and official regulations would be scrapped, private initiatives encouraged. The whole Social Democratic welfare state in Sweden would be demolished, just like the Berlin Wall.

The Left were also pleased. They no longer had to bear the yoke of Soviet Communism. Eastern Bloc socialism was after all the only real socialism in existence, however much they might want to distance themselves from it. Now they could create the kind of socialism they themselves wanted without having to listen to constant rants about the Soviet Union.

But society was heading in a different direction. Change was only partly to do with the winds of freedom versus socialist regeneration; it was rather more to do with economic crisis, racism, ethnic cleansing, refugees and even more racism.

Though it cannot actually be said that Swedish literature attempted to come to terms with this new reality. It had other ideals.

The 1980s was the decade of postmodernism. Young writers and critics rebelled against the politically committed literature of the 1970s that had been accused of ignoring concepts such as aesthetics, form and quality. The journal *Jakobs stege*, published by the former Trotskyist Rene Coeckelberghs, mounted a campaign against social realism. The journal *Kris*, whose tone was set by its regular contributors Horace Engdahl, Anders Olsson and Stig Larsson (Stieg's namesake of the same generation from Umeå), was extending the theory of postmodernism.

'Grand narratives' were dead, they argued. They meant both the all-embracing social and philosophical theories, Marxism, Freudianism, and traditional naturalistic literature.

Literature and reality were two entirely distinct grand concepts. Literature existed in the universe of texts and could fundamentally only refer to and engage with other texts.

The new Swedish literature of the 1980s had been moulded to a postmodernist pattern, as if a symbiosis between critics and writers had come into being. 'How many readers schooled in modernism want a writer whose texts are unambiguous, autobiographical, coherent and intimate?' asked the literary critic Johan Svedjedal in a presentation of Stig Larsson's writing in the journal *Artes*.

But perhaps the majority of readers were not schooled in modernism. They were quite happy to read coherent texts. Ten or fifteen years earlier many of them had been immersing themselves in Sven Delblanc's Hedeby saga, Kerstin Ekman's Katrineholm novels or Sara Lidman's railway epic – the lengthy sequences of novels from the 1970s that were both descriptive and coherent, and which through book clubs and reading groups reached an audience comparable in size to that enjoyed by Vilhelm Moberg in the 1950s.

The era of the realistic multi-volume narrative had passed, but in the early 1990s there was still a reality crying out to be portrayed. And there are usually writers ready to take up the challenge.

BOOKS CAN APPEAR too early or too late, or sometimes at just the right moment. There can be no doubt that Henning Mankell's *Faceless Killers* came at exactly the right moment.

In this novel an elderly couple are murdered on an isolated farm in Skåne. The dying woman is heard to say something that sounds like 'foreign', and that word is the spark that ignites a conflagration. A spate of xenophobic crimes erupts across the southern Skåne countryside.

Faceless Killers was an almost prophetic book. It was published in 1991, coinciding with a new reality which was exploding right in the face of the unprepared. The years 1990 and 1991 saw refugee camps being set ablaze in various parts of the country, the formation of the neo-Nazi White Aryan Resistance and the shooting of immigrants by the 'Laser Man'.

The book's author, Henning Mankell, had begun his writing career in 1973 with a typical working-class novel called *Bergsprängaren* (The Rock Blaster), and proceeded to write a number of realistic narratives with a politically radical subtext, published by Ordfront, one of the most distinctive publishing houses to emerge from the 1960s.

Faceless Killers was conceived as a sociological novel, but the story needed a policeman and the author found a suitable name, Kurt Wallander, in the telephone directory.

And Wallander was here to stay. Throughout the 1990s he drove on the back roads of the district around Ystad, squelching about in the muddy fields of Skåne, in constant pursuit of ruthless mass murderers, himself morose, obstinate and generally unpleasant, over the years increasingly a self-caricature.

Yet Kurt Wallander is without a shadow of doubt one of the best characterizations in Swedish crime fiction. He is a kind of Hamlet in 1990s dress, a man who, despite having chosen his profession of his own free will, has landed up where he doesn't want to be in life, in what always turns out to be deep shit. And he is the one who has to sort everything out on his own. Perhaps simply because it is his duty.

Wallander is as basically apolitical as Martin Beck. He notes the change in society but makes no protest. Whereas Beck can seek support from his colleagues and discuss situations with them, Wallander remains detached and fairly uncommunicative. He is not much bothered about Martinsson, Hansson, Svedberg, Höglund or the other detectives in Ystad. And, to tell the truth, nor is the reader. Sjöwall and Wahlöö needed their collective, but Mankell doesn't. Wallander takes over and creates all the roles himself. He is all the Sjöwall–Wahlöö characters in one: a depressive like Beck, a loutish rule-breaker like Gunvald Larsson, an overweight philosopher like Kollberg and a taciturn man of conscience like Einar Rönn.

By the mid-1990s, as the Wallander series was entering its second phase, Mankell's books were the biggest sellers in Sweden. He was the successor to Jan Guillou as the Swedish author consistently at the top of the bestseller lists. His murders were also becoming more and more spectacular and artfully contrived – victims were hacked to pieces or scalped in Red Indian mode, impaled on sharp stakes in an animal trap or burned to cinders in a transformer unit.

Kurt Wallander himself drives about in the hunt for his murderers on the periphery of a Sweden which itself is a remote corner of Europe, in its turn a small fraction of the world as a whole. The links criss-cross the globe – from Ystad in Skåne to Riga in Latvia, to Transkei in South Africa, to Santiago in the Dominican Republic, to Luanda in Angola. The globalized world seeks out Kurt Wallander, not the other way round. *The White Lioness*, which was the real breakthrough for the series, marked the beginning of the theme of Sweden and the world.

But Mankell does not preach in his crime novels the way Sjöwall and

Wahlöö did. He would never so explicitly posit Karl Marx as the final missing piece in the jigsaw puzzle of society. But he indubitably shares his predecessors' fundamental outlook, as is evinced in his depiction of the relationship between Sweden and the Third World, where he is out of step with the spirit of the times in Sweden and Europe. In the early 1990s the attitude towards the countries of the south had shifted from vaguely positive to an almost entirely negative one. What was called Third Worldism came under attack, and Swedish foreign policy underwent one of its greatest transformations ever as it was redirected towards Europe and the West. In the United Nations in the 1980s Sweden had often voted with Third World countries and against the West. From the next decade on this was almost never to happen.

When Mankell returned home to Sweden in 1989 from Mozambique, where he had been working in theatre in the capital, Maputo, and started on his first Wallander novel, his experiences were utterly unlike those of most Swedish authors. By and large he still retained the 1970s attitude that the important events and developments in the world were taking place in the poverty-stricken countries. In that respect he had a markedly divergent view of his native land and saw quite different things from the majority of Swedish authors, which was unquestionably one of the secrets of his success.

If Sjöwall and Wahlöö wrote with the winds of change at their backs, Mankell was tacking against the wind. But this did not mean that he was any less popular with the general public. On the contrary, his books sold far more successfully than theirs had ever done.

MANKELL BROUGHT ABOUT THE TRANSFORMATION. The status of the Swedish crime novel was raised at a stroke. Crime fiction prizes suddenly became interesting again and the potential of the genre more apparent.

Others soon followed in his wake. First up was Håkon Nesser, who had been a teacher for twenty-five years before he published his little-noticed debut novel. In 1993 he felt an impulse to write about crime: the result was *The Mind's Eye*, and then *Borkmann's Point*, a considerably more violent story about a serial killer who slits his victims' throats, apparently without motive. These were the beginnings of a new series about Detective Chief Inspector Van Veeteren and his colleagues Reinhart, Münster and Moreno, living and working in Maardam, a fictional town in an indeterminate northern European country. Van Veeteren has certain similarities to Wallander – he can be morose and surly and has an intuitive ability to read people's reactions and interplay, but is at the same time a more tragic figure, with a son who is a criminal and who eventually gets murdered.

Åke Edwardson had already published two freestanding crime novels when his *Dance with an Angel* introduced the series about Chief Inspector Erik Winter in Gothenburg. The sequence was planned as ten books, with a protagonist who was to differ substantially from the ageing Beck, Wallander and Van Veeteren. The young and upper-class Erik Winter is a man who smokes cigarillos and whose taste in whisky is for single malts, who wears bespoke suits, collects jazz records and barely knows what punk is despite having been born in the 1960s. Winter is an oddball, but his snobbishness is somewhat mitigated by his circle of mundane yet characterful Gothenburg police colleagues.

Both Nesser and Edwardson are stylistically conscious writers who have created settings typical of their times. Nesser's indeterminate Maardam is part of an ever more homogeneous Europe, in an EU which Sweden joined in 1995. Edwardson's plots are set with supreme assurance in the cosy small-town atmosphere of Gothenburg where the transition to cruel and menacing big city in a tough fin-de-siècle world is seamless.

In the second half of the 1990s the crime novel was establishing itself as a significant genre on the Swedish book market. Public demand seemed insatiable, Wallander fans were branching out to sample other detectives too and more or less every publishing house dreamed of finding its own detective superstar. The whole genre was still firmly anchored in the Swedish tradition of social realism, and provided an ideal form for throwing light into dark corners and portraying both the top and bottom of society in one broad sweep. This was to be reflected in the clearest fashion in the work of two of the most prominent but quite dissimilar new names at the end of that decade: Kjell Eriksson and Arne Dahl.

Kjell Eriksson's crime novels are set in the university city of Uppsala, but he himself is far removed from academe. As a former gardener and farm labourer he is the one who, together with Aino Trosell, has extended the tradition of the working-class novel into crime fiction. Eriksson has an unerring eye for ordinary people, including policemen, for their way of life, mode of expression, gestures and not least their surrounding environment; but just like Mankell, he also shows the wider world impinging on the smaller local world and changing it irrevocably.

Arne Dahl, a pseudonym for the established literary author Jan Arnald, wrote a succession of novels about what he called the A-Team, a special unit of hand-picked police officers charged with investigating 'violent crime with an international dimension'. Dahl's novels are plotted against a background of the major events in Sweden and the world in the years surrounding the turn of the millennium. What Sjöwall and Wahlöö identified in its infancy – a more organized and international criminality – has become full-blown reality in Arne Dahl's novels, with new kinds of threats, new types of villain, new political ideals – but perhaps still the same old class-ridden society.

Female Readers Demand Their Heroines

IN THE EARLY 1990S A BOOK appeared which was very different from all these series novels and did not really fit into the category of crime novel at all, yet which now stands out as one of the high points in Swedish crime fiction: Kerstin Ekman's *Blackwater.*

Ekman began her crime novels in the 1960s and was awarded the accolade 'Queen of Crime Writing' before she went over to rather more literary novels with ever-increasing success. In the 1970s she was one of the most lauded of Swedish novelists and was elected in 1987 to the Swedish Academy, although she resigned her active role after dissenting from the Academy's response to the Salman Rushdie affair.

The mystery in *Blackwater* bears many resemblances to a hair-raising real-life crime that occurred in the Swedish fells in 1984. A Dutch couple, Janni and Marinus Stegehuis, were camping on the shores of Lake Appojaure in Norrbotten when they were murdered in the night with multiple stab wounds through the canvas of their tent by an unidentified assailant.

Kerstin Ekman's novel is set in the fell village of Blackwater (from which the English-language edition took its title – the Swedish original is literally *Events by the Water*) and describes a similar murder and police investigation; but at a more profound level it is about the effect of the memories of the crime and all the events surrounding it seeping like a poison into people's lives. It is also about the devastation of nature by human beings, another kind of murder and one which rural dwellers are forced to live with and try to come to terms with.

The female perspective which is so discernible in Kerstin Ekman's books was not common in Swedish crime fiction at the time. More typical perhaps was the inclusion by the three big names, Mankell, Nesser and Edwardson, of a token woman police officer with a subsidiary role. But worse still, there were no female crime writers, which was quite odd. Great Britain had its Agatha Christie and Dorothy L. Sayers, who had more or less created the enormous public appetite for detective stories, and many successful women crime writers followed in their wake in Britain and North America, including P. D. James, Minette Walters, Patricia Cornwell, Elizabeth George and Sara Paretsky, the last two being particular favourites of Stieg Larsson. Norway had such bestselling names as Karin Fossum, Kim Småge and Anne Holt.

In the 1930s the best Swedish crime novel was written by a woman: Kjerstin Göransson Ljungman's *Tjugosju sekundmeter, snö* (Twenty-seven Metres per Second, Snow) – only a later novel of hers, *The Shining Sea*, was translated into English – and the 1950s were dominated by Maria Lang's murder mysteries. But now the female input had mysteriously dried up.

When the change came it was swift. Three Swedish crime novels written by women were published in the years 1995–7. The following year, 1998, there were ten titles from women writers.

Both new and experienced writers had decided to grapple with the genre. Inger Frimansson, for instance, already had eight books to her credit when she went over to thrillers with her *Good Night, My Darling*. Readers who were tired of police procedurals, crime scene investigations and the questioning of suspects found what they were looking for here, because in her books the suspense lay more in psychology than incident. And the foul deeds took place not in the urban jungle or among high-rise apartment blocks but where the readers themselves lived, in neat and tidy quiet middle-class suburbia.

That same year saw the publication of the first novel by Karin Alvtegen, who was also more interested in the individuals behind the crime than the crime itself. For her it is often people on the margins of society who commit desperate and dangerous acts motivated by a kind of heart-rending longing for reconciliation and love rather than by evil or aggressive tendencies.

THE SWEDISH CRIME WRITING ACADEMY thought the gender problem might be specifically to do with the police procedural, in that women are more inclined to read and write about clever Miss Marple characters than about shabby detective inspectors or police teams on night shift. So when a special prize was set up for a promising woman crime writer it was called the Poloni Prize, after the Swedish Agatha Christie acolyte Helena Poloni.

But it is difficult to imagine a crime novel heroine further removed from the widowed clergyman's wife Astrid Brunelius, Poloni's heroine, than Annika Bengtzon in Liza Marklund's debut novel *The Bomber*, which received the inaugural award: a stressed, foul-mouthed freelance reporter for a tabloid evening newspaper with a child to take to the nursery every day.

The book appeared, almost unnoticed, from the tiny imprint Ordup-plaget, which was run by the journalist Sigge Sigfridsson. He had taken it on condition that she write four more books and waive her advance in favour of an equal division of profits between publisher and author. She agreed. The print run was 4,000 copies, of which the book trade ordered only 300 in advance. Nor did sales take off after publication, so the entire project seemed stillborn.

But then she received the Poloni Prize, and the newspapers began writing about her, voting her the new Queen of Crime Writing that everyone had been waiting for, and when the paperback came out, with Marklund herself on the cover, the dam burst. *The Bomber* was paperback bestseller of the year, and the profit-sharing principle which had been a temporary expedient became a concept that was to transform the Swedish book trade.

When Jan Guillou and his common-law wife, the publisher Ann-Marie Skarp, left the publishing house of Norstedts and joined Sigfridsson's firm, the new Piratförlaget was formed. Its payment method was tempting for big-selling authors and in the course of just a few years it grew to become one of Sweden's largest publishers in terms of turnover. And Marklund's public success definitively broke the male domination of the Swedish crime fiction market.

There must have been a myriad unpublished women writers sitting at home putting the finishing touches to their crime novel manuscripts, because in less than a couple of years a veritable tide of female crime fiction authors swept in to flood the book market. It seemed there was a pent-up demand for simple, straightforward thrillers with realistic everyday settings, since over the next two or three years a host of new female writers joined the bestseller lists: Anna Jansson, Karin Wahlberg, Tove Klackenberg, Mari Jungstedt and Camilla Läckberg. Some of those who started writing around then, including Åsa Larsson and Eva-Marie Liffner, were to diverge into a more purely literary direction.

Åsa Larsson confirmed her position with her next novels as one of the best of Swedish crime writers. She evoked a fictional world in a distinctive and atmospheric setting – the northern Swedish landscape around Kiruna – with two strong but very disparate female protagonists, the policewoman Anna-Maria Mella and public prosecutor Rebecka Martinsson.

THE FEMALE CRIME WRITERS brought in new milieus and a different view of human relationships and the problems of everyday life, but also more serious themes such as discrimination in the workplace and abuse of women and children.

The sales success was not so surprising in the light of developments in reading habits in Sweden. It is an established fact that Swedish women are more avid readers than men, so it was only natural that books taking up issues with which women could empathize soon became popular.

Most popular of all is Camilla Läckberg. Her novels are set in the picturesque little west coast town of Fjällbacka, where her heroes, the writer Erica Falck and police officer Patrik Hedström, solve murder mysteries in the best Maria Lang style. Although she has frequently received glowing reviews abroad, her books are as damned by the critics in Sweden as they are loved by their loyal and ever-increasing hordes of readers.

The Läckberg phenomenon has puzzled some; others have tried to imitate her and hoped to achieve similar sales – but in vain. She has reached a position from which she will not easily be ousted: she has become the queen of the cosy thriller, the author who puts her readers' everyday thoughts and fantasies into novelistic form.

Läckberg has a very technical approach to her writing. She sees crime fiction as a craft and has herself laid out the basic techniques on her website. She decided early on to turn herself into a brand and so got in touch with an agent, Bengt Nordin. He transferred her from her initial small publisher to Forum, a house owned by the major publisher Bonniers, where there was a willingness to invest in marketing her. In three years she was established as one of the best-selling authors in Sweden.

Her career also reflects significant changes in the Swedish book market. While some of the major European countries like France and Germany still apply fixed prices for books, to protect literary values from the pressures of commercialism, Sweden, like Britain, has gone in the opposite direction. Since 1970, when its equivalent of the British Net

Book Agreement was abolished, the Swedish book trade has developed into one of the most commercialized in Europe. Alongside Norway, Sweden soon headed the list of the world's leading book club countries. Bookshops responded to the rise of book clubs by going in for active marketing, prominent displays and emphasis on blockbusters. Books also began to be sold in a wider variety of outlets: department stores, news-stands, supermarkets. Paperbacks, which had been edged out of the market in Sweden in the 1970s, made a remarkable comeback, and in the new millennium sales of low-price books really took off. Paperbacks were the typical impulse buy and so were integral to the surge in crime fiction sales.

When the Gothenburg Book Fair first started, in 1986, many people in the trade thought there would be no point in bringing in lots of authors. Who would want to go and see someone who had written a book when it was the actual book itself which was of interest? But it turned out to be exactly what the public did want. And the cult of the celebrity and focus on personality have continued to increase and are magnified a hundredfold nowadays in the echo chamber of the media.

Nor was it only the pricing of books which was deregulated. The national agreement between publishers and writers was also abolished. A window was opened for individual negotiations and for literary agents to fulfil a role they had never had before in Sweden – to represent authors in the British or American manner, including vis-à-vis publishers, to negotiate more generous royalties and advances for authors who were selling well, and to try much more energetically to sell foreign rights than the publishers had previously done.

Today agents switch authors between publishers, demand better advances, direct the marketing and place an author abroad before the books have even been published in Sweden.

A book is no longer just a book. It can be a film, a TV series, a serial, occasionally a comic strip. Crime novels have even become part of the Swedish tourist industry. All this can provide superlative publicity, though only for authors who have already made their breakthrough to real sales success. As the literary sociologist Johan Svedjedal has pointed out, it is now not so much a matter of selling books as of selling complete fictive worlds.

SJÖWALL–WAHLÖÖ, Mankell and many of their successors have raised the status of the thriller. Other forms of popular fiction such as chick lit have continued to be held in low esteem by the critics and the educated classes. When Jackie Collins came to the Gothenburg Book Fair in 1989 all the arts pages were united in giving her the thumbs down and the chair of the Swedish Writers Union protested at her invitation. But today's crime writers are now extremely welcome on the podium at the fair. They are taken seriously and reviewed in the media, and crime fiction as a whole has become more visible and found new readers.

But with the steady increase in numbers of titles published, the overall quality of books has gone down. And the critics complain of interminable series, poor style, stereotypical characters and hopelessly predictable plots. It also seems as if commercial pressure is making crime fiction, both Swedish and international, more explicitly violent, more inclined to glorify sadism, and this may in a few years induce a satiated public to give up and so hasten the end of the crime novel's current heyday.

But for the time being crime writing remains very strong commercially because it is giving a sizeable audience of readers exactly what they want. If the crime writers of the 1950s aimed at the optimistic middle classes and those of the 1990s at discontented radicals, current authors are writing for overburdened media consumers who require books with a declaration of content and as few surprises as possible.

OF COURSE, SUCH SWEEPING CRITICISM is not entirely fair. After all, the Swedish crime novel, or perhaps rather the thriller and popular literature in the broadest sense, has retained a good deal of its innovatory qualities. John Ajvide Lindqvist has picked up the horror story with his first book, *Let the Right One In*, and its sequels and made something of this traditionally despised category that has astonished both critics and the general public. Johan Theorin has been very effectively incorporating old legends and ghost stories in his crime novels set on Öland, off the east coast of Sweden. And the brutal side of present-day Stockholm found its voice when Jens Lapidus had a runaway success with his novel *Snabba cash* (Easy Money). He turned the traditional thriller on its head, doing away with the police and portraying society from the gangster's perspective. The world of inner-city Stockholm, where drug dealers from the suburbs, violent mafiosi, motorcycle gangs, celebrities and coke-snorting upper-class youth are all involved together in the pursuit of the only things that matter: money, luxury and status.

Then, in 2005, the writer appeared who would outstrip them all in commercial success. A fifty-year-old who had never written a novel before, who seemed to be writing in all the thriller genres and sub-genres simultaneously, and who tragically had died before his first novel was published.

Debut and Demise

IT WAS AT SOME POINT IN 2003 that Stieg Larsson decided to submit his two completed manuscripts to Piratförlaget. He was aware of their unconventional payment contract, profit-sharing between publisher and author, and found it eminently appealing. But instead of a response the package came back unopened; he sent it in again, telephoned them after a suitable period had elapsed and was told they had not yet got round to reading it. It was eventually returned with a standard letter of rejection.

Stieg was far more interested in writing than in selling himself on the book market. It had never occurred to him to get an agent, for instance, and he was not in any great hurry to look for another publisher.

Robert Aschberg, who had read the manuscript and seen its potential, felt this was the moment to intervene. 'Both Mikael Ekman and I used to keep nagging Stieg to get his backside out of the chair and take his books to another publisher, but he was absolutely unconcerned about it. I thought it ought to have a big publisher with a strong sales team, so I phoned Svante Weyler, who was then head of Norstedts and had published a couple of my own books, and told him I had a sure-fire hit for them if they could undertake to read it quickly.'

Weyler promised they would and two files labelled 'Men Who Hate Women' (the title of eventual publication of the first volume in Sweden) landed on Norstedts' desk.

Weyler, as managing director, and Eva Gedin, publisher, read one each, and passed both novels to Lasse Bergström, retired publisher-in-chief, who still used to read the most promising manuscripts for them.

Lasse Bergström said he had never heard of anything like it before: a writer unknown in the literary field finishing two complete novels before turning to a publisher, and with a third well on its way. So he read fast, over one weekend, and then wrote a comprehensive and enthusiastic report on the two books. He noted that the author had managed to hold together the most wide-ranging of plots and that he gave conscious and playful nods to a variety of thriller genres. The first book was an almost classic detective mystery, the second more of a police procedural. The third book would turn out to be a version of yet another genre, the spy thriller. In Lasse Bergström's opinion they would in all probability do very well.

Eva Gedin and Svante Weyler shared his view. This was an unusually mature beginner who really was master of his chosen vehicle, and readers were certain to fall for the Blomkvist/Salander duo.

From that point on, things moved fast. The publishers rang the author and fixed a meeting. A delighted Stieg Larsson told them that the third volume was nearly ready and that he saw the books as a trilogy about the life of Lisbeth Salander. And there would be more to come. He had in mind a series of ten. His message was, 'If you can market them professionally, I can write them.'

When he later read Lasse Bergström's report he chuckled contentedly, especially at the final comment – 'Eat your heart out, Jan Guillou!' – and thought he really might be going places.

Eva Gedin saw Stieg as a typical man from Norrland: laid-back, laconic, but perfectly sure of himself. He was quite simply convinced that what he had written was good. He said he found everything about novel writing fun and so had just carried on writing without giving much thought to publication, and suddenly found he had near enough three volumes under his belt.

Norstedts proposed a three-book contract, to include paperback rights, an unprecedented deal for them with a totally unknown writer. Stieg would receive an advance of 600,000 kronor. That was an unusually high lump sum for a new author, albeit not enormous in respect of three titles.

FROM A MARKETING ANGLE, the publishers were in an excellent position with an author who, although unpublished, had shown himself to be an exceptionally fluent writer of suspense. They had three manuscripts almost ready and so were able to plan for a high-profile launch with a series name, a distinctive design and uniform covers, and plenty of time to consider every aspect of the marketing campaign. Stieg himself came up with the idea of an interactive website under the name Millennium, and that triggered the notion of the series title.

Norstedts decided to wait until the summer of 2005 to allow themselves scope for proper planning. During April 2004 Eva Gedin and Stieg Larsson had general discussions about publication and the main outline of the books.

'One thing that was really striking,' Eva Gedin remembers, 'was that he had the entire plot in his head, despite its complexity. He never lost sight of any character and never confused a name. But he had questions he was keen to air, such as what Salander should look like, how she should speak and what her weight might be.'

'I've very nearly asked girls on the tube what they weigh, but then thought better of it,' Stieg wrote in an email to the publishers, 'but 42 kilos sounds about right, I think.'

There was really only one matter on which they disagreed. Eva Gedin's immediate reaction to the title *Men Who Hate Women* was that it sounded cold and might even repel some readers. But Stieg, who was otherwise open to discussion on everything, would not compromise on this. And in the end he got his way.

Throughout this period he was working incredibly hard and it was not that easy to get in touch with him. He was sometimes under so much pressure that he barely knew where he was.

At the end of April he wrote in an email to the publisher, 'Just realized it's Walpurgis Night. I'd utterly forgotten about it. My younger colleagues are grumbling and want to go home or out for a beer, so I've promised they can go at nine tonight. Poor old Daniel Poohl, our editorial secretary, has been sleeping in the office for two weeks now. And they're even starting to talk about unionizing. Hmm.' (Walpurgis Night in Sweden is an occasion for bonfires and celebrations.)

Eva Gedin asked him once how he ever found time to write novels.

'I don't need that much sleep,' was his response. 'I write at night.'

After the summer break, more or less as Stieg delivered the manuscript of the third book, the publishers were starting work on the first. Elin Sennerö was appointed Stieg's editor and she went through the text in detail with him.

'He was very sure about what he thought was good and bad, and he radiated great self-confidence. There were huge numbers of facts in the books, but Stieg had an incomparable grasp of all the areas he had written about.'

During the summer Eva Gedin had gone round bookshops examining crime novel book covers, because she was certain they ought to do something quite special for this series. A concept eventually took shape of creating a magazine-like layout with the series name Millennium as a magazine title at the top and beneath it a few puffs for the book itself. The effect would also be to partially conceal the title in the mass of information, while the author's name would stand out loud and clear.

THE EDIT OF THE FIRST VOLUME was completed in October. It coincided neatly with the annual Frankfurt Book Fair, the prime venue for the international book trade to buy and sell publication rights from country to country. Norstedts Agency, the foreign rights department, had decided to make an initial test of the market at Frankfurt to assess potential foreign interest in the series. A synopsis of the first two volumes was prepared as a basis for presentation and discussion with selected publishers.

Magdalena Hedlund, of Norstedts Agency, who had been dealing with Stieg Larsson from the outset, hoped to be able to use the fair to spread the word about the forthcoming titles. It proved easier than anticipated. They soon had a small queue of publishers wanting to read the synopsis, and they had an instant offer during the course of the fair for all three books from the German publisher Heyne, who had had a hot tip from their scout in Sweden. Norstedts accepted after a brief discussion, partly because they thought it was a very satisfactory offer from a large and respected publisher, but also to be able to boast that they had sold the titles immediately to one of the most important countries in Europe. So Norstedts was able to ring Stockholm and break the news of the first foreign sale.

'It was typical of Stieg,' Eva Gedin reminisces, 'that he knew that Heyne belonged to the Bertelsmann empire. And he knew that Bertelsmann owned the American Random House, who had published many of his own favourite authors. So here, he reasoned, could be a chance to get the books out in the USA too. That's exactly what happened, but he didn't live to see it.'

Word of the forthcoming trilogy spread beyond the book trade and enquiries began coming in from film companies. Norstedts consulted Stieg about film and film rights in general. One of his express wishes was that Strix Television and Robert Aschberg, their board chairman, should be invited to take part in negotiations.

Norstedts and Stieg Larsson held a meeting with Aschberg and his colleagues, who presented their concept of a film version.

'I rang Stieg afterwards to ask what he thought,' says Magdalena Hedlund, 'and he felt they had some valuable ideas, but he wanted Norstedts to offer the rights to other likely film companies too.'

That was 8 November 2004. Stieg Larsson knew by now that all three books would be published in Sweden and then in a number of other countries and that they would in all probability be filmed. He had had the first indications that they were indeed good and of interest to a wider market than just the Swedish. That was all he ever knew.

THE NEXT DAY, 9 NOVEMBER, Robert Aschberg contacted Norstedts again, but this time with harrowing news. He told them Stieg had just died of a heart attack in St Göran's hospital.

'It was such a colossal shock and at such a critical stage,' says Eva Gedin. 'Everything was set up, it was all on course, and then Stieg dies so unexpectedly. We more or less stopped work on hearing of his death. We met the family, then there was the funeral. But there was never any question about whether we should carry on. We all agreed the books had to be published. But it was a massive challenge. How would we launch these novels without having the author with us?'

Eva Gedin emailed the foreign publishers and told them what had happened. There was a general feeling of gloom, naturally enough. But the majority were of the opinion that the project should proceed as planned. The greatest hesitation was in the countries with whom Norstedts had not worked much before, but also in Britain and North America, where initially the absence of an author induced an element of doubt.

Within Norstedts the editorial work proceeded on volumes two and three. 'It was fortunate that we had gone through the first book so carefully,' says Eva Gedin. 'I had also talked over the second and third with Stieg, so we had laid a solid foundation for the continuing edit.'

Elin Sennerö thought the second and third needed less editing than the first. Many questions and problems had been resolved in the first book and she knew what sorts of changes Stieg had accepted without argument.

Men Who Hate Women (*The Girl with the Dragon Tattoo*) came out for the summer of 2005. Expectations were high and many feared that it would all end in a real anticlimax. But there was no need to worry. Norstedts' aim had been to sell 20,000 copies, but the book achieved more than double that figure. Before the year was out they had distributed over 50,000 copies.

But it was not until the second volume that sales really took off. They sold 100,000 copies of the hardback edition of *The Girl Who Played with Fire* in year one. And that was just the beginning. Volume three sold 400,000 in its first year.

Negotiations were proceeding simultaneously for the film rights to the trilogy, and they finally went to Yellow Bird, a company set up by Henning Mankell, Lars Björkman and Ole Søndberg, mainly with the intention of filming the Wallander series, but from 2007 owned by the production company Zodiac Television. Norstedts said Yellow Bird had put in the best offer and was the most suitable to produce the films, a decision which annoyed Aschberg considerably, since he felt he could have upped his own bid substantially if he had been given the opportunity.

An International Phenomenon

THE MILLENNIUM BANDWAGON WAS NOW rolling in country after country. 'The "Welcome to Sweden" sign at Arlanda airport ought to feature Stieg Larsson's portrait rather than the king and queen,' was the view of British publisher Christopher MacLehose. It certainly is Larsson and his Millennium Trilogy that represent Sweden for most foreign visitors today.

But just as Stieg Larsson's books were about to appear it was beginning to look as though the crime fiction wave had peaked. European publishers, and Germany in particular, had bought the rights to a great number of Swedish crime writers. Some had achieved commercial success, but others had failed to live up to expectations. There was talk of the European market becoming saturated with Swedish crime novels.

Ten years earlier international interest in Swedish fiction had been no more than moderate. It had only ever been children's books, especially Astrid Lindgren's, that had given Sweden a truly distinctive profile in the wider context.

The Sjöwall–Wahlöö books had been quite successful in the USA and Europe in their day, but the real breakthrough came with Henning Mankell's novels in Germany. The Wallander books were published by a small German imprint but did not at first meet with much favour, despite their overwhelming popularity in Sweden. It was only when the major publishing group of Carl Hanser in Munich purchased the rights and relaunched the series through their subsidiary imprint Paul Zsolnay in the autumn of 1998, backing it up with a huge marketing campaign and attention-grabbing jackets, that the titles took off. Mankell quickly became the biggest-selling author on the German market, and each new book went straight to the top of the bestseller lists in *Der Spiegel*.

There was something in Mankell's stories about an isolated Sweden on the edge of Europe and in his portrayal of the morose but conscientious Kurt Wallander that had great appeal for the German public. The media also gave Mankell a lot of coverage in Germany, fascinated by a writer who was so different from the usual purveyors of bestsellers: he lived for much of the year in Africa, was overtly political, and dared to speak out on serious matters like the Aids catastrophe and the injustice of the global economic system.

A sequence of Swedish and Scandinavian authors then followed in Mankell's footsteps in Germany. They were mostly crime writers, including Edwardson, Marklund, Nesser, Leif G. W. Persson and others, though the one who became the biggest seller, Marianne Fredriksson, wrote novels with no crime mystery element at all.

Swedish detective stories suddenly had fans, just like football teams, and Swedish crime fiction became a concept, with its own website on the Internet, under the newly coined term *Schwedenkrimi*.

Germany became the gateway Swedish writers had to pass through on their way to international success. They could then go on to Holland, France, perhaps Spain and Italy – and in a few lucky cases even to Britain and America.

So when it came to launching Stieg Larsson at Frankfurt in 2004 the platform already existed. He was simply one of many surfing the wave of Swedish thrillers. Nowadays of course the situation is the reverse: it is Larsson who is the driving force, bearing more and more Swedish books with him and opening doors to more and more countries. Now everyone pays attention when a new Swedish crime writer is mentioned. Bonniers, for instance, sold *The Hypnotist* by the pseudonymous Lars Kepler to more than twenty countries before it had even been published at home.

Sweden, for decades known for producing serious novels with neither suspense nor plot, had become the pre-eminent source of bestsellers in Europe.

By April 2010 Stieg Larsson's books had been sold to forty-four countries and achieved sales of 26 million copies. Henning Mankell and Astrid Lindgren still remain far above that figure in total sales, but no Swedish writer has ever accomplished so much in such a short period and with so few titles as Stieg Larsson.

In 2009 he was one of the two or three top-selling authors in the world. A conflation of the figures from the principal book trade journals places him at number one in Europe. The Millennium Trilogy ranks alongside the other bestselling phenomena of the past decade: J. K. Rowling's Harry Potter books, Dan Brown's *Da Vinci Code*, Khaled Hosseini's *The Kite Runner* and Stephenie Meyer's Twilight books.

IN RETROSPECT EVERYTHING SEEMS SELF-EVIDENT. But when the books started to sell internationally no one knew for sure whether they would be a triumph or a failure. Numerous publishers had rejected them. There was particular reluctance in Britain and the USA.

'I must have been about the eighth publisher in Britain to consider the books,' says Christopher MacLehose, head of the eponymous press within Quercus Publishing, who was the one who finally took the trilogy.

By that stage there was already a complete translation by Stephen T. Murray, done on the assumption that the books would eventually be published in the English-speaking countries. The Swedish film company Yellow Bird also had a vested interest, since they wanted to release the films in Britain and the USA.

'As far as I was concerned, there was no doubt at all when I'd read them,' says MacLehose. 'They were absolutely impossible to put down, and they just got better and better from one volume to the next.'

There were three basic reasons for the hesitancy, MacLehose thinks: 'The author was Swedish, he was dead and there were only three books to be published.'

Authors often have to wait for the fourth or fifth book before they make their breakthrough, so it was not such an attractive proposition if one knew that three were all there were ever going to be. But that wisdom too was overturned. The translations in Britain and North America were published later than in most other Western countries, but when sales picked up speed it was with the same momentum as everywhere else. In the spring of 2010 *The Girl Who Kicked the Hornets' Nest* was the top-selling book in Britain and the trilogy had sold 5 million copies in total. When this third volume was released in the USA in May it was printed in a first edition of half a million.

In Germany, the Swedish crime novel's second home, the breakthrough was surprisingly slow to come, but accelerating sales of the paperback editions have brought total sales to over 4 million copies. And not far behind are France and Spain, countries where Swedish literature has normally found it hard to reach a wider audience.

IT IS OBVIOUS THAT STIEG LARSSON is not only riding on but cresting a wave of change in the international book trade. It is already a fact that the most interesting literary novels are increasingly coming from the Third World or countries on the periphery of Europe. Now the same trend seems to be happening for bestsellers.

'Swedish crime, headed up by Larsson and Mankell, was the flavour of the year in Europe,' the *Guardian* reported in an article on 29 April 2009, referring to a survey carried out by the literary sociologists Miha Kovac and Rüdiger Wischenbart which had made a special study of fiction bestseller lists in seven European countries in 2007 and 2008. Their European rankings, based on how long the various authors' books had been on each country's list, showed Sweden with the most titles of all. Larsson came out top, Mankell a little lower, but also Liza Marklund, Jens Lapidus, Mark Levengood, Jan Guillou, Åsa Larsson and Johan Theorin. And way down, below all the Swedes, were American big-name bestsellers like James Patterson and Mary Higgins Clark.

'Wischenbart and Kovac predict that the Europe-wide success of the Mikael Blomkvist and Kurt Wallander creators may soon be followed by Swedish fiction writers who are already making an impact on the top 40,' the *Guardian* added.

This is not just a Swedish crime fiction phenomenon but reflects a broader process on the book market, a shift away from English-language dominance. On this pan-European booklist only thirteen authors are English-language writers; the remaining twenty-seven write in other languages.

It is also noteworthy that the new titles and authors that are selling well have come from a surprising mix of small, medium and large publishers, while the established names are almost all from the major publishing conglomerates. In an international book market where crisis is ever more in evidence, much of the hope of regeneration, both literary and commercial, lies in innovative independent publishing houses, which of course may be found anywhere in the world.

A CLOSER EXAMINATION of Stieg Larsson's publishers internationally reveals that it is those belonging to the big national or international media conglomerates which have taken on the trilogy in countries like Germany, the USA, Spain and the Netherlands, as well as Norway and Finland. But in Denmark, France and Great Britain, for example, it is medium-size independent publishers which have acquired the rights to the Millennium books.

Denmark, with its 5.5 million inhabitants, is probably the country to have sold the greatest proportionate number of Larsson books after Sweden. The formerly alternative press Modtryk had distributed 1.6 million copies of the Millennium Trilogy to Danish readers by the spring of 2010.

Modtryk started out as a true child of the 1960s, with a list of progressive political books. But they gradually had to find more titles that would provide an income and ensure the firm's survival. Their publishing director, Ilse Nørr, explains: 'Everyone connected with Modtryk had read Sjöwall–Wahlöö in the 1970s and realized that crime fiction could be more than mere entertainment. It was a genre which could also provide a critique of society and maybe even contribute to changing it, and that suited Modtryk perfectly.'

They established their crime list, and with interest among the larger publishers for buying foreign rights and translating crime novels from abroad lukewarm to say the least, Modtryk was able, as soon as the Swedish crime novel started gaining momentum, to lay their hands on a whole line-up of the thriller writers they liked best: Jan Guillou, Leif G. W. Persson, Håkan Nesser, Arne Dahl, Åsa Larsson, Jens Lapidus.

So they also pricked up their ears when Agneta Markås and Magdalena Hedlund told them about Stieg Larsson, and were quick to read the manuscript of the first book.

'I remember three things we noted,' says Ilse Nørr. 'That there was a fantastic pace to the novels, spurring you on to read more, that we fell in love with Salander and that the subject matter raised important issues.'

By this time, however, the tepid interest of the big Danish publishers for Swedish thrillers had warmed up quite considerably and the titles went to auction. But since Modtryk had well-filled coffers after earlier successes in the genre, and was the most highly motivated, they were able to put in the highest bid. They did not regret it. They soon realized that Larsson would far exceed all the other crime fiction successes they had had.

'This was a phenomenon that just grew and grew, and some time in 2007, when the second book was out, the media started making comparisons with Harry Potter. When the original Swedish edition of The Girl Who Kicked the Hornets' Nest appeared in October 2007, it was said that only the Swedish Hymnal had ever had a bigger print run.'

❖

IT WAS WHEN THE PUBLIC'S ENTHUSIASM for Stieg Larsson's books reached fever pitch in France that it became clear that the Millennium Trilogy would be a unique phenomenon in the Swedish 'crime wave'. Here too the books had gone to a publisher outside the big media conglomerates: Actes Sud in the Provençal town of Arles. And the man behind their decision was someone with a long-standing commitment to Swedish literature in France: Marc de Gouvenain, freelance publisher and translator.

Marc de Gouvenain had lived a varied life before literature took over. He had travelled the world, worked in Ethiopia and Morocco, run a travel agency and written his own travel books. In the 1960s he began visiting Sweden regularly, was employed as a cleaner by the Swedish Environmental Protection Agency and as a metal-worker at a steelworks in Malmö, and met Lena, the Swedish woman he was to marry. Back in France again, he was encouraged to translate Swedish novels by C. G. Bjurström, the legendary link-man on the Franco-Swedish literary scene and introducer of each country's literature to the other.

Marc de Gouvenain started working for Actes Sud and edited on their behalf a Scandinavian literary series, *Domaine Scandinave*, with a list of writers that has included Torgny Lindgren, Kerstin Ekman, P. O. Enquist, Göran Tunström, Christine Falkenland and Peter Kihlgård.

He initially heard of Stieg Larsson's books as he was walking to a Norstedts publisher's party with Agneta Markås one evening in December 2004 on a visit to Stockholm. 'I have always relied totally on her judgement, so I hurried to read the manuscript of the first book and felt that we must take it, and the contract was signed in January 2005.'

He rang the head of Actes Sud and said he had bought a brilliant title and that perhaps the time had come to embark on the crime fiction series that they had talked about for so long. Although he had not wanted to carry on translating, Stieg Larsson's books made him change his mind. He liked the Millennium novels, and though they were not his absolute favourites in Actes Sud's crime series, they were definitely good, and since he thought they had commercial potential and might sell some 20,000–30,000 copies, he might be able to earn a worthwhile sum as translator. (In France, as in Britain, translators have a percentage of royalties, though few books achieve sales high enough to recoup the advance payment made for the translation, normally based on a rate per 1,000 words.) So he decided to undertake the translation himself, together with his ex-wife Lena Grumbach.

The first book came out in June 2006 and the second in the autumn of the same year. But hopes and expectations were not fulfilled. They were well received but sales remained modest.

The publishers realized in early 2007 that the chances of achieving high sales were fast evaporating. So the marketing department decided to mount a publicity campaign. The publication date of the third volume was brought forward. Influential people in the media were told of these remarkable Swedish books and the trilogy was relaunched as 'the cult series already read by millions'. And now at last they began to fly off the shelves: '*la mayonnaise a pris*'. From almost having come to a standstill, the sales curve rose exponentially at the end of 2007 and continued on a similar trajectory throughout 2008.

LARSSON FEVER IN FRANCE, AND ALSO IN SPAIN, has gone hand in hand with and driven increased sales of crime fiction as a whole, and even given rise to a new form of marketing in the French book trade. FNAC, the largest bookshop chain, has put up signs announcing '*Polars suédois*' or '*Polars scandinaves*', a term now virtually synonymous with crime thrillers in general. (The word *polar* is actually derived from *policier* but applied to all forms of the thriller.)

So Stieg Larsson's reach extended far beyond the Swedish crime novel's usual core countries – Scandinavia, Germany and the Netherlands. Spain followed in the wake of France. Destino came upon the books via the French translation and decided to go for them in a big way, and there, as in France, sales absolutely exploded when the third volume was published. Destino sold 200,000 on publication day alone, and in total they have sold the same number as in France: 3.5 million copies of the three books by the spring of 2010.

In a Spanish book market severely dented by the financial crisis, Larsson is the chief attention-grabber and publishers are looking feverishly for new Swedish crime authors to translate. Everything to do with the Millennium Trilogy has become a cult. Prime Minister José Luis Zapatero has admitted to being an admirer of Stieg Larsson and took the opportunity of going on one of the Millennium tours arranged by Stockholm City Museum when he was visiting the Swedish capital. In Spain particular emphasis has been laid on the more socio-political themes in the books, not least the subject of male violence towards women.

What is the secret behind the phenomenal success in one country after another? From the reader's perspective it is an easy question to answer. The books have a unique heroine.

Cyberpunk Pippi

ONE FINE SUMMER'S DAY, in the most famous of Astrid Lindgren's children's books, Pippi Longstocking moves into Villekulla Cottage. Nobody knows her background. She seems to have no parents and no friends. Pippi Longstocking is alone in the world.

That is the way Lisbeth Salander had first turned up at the offices of Milton Security, as we learn in Chapter 2 of the first Millennium novel. No one knew who she was and she was not forthcoming with information. She wanders around the premises like a lost dog and is called 'the girl with two brain cells, one for breathing and one for standing up'. They might be able to use her at most for making the coffee and dealing with the mail.

Actually her situation is even worse. For though she may have few or no friends, she has plenty of powerful enemies. But just like Pippi, who can lift her horse high above her head, Lisbeth is equipped with almost super-human powers. She has a photographic memory, can solve Fermat's theorem and can fell a 100-kilo biker with a single karate kick. She can also find out anything about anybody. But most important of all, her uncommunicativeness is her greatest strength. In extreme situations of vulnerability she shuts out the external world, constructs her own inner world of strictly logical rules and then acts, takes her revenge and frees herself.

AN AUTHOR DECIDED TO LET LOOSE a children's book heroine from literary history and have her walk into the present, now grown up and transformed into a Goth girl with dyed black hair, tattoos, pierced eyebrows and T-shirts bearing admonitory slogans such as 'I am also an alien' or 'Consider this fair warning'. When Stieg Larsson told his friends and acquaintances about her as he was writing the books, some of them wondered what on earth he was playing at.

In 2002, with Stieg still composing his narrative of Lisbeth Salander, Astrid Lindgren died. Even before her death she was almost a national saint, and Pippi Longstocking was one of the best-loved children's book characters in the world. It was difficult to imagine a less controversial model for the heroine of a novel.

But that had certainly not always been the case. Astrid Lindgren knew when she submitted her manuscript to Bonniers in April 1944 that she had written a provocative story. A book about a girl who was 'independent of all adults and lives her life exactly as it pleases her' would be hard for a lot of people to swallow. And indeed after a long delay the manuscript was returned with a rejection. The publisher, Gerard Bonnier, admitted later that he was the one who had turned it down. 'Sugar all over the floor and chaos in the nursery. No, I wasn't willing to be responsible for that . . .' But the book was published anyway, by Rabén & Sjögren. The story of what Astrid Lindgren herself called 'a little Übermensch in the person of a child' won first prize in a children's book competition, was praised in the newspapers and sold like hot cakes.

It might have seemed as if no one was against Pippi. In fact almost the opposite was true. When the second book appeared, the storm broke. One of the country's most renowned professors of literature, John Landquist, declared that Pippi's way of eating cake and throwing sugar over the floor was 'reminiscent of the imaginings of a mental defective, or of some pathological obsession'. The book about Pippi was badly written, cynical and offensive. 'This unnatural girl and her distasteful adventures in Lindgren's book will linger in the memory, if remembered at all, as a very unpleasant experience, as a minor irritant at the back of the mind.'

Perhaps posterity should be grateful to John Landquist. The subversive influence of the Pippi character would certainly never have made such an impact had it not been for him. Because after his intervention the expected torrent of criticism hit the letters pages of the newspapers and the educational press. It was all about educational theory and methods of upbringing. About order and discipline as opposed to freedom and child-centred values. And it went on right up to 1995, when Carin Stenström, columnist and Christian Democrat, wrote in *Svenska Dagbladet* that 'Pippi adulation has turned everything upside down, school, family life, standards of behaviour [. . .] It has glorified self-centredness, egotism, lack of consideration for others and escapism.'

Astrid Lindgren did not herself rush to respond to all the criticism. But she knew that her Pippi had given encouragement to many repressed children – especially girls. She wrote in an article in *Aftonbladet* a few days later, in March 1995, '[The reaction] is understandable, since it has been boys, boys, boys all through the ages – and now along comes a girl. It stands to reason girls are going to start thinking maybe I can too.'

IN ITS WAY *PIPPI LONGSTOCKING* was what the Swedes call a novel of ideas, the French a *roman à thèse*, expounding a social theory. It appeared just as the Second World War was ending and a new epoch was dawning. The jackboot tyranny had been vanquished and all authoritarian structures should likewise be repudiated. A fairer social order needed to be introduced and children especially, as the weakest members of society, regarded as people in their own right.

These ideas had actually been around for a long time. They formed the basis of the British child psychologist Alexander Neill's experimental school, Summerhill, in the 1920s, and Gustav Jonsson's Swedish counterpart, Barnbyn Skå, in the 1940s. Though beyond enlightened radical circles, society at large between the wars remained uncompromising and unforgiving; social deprivation was no respecter of persons, least of all children. Yet somehow society had to intervene and alleviate all the misery out there. A strategy had to be found to tackle the problems. The prevailing view in the first half of the twentieth century was that children who became delinquents were either badly brought up or of a degenerate disposition. In the latter case they themselves were the problem.

The 'degenerate' label gave society complete discretion to take children into care and place them in an institution without having to prove that any wrongdoing or criminal offence had been committed; and wardship could be extended to cover the whole of their youth if so desired.

'Institution' did not sound a very attractive term, so the word 'home' was used. It was a place where society's unfortunate children might experience security and some care and attention. Pippi must have been a problem child such as those described in official reports and institutional rules. She was presumably a case of inadequate upbringing, since her only parent was ruling over a desert island in the South Seas instead of teaching his daughter how to behave. She was most definitely degenerate, so it would be logical to put her in a children's home.

ADMITTEDLY, SOCIETY HAD IMPROVED in many ways in the post-war years, seen by Swedes as the era of reaping the benefits of prime minister Per Albin Hansson's 'people's home' concept. But the forces of oppression were still there, merging with new forms of bureaucratic, political and commercial power.

How would life have gone for Pippi if she had remained anarchistically antisocial into her twenties and been alive today? Certainly an army of doctors, behavioural therapists, psychiatrists, career guidance counsellors, life coaches and physiotherapists would have been on hand to support her. A great many diagnoses would have been applied, in various combinations of letters – DAMP, ADHD, ADD – but she would have finished up in an institution anyway, locked in, isolated, given sedatives. And there the story might have ended.

But it doesn't. Because Stieg Larsson's Pippi is quite different from a maladjusted self-destructive girl whose resistance and anger are ground down by the millstones of bureaucracy. The basically good-humoured story of Pippi Longstocking has been revived as a tale of evil, a feverishly heightened fantasy about unprecedented conspiracies and vicious power-hungry men.

From the very first instant, even while still in the womb, Stieg Larsson's Pippi, Lisbeth Salander, is categorized and rubber-stamped, classified as an enemy of the state. And the moment she emerges into the world she must be removed from it. So she is declared psychologically disturbed by a malevolent psychiatrist and locked up in a care home. Having been deprived of her rights, she then becomes a victim of further abuse and is exploited and raped even by those who are meant to be protecting her.

In the objectively narrated and richly detailed Millennium Trilogy the story of Lisbeth Salander breaks its own bounds. The narrative goes beyond the credibility associated with the realistic crime novel. Yet it remains firmly anchored in a reality which had actually existed in Sweden. It functions as a true account of the dark underbelly of the beneficent welfare society, of the way individuals, often the most vulnerable, can be ill-treated and lose all their legal rights.

There in the background are echoes of the corrupt legal practices of the 1950s, when Vilhelm Moberg acted as tribune of the people, for example on behalf of the artist Gustaf Unman, who was interned in a mental hospital while his allotted guardian, Folke Lundquist, embezzled his money, with Unman's own protests going unheeded because he had been certified as not responsible for his actions. There too is a reminder of the abuses that occurred in foster home placements and enforced detention in reformatories and children's homes. Modern retrospective investigations reveal a shocking picture of how institutionalized children suffered. Neglect and ill-treatment were common, as were sexual abuse, incarceration, threats and humiliations, which, especially in the case of girls, had sexual overtones.

There in real life were the educationally subnormal in an institution in Skåne who were used as human guinea pigs as part of an investigation into the role of sugar in causing caries, made to eat a specially manufactured toffee until their teeth completely rotted.

And then perhaps the most disturbing mass abuse of the weak and vulnerable in modern Swedish history: the sterilization imposed over a period of forty years, between 1935 and 1975, on some 60,000 people, the aim of which was to prevent the mentally deficient and other 'social parasites' from reproducing. The historian Maija Runcis demonstrated in an academic thesis that it was predominantly the most socially vulnerable women who were subjected to the more or less obligatory sterilizations. And the decisions were frequently based on very vague, prejudiced and moralizing judgements. Runcis writes of a provincial doctor putting in a request to the children's care board for a fifteen-year-old girl who is regarded as having learning difficulties to be sterilized, 'because she is reported to have attended dances and shown a great interest in boys; it is this potentially improper mingling with boys which prompts the present application'.

In Stieg Larsson's novels the weak individual lacks legal redress. Authority is inaccessible, totalitarian. But he avoids extending his analysis into a general plea for social reform. One of the unequivocally positive male characters in the novels, Salander's 'good' guardian, Holger Palmgren, is said to be 'a peculiar mixture of jurist and social worker [. . .] a crazy Social Democrat who had worked with troubled kids all his life'.

Abuses, in fiction and in reality, are perceived to have other causes. They relate to the authoritarian tradition, a tradition not so unlike fascism, which ought to have vanished with the end of the Second World War but didn't, and to contempt for women.

STIEG LARSSON LETS PIPPI OUT OF THE children's home: releases Salander from compulsory sectioning. But not to proper freedom. From society's viewpoint Lisbeth Salander is only conditionally discharged. She is placed under guardianship, what was once called a declaration of incapacity: she cannot do as she wishes with her life or her possessions. The range of activities she is permitted by the authorities is extremely narrow. But since she doesn't intend to obey any such restrictions she constructs her own freedom of action. With talent and single-minded perseverance she has developed into a world-class hacker, and with the aid of computers she operates at will in digital space and so nullifies the limitations imposed on her. She also ignores conventional sexuality, making love with both men and women, and discards her boyish figure in favour of more voluptuous breasts. In the end she frees herself even geographically and goes to Pippi's South Seas, or in her own case to the West Indies, along with her virtual chest of gold which she has expropriated from the financial scoundrel Wennerström by a brilliant piece of hacking.

She is also a true child of the pirate generation. When Stieg was writing his Millennium books, the Pirate Bay had just hoisted its flag. This Swedish file-sharing website, where private individuals could download music, films, digital books and the like, was the largest of its kind in the world, digital entertainment's equivalent of Ikea, except that the prices were not so much low as non-existent. For the established entertainment industry, the site was indeed a pirate, and in 2006 the long arm of the law closed down all its servers. But the legal cases against it in 2008–9 and the formation of the Pirate Party indicated that something had been happening over the course of that decade which was way beyond the control or understanding of politicians, big business or ordinary citizens. There proved to be thousands of Lisbeth Salanders out there.

But it was inconceivable that Salander should join any party, pirate or otherwise. She is more like a member of Anti-Fascist Action: fanatically moral and a committed activist, and so autonomous that she is not willing to cooperate with anyone. Yet that is exactly what she does when she meets Mikael Blomkvist – about whom she already knows all there is to know, because she has checked his personal details and hacked into his computer.

So the Blomkvist–Salander partnership is established. They are not just an ill-matched pair: they are two people from completely different worlds. Salander is at the extreme of the fictional range, a fairy-tale character, while Blomkvist is a realistic, conventional detective story figure. A bit boring, perhaps, but a good bloke. He has a quite extensive, undemanding and apparently untroubled love life which in the usual male way he believes is free of prejudice, but which is actually very male chauvinist. He gives only the most fleeting occasional thought to his ex-wife and daughter. He is a typical urban man of the twenty-first century, someone who moves easily from one milieu to another, who chooses his acquaintances and his projects, but avoids long-term commitment; a hyper-individualist but with idealistic traits.

The portrayal of Blomkvist does not present him as an original; he has other functions in the novels. His personality is fairly incompatible with that of Salander, which complicates their work together and is thus an advantage for the plot. The dramatic tension of the books derives from the fact that pace and suspense are created by maximum resistance.

And by being a man without qualities Blomkvist enhances the prominence of the only real hero of the story on whom all light must shine: Lisbeth Salander.

Mikael Blomkvist compliantly accepts the subsidiary role he has to play. He lacks the typical male attributes of prestige and desire for power. So he constitutes no threat to Salander and she gradually becomes aware, to her own surprise, that she likes and even trusts him.

DESIRE FOR POWER AND THE EXERCISE OF POWER ARE, however, the essential characteristics of the gallery of male rogues who appear in the books. The trilogy is not least an exposition of female suppression as society's permanent legacy, perpetuated by those in positions of respectability or authority, like the three brothers in the Vanger industrialist family or Bjurman the lawyer; and of the everyday disparagement of women, which has the potential to flare up into outbursts of raging hatred.

Whenever Stieg Larsson encountered objections that the murders of women depicted in the first book in particular are so brutal as to be unbelievable, his response was always that the reality was far worse. He had himself systematically perused hundreds of police reports and court proceedings, and written about the cases of Melissa Nordell and Catrine da Costa, who were murdered in a bestial and almost ritualistic manner. And for Stieg, who had studied fascist ideology for many years, it seemed obvious that it had to do with a distorted view of humanity. Nazi thought is completely permeated by an identification with power, according to Harald Ofstad in his classic book *Our Contempt for Weakness*: 'A real man cannot ever have profound contact with a woman. Her world is totally different from his. Real men can only have contact with men – as in the SS and other male groups. Real men are bound to one another in comradeship and loyalty to the leader.'

A German author, Klaus Theweleit, published an extensively

reviewed book in the late 1970s entitled *Male Fantasies* (English translation 1987), based on letters, diaries and literary works by people in the so-called Free Corps, armed squads set up at the end of the First World War to quash the German left-wing revolution of 1918–19. They developed into self-ruled and ill-disciplined groups with a strong sense of solidarity, and it was from them that the Nazi fighting units grew, especially the SA.

What Theweleit was chiefly interested in was men's attitude to sex and their complex relationship with women and women's bodies. How their concepts of purity and motherhood were at odds with a compelling and anxiety-ridden sexuality: everything that they cannot admit, cannot talk about, but that bursts out in extreme situations of violence and lack of social inhibition in which these men find themselves, expressed in abusive fantasies directed at those defined as the enemy, and most especially at women.

THE DEFENCELESS TRAPPED IN THE CLAWS of the powerful have usually had no other choice than to submit. But for Salander the whole point is not to submit under any circumstances. Her story is a fantasy on how the most oppressed and abused can become invincible if they do not allow themselves to be broken. Salander's way is the way of the individual, the way of vengeance. In this she is typical of her times. The Danish writer Carsten Jensen surmises that the incredible popularity of the Millennium books stems from revenge fantasies on the part of a new middle class 'with a low frustration threshold and a head full of imaginary insults that demand immediate redress [. . .] Lisbeth Salander, a dream of omnipotence in the shape of a victim of violence, starts out as a Pippi Longstocking for the digital age and ends as a Christ figure, complete with burial and resurrection.'

Lisbeth can of course also be seen as an over-explicit representative of the new breed of female warriors who are called ninja feminists and appeared in the 1990s in novels such as Helen Zahavi's *Dirty Weekend* or Anja Snellman's *The Geography of Fear*, or films like *Thelma and Louise*, *Nikita* and *Kill Bill*.

In a cynical and brutalized society there are only two roles to choose from: victim or executioner. And Bella, the threatened protagonist in Zahavi's book, has no doubt about her own. When she goes out on the town she no longer packs a lipstick in her handbag but a pistol.

'There is a feminist strength in the women whom I regard as cynicism feminists,' writes Nina Björk in her book *Under det rosa täcket* (Under the Pink Duvet). 'Protest as liberation, the enjoyment of seeing and reading about women who have encountered repression that I as a woman recognize, and who refuse to accept it. But they also embody a fundamental human failure: not allowing any room for weakness.'

Stieg Larsson inserts historical epigraphs in *The Girl Who Kicked the Hornets' Nest* about female warriors always having existed. They were present even though society has suppressed information about them.

In a contribution to the discussion about military conscription for women in *Internationalen* which Stieg wrote (under his pseudonym Severin) back in 1983, he points out that there is no proof that women are physically weaker than men or that women have been more peaceable over the course of history:

Women should not be required to do military service, because it is against their nature to fight. Their traditional role in this vale of tears is to create peace, heal wounds and provide tender loving care. I have met many women who represent all of the above. Equally I have met many men in the same roles. But I have also met women who have been bellicose, militant and aggressive, who have taken part in war as fully armed soldiers and who have trained and fought alongside men. Of course women must work for peace, but not by giving currency to a new mythology of women.

Salander's violent rampage can also be seen as a kick in the teeth for what might be called 'separate species feminism'. Fundamentally men and women are the same. Equally physically expressive and equally introverted, equally inclined to violence and equally peace-loving. Men have had the upper hand and exploited it, including the use of physical force as their weapon. Would everything be different if the roles were reversed? We cannot know, of course.

Coming in from the Cold

STIEG LARSSON WAS THE CRIME writer who came in from the cold. He lived his early years among the forests of northern Sweden, but when he became a storyteller his tales were of the capital city, Stockholm, of the twenty-first-century urban middle classes working in the media, buying expensive apartments on Södermalm and socializing in cafés and restaurants.

He was an avid consumer of thrillers and light-entertainment films, and an instinctive opponent of cultural snobbery, who after his death was praised and analysed – and also criticized – by some of the biggest names of the literary world, including Mario Vargas Llosa, Christopher Hitchens and Carsten Jensen.

He has reinvigorated the Swedish crime fiction tradition of social criticism, but declared that he himself only read crime novels from the USA and Britain, since the Swedish ones were not worth reading.

Stieg grew up with and continued to believe in cooperation and solidarity. But in his books the painstaking teamwork of the police has been ditched. His two protagonists, Salander and Blomkvist, hunt on their own, disengaged from the police or other authorities, and almost independently of each other – a striking picture of the extreme individualism of our new century. Nor is he as a crime writer much interested in which aspects of society today are the causes of crime; the important thing is to find the villains, pursue them, nail them.

He was a conscious feminist with a female heroine who really stands on the barricades, does battle with the networks of malevolent males and is herself both 'queer' and 100 per cent gender correct. But he has a male protagonist who lives the typical male dream of wishful thinking where all women are in love with him, while he himself maintains his independence, his amicable distance and really loves only his job.

Everywhere this duality. Perhaps it is part of the secret. Giving the books their feeling of modernity without the superficiality, cynicism or ego-trip quality of so many other contemporary violence-fixated crime novels. And attracting so many different kinds of readers. Everyone finds something to identify with in these books.

CAN A NOVEL BE FLAWED AND EXCEPTIONAL at the same time? That is a question posed by the Peruvian novelist Mario Vargas Llosa. His answer is: yes, indeed it can. Stieg Larsson's novels are not conspicuously well written, and their structure is far from perfect, but such remarks are irrelevant because there is something else at work, a sort of primeval narrative force drawing the reader into all these unexpected and enchanting tales and tangents, these stories of oppression and revenge. It is like the classic nineteenth-century novels of Dickens, Dumas, Victor Hugo: you read for the sake of reading, because you don't ever want it to come to an end.

How could a first-time novelist achieve this? That question may never be answered.

Nevertheless it is possible to see how his life and his anti-racist work are very consistent with his thrillers even beyond the actual subject matter. How his minutely detailed surveys of extremist right-wing organizations are transformed into intricate and encyclopedic plots in which all the pieces of the puzzle fit exactly, where no threads are lost and no names forgotten. As in the novels of his predecessor Frederick Forsyth, the books can be read as a sort of carefully researched reportage in novel form, where the reader is persuaded that every single particular is correct and that every fact has been checked. Yet that is not the point, nor indeed the secret behind the books' success. An author can devote infinite time and trouble to researching the facts, hunting through archives, conducting interviews, but that does not necessarily produce a book the public will actually want to read. There have to be other ingredients to make a book so loved.

Even as a teenager Stieg would sit in his rented room fantasizing and writing science fiction. He wrote a short story in the very amateurish fanzine *Sfären* about a girl with remarkable telepathic gifts who was extremely shy and never spoke to anyone. He himself obviously retained that special ability to live in his own imagination and to wonder about people whose behaviour differed from the norm. When he started work on the Millennium books he let all this blossom. Novels were easy because now he was writing for pleasure and could say whatever he liked.

So he really let the monsters emerge from the depths of the forest. His pages are filled with all the evils in contemporary society: abuse, rape, trafficking, drug dealing, tangled conspiracies.

Is it all believable? Yes, you have to believe it or the whole narrative structure would collapse like a house of cards. That is the reason for all those precise pedantic facts scattered through the 2,000 pages of the trilogy. The reader has to be convinced that the secret reactionary Freemason-like group within the Security Police, keeping its dragon-like watch over the critical dangerous secrets about Salander and her father, could exist in real life. Hence the meticulous account of the development of the Swedish intelligence services after the Second World War. Credible or not – that is for the reader to decide. The majority have clearly chosen to suspend any disbelief.

Stieg Larsson's books are a balancing act between wild fantasy and a near-fetishistic urge for facts. As novels, they occupy the nexus between real life and the imaginary. And he had indeed encountered evil himself, looked danger in the eyes, received countless death threats. How many crime writers can say that of themselves?

Could Stieg Larsson write? The answer is a resounding affirmative. He spent all his life writing: articles, stories, socio-political books, emails. This is what he tapped out on his typewriter as a nineteen-year-old: 'Let me tell you about Annie Johnson. Let me tell you what really happened. You probably won't believe me, and I don't blame you. No one else believes me either.'

There was much more to come. Not least three of the most read novels of our time.

The Inheritance Dispute

STIEG SIGNED OFF HIS UNWITNESSED and thus invalid will in the 1970s, 'Go and treat yourselves to a coffee together somewhere. Live life to the full and have fun.'

And life has indeed gone on since his death. But hardly in a spirit of amity and reconciliation. Instead it has been a tragic conflict between those closest to him, increasing in hostility in correlation with the escalating success of the novels.

Stieg Larsson and Eva Gabrielsson never married. Eva has said that they had planned several times to formalize their relationship, but what dissuaded them primarily were Stieg's anti-Nazi activities and all the threats he received. The violent Nazi groups made full use of public records to locate and harass their opponents, but because Stieg was not registered at his home address and was not in the register of marriages, he was not easy to find.

He never wrote another will. After Norstedts took on the novels, Eva says, he had intended to form a company jointly with her into which the income from the books would be paid. She thought Norstedts were going to set up and manage such a company for them, whereas Norstedts insist there must have been a misunderstanding, since they have never run companies on behalf of authors.

It was quite clear very soon after Stieg's death how the inheritance would be divided. Swedish law in respect of cohabitation gives very little protection for unmarried partners in the event of the death of one of them. The surviving partner is not the heir of the deceased, but simply has a right to a half-share of the household goods and joint residence – irrespective of how long the couple have lived together.

So when the division of property was made in the spring of 2005, Stieg's inheritance, plus the copyright in his literary works and half of the joint residence, went to his father, Erland, and his brother, Joakim, the latter through the inheritance of Stieg's deceased mother, Vivianne. So Stieg's common-law wife of more than thirty years was in effect left nothing.

When the Millennium Trilogy became such a success in one country after another, everyone could see that the income from the literary rights would be far more than the publisher's advance of just over half a million kronor. However, copyright law is not only about who will receive the money but also about who decides on how the works are to be exploited: where they are to be placed, what use can be made of them in other media, what contracts can be signed, what revisions can be made.

Since the copyright passed to Stieg's father and brother, Norstedts had to liaise with them on all matters pertaining to the future of the books. Numerous contracts were signed in 2005 and 2006, for translations into various languages, different editions, and also a film option and then firm contract with Yellow Bird.

Erland and Joakim Larsson felt that the circumstances obliged them to take responsibility for overseeing the process and ensuring that new projects continued.

Eva Gabrielsson wanted to take over control of all the literary work herself. She maintained that that was more important than the money. She felt it was logical because she was the one who knew Stieg's intentions with his writing. The then chairman of *Expo* drew up a draft contract to this effect, separating the financial aspects of copyright from the intellectual ones and allocating the latter to Eva, who would receive appropriate remuneration.

The Larssons, however, were not prepared to relinquish full responsibility for control of the literary estate and rejected the proposal.

In the situation that developed from the autumn of 2005, as interest in Stieg Larsson's books and the commercial pressures kept on growing, and more and more international contracts were signed and plans for the filming began, what had seemed a problematic scenario at the beginning now developed into open conflict and total breakdown of trust between the two parties.

One element of disagreement concerned the uncompleted manuscript of the fourth volume of the series which was in Stieg's computer when he died. In formal terms the computer was the property of *Expo*, and Daniel Poohl had checked through it directly after Stieg's death to see whether it contained any important *Expo* matters. He was not interested in whatever literary texts might have been there. Where the computer then went has remained a secret. The incomplete text has been assumed to be somewhere in the region of 150 to 300 pages in length. Joakim Larsson says that Stieg had written in an email shortly before he died that the book was almost finished.

Eva Gabrielsson wanted to have the manuscript, as part of an agreement on the control of the works, in order to ensure its completion if necessary; whereas Erland and Joakim thought it should be handed over to Norstedts, so that the publisher could decide whether it was viable, and so that any income from sales would go to *Expo*, as Stieg had wished.

In the autumn of 2005, Erland and Joakim Larsson's lawyer sent a draft division of inheritance agreement to Eva Gabrielsson. It proposed that they would transfer Stieg's half of the apartment to her, and that she would hand over the computer and the fourth manuscript. After that, negotiations could begin about financial recompense or a royalties percentage for her from any forthcoming book. The lawyer later informed her that they were considering going to court for an order to produce a document (i.e. the manuscript), which Eva regarded as blackmail – she would only be allowed to keep the apartment if she handed over the computer. Joakim Larsson has asserted that he sent an email to Eva explaining that they were not going to pursue this course and told her to delete the clause about the computer if she so wished. They intended to give her the other half share of the apartment anyway – as indeed was subsequently done.

THE CONFLICT HAS INTENSIFIED over the last few years, and the media have reported every step taken by both sides, with all the various initiatives and counter-proposals.

The inheritance battle has become an integral element of the Millennium mythology. There is no suggestion that either faction is motivated by ill-will, and both have expressed their desire to reach an agreement, but it has so far proved impossible. Erland and Joakim Larsson have announced that they are willing to give a specified sum from the inheritance to Eva Gabrielsson and that they are prepared to discuss how control of the works can be shared, but this presupposes that the two sides can talk to each other. Eva has insisted that the vital element for her is the sole trusteeship of Stieg's literary legacy in its entirety, and that she would be prepared to undertake that in return for a low percentage of the royalties.

The parties announced in early 2008 that they had agreed not to publish the fourth Millennium novel. So it seemed that the most remarkable of all Swedish thriller series had been brought to a conclusion. But to what extent that decision is set in stone is another matter entirely.

What is beyond question, however, is that Salander and Blomkvist live on in the reader's imagination. As with all literary creations, they are the ones who are ultimately the trustees of Stieg Larsson's literary legacy.

REFERENCES

p. 1 Quotation Bjursele. Stieg Larsson: *The Girl with the Dragon Tattoo.* London: MacLehose Press, 2008, pp. 324–5.

p. 5 Quotation. Per Olov Enquist: *Ett annat liv.* Stockholm: Norstedts, 2008, p. 38.

p. 6 Västerbotten authors. Åke Lundgren: "Det litterära arvet." *Svenska Turistföreningens årsbok 2001.* Västerbotten, p. 78ff. **Quotation.** Åke Lundgren: *Svenska Turistföreningens årsbok 2001,* p. 80. **Quotation.** ibid., p. 82.

p. 8 Erik Lidman. See Birgitta Holm: *Sara Lidman—i liv och text.* Stockholm: Bonniers, 1998, p. 22ff.

p. 9 Rönnskärsverken. *Guld och döda skogar. Rapport från Rönnskärsverken— Sveriges skitigaste industri.* Pockettidningen R. Stockholm: Prisma, 1978, p. 8ff.

p. 10 blood on the handkerchief p. 28ff.

p. 15 Quotation. Eva Gabrielsson: "Stieg ville inte bli kändis, allra minst som deckarförfattare," *Norra Västerbotten,* October 4, 2007. **Work companies.** Karl Molin: *Hemmakriget. Om den svenska krigsmaktens åtgärder mot kommunister under andra världskriget.* Stockholm: Tiden, 1982. See also Tobias Berglund and Niclas Sennerteg: *Svenska koncentrationsläger i Tredje rikets skugga.* Stockholm: Natur & Kultur, 2009.

p. 17 Quotation Bosse Lindh. Article series by Hans Forsman, *Västerbottens Folkblad,* February 26, 2009. **Quotation Haga school.** ibid.

p. 21 Quotation Ingela Mattsson-Löfbom. ibid.

p. 23 Anti Vietnam War movement. See Åke Kilander: *Vietnam var nära. En berättelse om FNL-rörelsen och solidaritetsarbetet i Sverige 1965–1975.* Stockholm: Leopard Förlag, 2007.

p. 24 Sara Lidman: *Samtal i Hanoi.* Stockholm: Bonniers, 1966; *Gruva.* Stockholm: Bonniers, 1968.

p. 26 On Trotsky. See Isaac Deutscher: *The Prophet Armed: Trotsky 1879–1921; The Prophet Unarmed: Trotsky 1921–1929; The Prophet Outcast: Trotsky 1929–1940.* London and New York: Oxford University Press, 1954, 1959, 1963.

p. 27 Trotskyism in Sweden. See Kjell Östberg: "Det är något visst med en trotskist" in *Människan i historien och samtiden.* Festskrift till Alf W Johansson. Stockholm: Hjalmarson & Högberg, 2000, p. 310ff.

p. 34 Ethiopia–Eritrea. See Ryszard Kapuscinski: *The Emperor: Downfall of an Autocrat.* London: Quartet, 1983; Lars Bondestam: *Eritrea: Med rätt till självbestämmande.* Stockholm: Clavis, 1989.

p. 36 Female guerrilla soldiers. *Aftonbladet,* June 6, 2007; Stieg Larsson: *Autisterna.* Stockholm: Alba, 1979.

p. 41 Quotation. Stieg Larsson: *The Girl Who Played with Fire.* London: MacLehose Press, 2009, p. 7.

p. 42 Grenada. See Beverly A. Steele: *Grenada: A History of Its People.* London: Macmillan, 2003, p. 11ff.; *Forward Ever!: Three Years of the Grenadian Revolution. Speeches of Maurice Bishop.* Atlanta, GA: Pathfinder Press, 1982.

p. 45 Quotation. "Så firas revolutionen på Grenada." *Internationalen* 13/1983.

p. 49 Report on the coup. Roland Eliasson, Eva Gabrielsson, Stieg Larsson: "USA ut ur Grenada," *Internationalen* 43/1983.

p. 53 Quotation. Stieg Larsson: "CIA bakom militärkuppen," *Internationalen* 44/1983.

p. 54 Coard freed. *Grenada's last 1983 rebels free.* BBC Online. September 5, 2009. *Internationalen* website, November 2, 2009.

p. 56 Quotation. Anders Hellberg: "Stieg Larsson kunde inte skriva," *Dagens Nyheter,* January 21, 2010. **Quotation.** Severin: "Vidskepelsens världsbild," *Internationalen* 39/1983.

p. 59 Quotation. Per J. Andersson: *När Vagabond skickade Stieg Larsson till Kina.* www. vagabond.se/Redaktionellt/Resmal/Ovrigt-om-resor/Litteratur/Nar-Vagabond-skickade-Stieg-Larsson-till-Kina. Published September 21, 2009.

p. 61 Quotation. Stieg Larsson and Per Jarl (photog.): "9001 kilometer till Beijing," *Vagabond,* February 1987. **Quotation.** Kenneth Ahlborn: "Stieg Larsson var ingen kitslig wannabe," *Dagens Nyheter,* January 19, 2010.

p. 63 Swedish National Association. Stieg Larsson: "SNF. Extremhögerns gubbmaffia," *Expo* no. 1/1997.

p.64 Christopher Jolin: *Vänstervridningen. Hot mot demokratin i Sverige.* Stockholm: Vox/ Bernces, 1972.

p. 66 *Strindbergsfejden:* *465 debattinlägg och kommentarer utgivna av Harry Järv I–II.* Stockholm: Cavefors, 1968. **Quotation Strindberg.** August Strindberg: "Faraon-dyrkan," *Strindbergsfejden,* p. 17ff.

p. 67 Quotation Kjellén. Rudolf Kjellén: "En tornering. Sven Hedin mot August Strindberg," *Strindbergsfejden,* p. 328ff. and 358ff. **New conservatism.** See Nils Elvander: *Harald Hjärne och konservatismen. Konservativ idédebatt i Sverige 1865–1922,* p. 257ff. **Quotation Kjellén, Strong man.** Rudolf Kjellén: *Politiska essayer.* Studier till dagskrönikan II, Stockholm: Gebers Förlag, 1915, p.19. **People's home.** A metaphor used by many speakers of various political persuasions. Best known among the first users of the term was Rudolf Kjellén: see his *Politiska essayer,* p. 56.

p. 68 Quotation national socialism. Kjellén: *Politiska essayer,* p. 22. **Swedish nazism before and during WW2.** See Heléne Lööw: *Nazismen i Sverige 1924–1974. Pionjärerna, partierna, propagandan.* Stockholm: Ordfront, 2004, p. 13ff.; Stieg Larsson and Anna-Lena Lodenius: *Extremhögern,* Stockholm: Tiden, 1994, p. 77ff. **Herman Lundborg and the National Eugenics Institute.** See Maja Hagerman: *Det rena landet. Om konsten att uppfinna sina förfäder.* Stockholm: Prisma, 2006, p. 370; Gunnar Broberg and Mattias Tydén: *Oönskade i folkhemmet. Rashygien och sterilisering i Sverige.* Stockholm: Dialogos, 2005; Herman Lundborg: *Svensk raskunskap.* Stockholm: Almqvist & Wiksell, 1928.

p. 69 Nazism in the military. See Karl N A Nilsson: *Svensk överklassnazism 1930–1945,* Stockholm: Carlssons, 1996, p. 59ff., p. 197ff. **Hitler's birthday congratulations.** *ibid.,* p. 146ff.

p. 70 Swedish accession to German demands. See Maria-Pia Boëthius: *Heder och samvete. Sverige och andra världskriget.* Stockholm: Ordfront, 1999. **Vanger brothers.** Stieg Larsson: *The Girl with the Dragon Tattoo.* p. 158.

p. 71 Quotation. Stieg Larsson: *The Girl with the Dragon Tattoo,* p. 79. **Hallberg-Cuula.** See Larsson and Lodenius: *Extremhögern,* p. 82.

p. 72 Hibernators. See Heléne Lööw: *Nazismen i Sverige 1924–1974*, p. 121ff. **C E Carlberg.** See Larsson and Lodenius: *Extremhögern*, pp. 81, 102; Karl A. Nilsson: *Svensk överklassnazism*, p. 135ff.

p. 73 Quotation Sastamoinen. Armas Sastamoinen: *Nynazismen*. Stockholm: Federativs Förlag, 3rd ed., 1966, p. 5.

p. 74 Sture Eskilsson. *Motvind, medvind. Artiklar av Sture Eskilsson 1958–1989 i urval*. Stockholm: Timbro, 1990; Stefan Koch: *Höger om! En svensk historia 1968–98*, Stockholm: Ordfront, 1999.

p. 77 Quotation. Stieg Larsson: "Fascisterna kring Margaret Thatcher," *Internationalen* 43/1984.

p. 78 Notting Hill. After 44 years secret papers reveal truth about five nights of violence in Notting Hill. *The Guardian*, August 24, 2002; Maj-Britt Morrison: *Jungle West 11*. London: Tandem Books, 1964.

p. 79 Maurice Ludmer. See Institute for Race Relations. www.irr.org.uk

p. 80 Ray Hill. *Searchlight* no. 152/1988, Ray Hill and Andrew Bell: "The Other Face of Terror. Inside Europe's Neo-Nazi Network." London: Collins, 1988.

p. 81 Nordic National Party, Umeå. "På barrikaden för demokratin," interview with Stieg Larsson in *Humanisten* no. 3–4, 2002. Frederick Forsyth: *The Odessa File*. London: Hutchinson, 1972.

p. 82 Quotation. *Humanisten* no. 3–4, 2002.

p. 84 Cable Street. Audrey Gillan: "Day the East End said 'No pasaran' to Blackshirts," *The Guardian*, September 30, 2006. **Mosley.** See Robert Skidelsky: *Oswald Mosley*. London: Macmillan, 1981.

p. 85 National Front. See Lodenius and Larsson: *Extremhögern*, p. 147ff.

p. 87 Reagan. Stieg Larsson: "Reagan i nazihärva," *Internationalen* 35/1984.

p. 88 WACL. Lodenius and Larsson: *op. cit.*, p. 266ff. See also Scott Anderson and Jon Lee Anderson: *Inside the League*. New York: Dodd, Mead & Co., 1986.

p. 89 Singlaub. Stieg Larsson: "Mannen bakom den internationella högerterrorn," *Internationalen* 1/1985; Stieg Larsson: "De nya kannibalerna," *Internationalen*, March 1985.

p. 92 Ian Stuart and White Power music. See Heléne Lööw: *Nazismen i Sverige. 1980–1997*, p. 173ff.; Lodenius and Larsson: *Extremhögern*, p. 322ff., 333ff.

p. 94 Blücher quotation. *Nordic Order*, February 1985; Larsson and Lodenius: *Extremhögern*, p. 320.

p. 95 BSS. Lodenius and Larsson: *op. cit.*, p. 17ff.; Stieg Larsson and Mikael Ekman: *Sverigedemokraterna: Den nationella rörelsen*. Stockholm: Ordfront 2001, p.61.

p. 97 Per Engdahl: *Sverigedemokraterna—Den nationella rörelsen*, p.66; *Vägen framåt*, March 1979.

p. 98 Stop Racism. *Tidningen Stoppa Rasismen*, January 1983.

p. 99 Delle Chiaie. Stieg Larsson: "Svarta orkesterns dirigent," *Stoppa Rasismen* 2, March–April 1987.

p. 101 Progress Party. Lodenius and Larsson: *Extremhögern*, p. 89ff.

p. 102 Sweden Party. Larsson and Ekman: *Sverigedemokraterna*, p. 83f.

p. 106 Quotation Bidney. Stieg Larsson: "Fascisterna kring Margaret Thatcher," *Internationalen* 43/1984.

p. 109 New Democracy quotation. Lodenius and Larsson: *op. cit.*, p. 73. **Laser Man attacks.** See Gellert Tamas: *Lasermannen. En berättelse om Sverige*. Stockholm: Ordfront, 2002, p. 13ff.

p. 110 Sveg trial. See Gellert Tamas: *Lasermannen*, p. 235ff.

p. 111 Demonstrations. See Kurdo Baksi: *Stieg Larsson, My Friend*. London: MacLehose Press, 2010; Gellert Tamas: *Lasermannen*, p. 324ff. **Rinkeby.** See Gellert Tamas: *Lasermannen*, p. 302ff.

p. 115 Press Club. Consultant. Interview *Humanisten* no. 3–4, 2002.

p. 116 *Expo, Demokratisk Tidskrift*, Stockholm, January 1995.

p. 120 Quotation. *Dagens Nyheter* 23/10/1995, *Aftonbladet*, October 30, 1995.

p. 125 Quotation. Stieg Larsson: "Oklahomamassakern kan ske i Stockholm,"

Expo, January 1/1995. **On William Pierce and *The Turner Diaries*** see Leonard Zeskind: *Blood and Politics: The History of the White Nationalist Movement from the Margins to the Mainstream*. New York: Farrar, Straus & Giroux, 2009, pp. 17, 29.

p. 128 Schmidt quotation. Michael Schmidt: *Nynazismens ansikte: En rapport*. Stockholm: Bonnier Alba 1993, p. 66.

p. 129 White Power music. Sara Björk: 'Musiken—extremhögerns nya inkomstkälla," *Expo*, January 1995; Andreas Rosenlund: "Ultima Thule," *Expo*, February 1995; Jonas Hellentin: 'Imperiet Nordland," *Expo*, June 1996.

p. 131 Quotation Fridolin. Gustav Fridolin: *Blåsta. Nedskärningsåren som formade en generation*. Stockholm: Ordfront, 2009, p. 191. **Icehouse.** Andreas Rosenlund: "Myten om fryshuset," *Expo*, February 1995.

p. 133 Quotation. "Nationella Alliansen – nazismens enade front," *Expo*, February 1996.

p. 134 Attacks. *Expo*, March 1996, 'Expoaffären," *Expo*, April–May 1996.

p. 136 Co-publication with *Svartvitt*. Kurdo Baksi: *Stieg Larsson, My Friend*, p. 40.

p. 137 Meeting Nordland, Blood and Honour, etc. *Aftonbladet*, February 9, 2000. **IT-boom.** See Björn Elmbrant: *Dansen kring guldkalven—så förändrades Sverige av börsbubblan*. Stockholm: Atlas, 2005.

p. 139 Dear Mr Norén. See Elisabeth Åsbrink: *Smärtpunkten: Lars Norén, pjäsen Sju tre och morden i Malexander*. Stockholm: Natur & Kultur, 2009, p. 20.

p. 141 Tony Olsson. See Elisabeth Åsbrink: *Smärtpunkten*, p. 27. **Quotation shoot-out.** Stieg Larsson: "Tryggheten dog i Nacka," *Expo/Svartvitt* no. 3, April 1999.

p. 142 Quotation Up with Malexander. *Aftonbladet*, February 2, 2000.

p. 143 Quotation Nacka car bomb. Stieg Larsson: "Tryggheten dog i Nacka," *Expo/Svartvitt* no. 3, April 1999. **Murder of Björn Söderberg.** Stockholms tingsrätts dom, April 14, 2000, Svea hovrätts dom, July 14, 2000 (Stockholm District Court and Court of Appeal proceedings).

p. 145 Four newspapers on Nazi threat quotation. Stieg Larsson: 'Nazister i massmedia,' *Expo*, January 2000.

p. 146 Terrorism. Stieg Larsson: "Terrorism som folkrörelse," *Expo/Svartvitt* 3–4/1999.

p. 147 Stieg Larsson: *Överleva deadline. Handbok för hotade journalister.* Stockholm: Svenska Journalistförbundet, 2000.

p. 148 Erika Berger, security procedures. Stieg Larsson: *The Girl Who Kicked the Hornets' Nest.* London: MacLehose Press, 2009, p. 414.

p. 149 Anti-AFA. David Lagerlöf: "Anti-AFA—nazisternas SÄPO," *Expo/Svartvitt*, March–April 1999; "Nazister kartlade kända svenskar," *Aftonbladet*, September 11, 2001.

p. 153 Sweden Democrats. Stieg Larsson and Mikael Ekman: *Sverigedemokraterna: Den nationella rörelsen.* Stockholm: Ordfront 2001.

p. 154 Le Pen och National Front. See Bim Clinell: *De hunsades revansch: En resa i fascismens Frankrike.* Stockholm: Ordfront, 2003.

p. 166 Millennium. Stieg Larsson: *The Girl with the Dragon Tattoo*, p. 46.

p. 167 Quotation. Jon Voss: "Föraktet för det svaga är huvudsakligen föraktet för den egna svagheten," *Expo*, January 1995. **Nazis and homosexuality.** David Lagerlöf: "Dubbelliv som livsstil," *Expo*, January 2003.

p. 168 Leader quotation. Stieg Larsson: "Terrorn vi blundar för," *Expo*, January 2003.

p. 169 Francis Fukuyama: *The End of History and the Last Man.* New York: Free Press, 1992.

p. 170 Naomi Klein: *No Logo.* Toronto: Knopf, 2000. **Gothenburg events.** See *Vad hände med Sverige i Göteborg?* Eds. Mikael Löfgren and Masoud Vatankhah. Stockholm: Ordfront, 2001; Erik Wijk: *Orätt: rättsrötan efter Göteborgshändelserna.* Stockholm: Ordfront 2003.

p. 171 AFA:s view. See Jonathan Pye: "Stenkastandets logik," in *Vad hände med Sverige i Göteborg*, p. 105f.

p. 172 Quotation. Stieg Larsson. *Humanisten* no. 3, April 2002.

p. 173 Samuel P. Huntington: "The Clash of Civilizations," *Foreign Affairs*, 72(3), 1993. Jimmie Åkesson: "Muslimerna är vårt största utländska hot," *Aftonbladet*, October 19, 2009.

p. 174 Proud friends of Israel. See Sweden Democrats' general secretary Björn Söder's website. www.bjornsoder.net. **Progress Party.** See Magnus E Marsdal: *Frp-koden: Hemmeligheten bak Fremskrittspartiets suksess.* Oslo: Forlaget Manifest, 2007.

p. 176 Ethnic purity. See Maja Hagerman: *op. cit*, p. 10ff.

p. 178 Salem march. See *Expo* no. 4, 2004, p. 16.

p. 180 Salander's hacking technique. 'Visst funkar det," *Ny Teknik*, May 5, 2007.

p. 181 *Debatten om hedersmord. Feminism eller rasism.* Eds. Cecilia Englund and Stieg Larsson. Stockholm: Svartvitt & Expo, 2004, p. 6.

p. 182 Quotation. ibid., p. 43ff. **Quotation.** ibid., p. 102.

p. 184 Quotation. Lasse Winkler: "En man för historieböckerna," *Svensk Bokhandel.* www.svb.se, November 9, 2004. **Bigger than Mankell.** Markus Wilhelmson: "Mannen som lekte med elden," *Magasinet Att:ention*, November 2006.

p. 190 Quotation Writing thrillers is easy. *Svensk Bokhandel*, www.svb.se, November 9, 2004.

p. 192 Crime statistics. BRÅ: *Brottsutvecklingen i Sverige fram till år 2007.*

p. 194 'Dirty books'. Ulf Boëthius: *När Nick Carter drevs på flykten. Kampen mot 'smutslitteraturen' i Sverige 1908–1909.* Stockholm: Gidlunds, 1989.

p. 195 FIBs Popular Books. Lars Furuland and Johan Svedjedal: *Svensk arbetarlitteratur.* Stockholm: Atlas, 2006, p. 506ff. **Johan Hansson and crime fiction.** From N&K's foundation charter: "A basic principle of the Foundation's publishing programme shall be that no book will be published which does not merit binding. So bridge manuals and crime fiction will not normally be considered." Quoted from Carin Österberg: *Natur och Kultur: En förlagskrönika.* Stockholm: Natur & Kultur, 1987, p. 255.

p. 196 H-K Rönblom: *Endast för de segervissa: Meningar om mord.* Ed. Jan Broberg. Stockholm: Cavefors, 1968, p. 27.

p. 197 Quotation. Per Wahlöö, **rip open the belly** quoted from Bo Lundin: *Spårhundar, spioner och spännande personer.* Stockholm: Carlssons, 1993, p. 150. **Quotation.** Lasse Bergström: *Bokmärken.* Stockholm: Norstedts, 1998, p. 314.

p. 199 Maj Sjöwall & Per Wahlöö: *Roseanna.* London: Gollancz, 1965. **Quotation.** Maj Sjöwall & Per Wahlöö: *The Abominable Man.* London: Gollancz, 1971.

p. 201 Quotation. Maj Sjöwall and Per Wahlöö: *The Terrorists.* London: Gollancz, 1975.

p. 203 Quotation. Lars Lönnroth and Sverker Göransson: *Den svenska litteraturen: Medieålderns litteratur.* Stockholm: Bonniers, 1990, p. 257.

p. 204 IB Affair. *Folket i Bild/Kulturfront* no. 9/1973; Peter Bratt: *Med rent uppsåt.* Stockholm: Bonniers, 2007. See also *Rikets säkerhet och den personliga integriteten: De svenska säkerhetstjänsternas författningsskyddande verksamhet sedan år 1945.* SOU 2002:87. Stockholm: Statens Offentliga Utredningar, 2002. **Quotation.** Jan Guillou: *Ordets makt och vanmakt.* Stockholm: Piratförlaget, 2009, p. 271.

p. 207 Quotation. Per Olov Enquist: *Kartritarna.* Stockholm: Norstedts 1992, p. 138ff.

p. 209 Quotation. Johan Svedjedal: "Berättaren Stig Larsson," *Artes*, February 1989.

p. 210 Henning Mankell: *Faceless Killers.* London: Harvill, 1997.

p. 212 Swedish foreign policy. See Douglas Brommesson: *Från Hanoi till Bryssel: Moralsyn i deklarerad svensk utrikespolitik 1969–1996.* Stockholm: Santérus 2007, p. 165ff.

p. 213 Håkan Nesser: *Borkmanns Point.* London: Macmillan, 2006.

p. 215 Kerstin Ekman: *Blackwater.* London: Chatto, 1995.

p. 216 Kjerstin Göransson-Ljungman: *Tjugosju sekundmeter, snö.* Stockholm: Bonniers, 1939. **Inger Frimansson**: *Good Night, My Darling.* New York: Pleasure Boat Studio, 2007.

p. 217 Liza Marklund: *The Bomber.* London: Pocket, 2002.

p. 221 Quotation Johan Svedjedal: 'Fiktionsvärldar," *Svensk Bokhandel* no. 20/2009, p. 10.

p. 222 John Ajvide Lindqvist: *Let the Right One In.* London: Quercus, 2007. Jens Lapidus: *Snabba Cash.* Stockholm: Wahlström & Widstrand, 2006.

p. 233 Quotation. *The Guardian* 29/4/2009. **Miha Kovac and Rüdiger Wischenbart**: *Bestselling Fiction in Europe 2008/2009.*

REFERENCES

p. 240 Quotation. Letter to publisher. Margareta Strömstedt: *Astrid Lindgren: en levnadsteckning*, 4th ed., Stockholm: Norstedts, 2003, p. 252. See also Ulla Lundqvist: *Århundradets barn: Fenomenet Pippi Långstrump och dess förutsättningar*. Stockholm: Rabén & Sjögren 1979. **Quotation. Sugar all over the floor.** Margareta Strömstedt: *op. cit.*, *p. 252.* **Quotation. John Landquist:** 'Dålig men prisbelönt," *Aftonbladet*, August 18, 1946. **Quotation.** Carin Stenström: "Dags pensionera Pippi Långstrump," *Svenska Dagbladet*, March 8, 1995.

p. 241 Quotation, boys, boys. *Aftonbladet*, March 10, 1995. **Problem children.** See Kerstin Vinterhed: *Gustav Jonsson på Skå:*

Visionen. Stockholm: Marieberg 1980, p. 56ff.

p. 243 Unman. Vilhelm Moberg: *Komplotterna: Affärerna Unman och Selling.* Stockholm: Bonniers, 1956.

p. 244 Sterilizations. Maija Runcis: *Steriliseringar i folkhemmet.* Stockholm: Ordfront, 1998, p. 124. **Quotation Palmgren.** Stieg Larsson: *The Girl with the Dragon Tattoo*, p.145.

p. 245 Pirate Bay. Se Anders Rydell and Sam Sundberg: *Piraterna: De svenska fildelarna som plundrade Hollywood.* Stockholm: Ordfront 2009.

p. 247 Quotation. Harald Ofstad: *Our Contempt for Weakness: Nazi Norms and Values and Our Own.* Stockholm: Almqvist & Wiksell, 1989. Klaus Theweleit: *Male Fantasies.* Minneapolis: University of Minnesota Press, 1987. (Original German publication 1977.)

p. 248 Quotation. Carsten Jensen: "Lisbeth Salander och vår längtan efter hämnd," *Dagens Nyheter*, December 20, 2009. **Female warriors.** See Nina Björk: *Under det rosa täcket: Om kvinnlighetens vara och feministiska strategier.* Stockholm: Wahlström & Widstrand, 1996, chapter "Läppstiftet som blev en pistol," p. 127ff. Female avengers can also be found in e.g. Henning Mankell's *The Fifth Woman* och Håkan Nesser's *Woman with Birthmark*, both originally published in 1996, and in *Good Night, My Darling* by Inger Frimansson. Crime fiction characters taking the law into their own hands are discussed in Jan Broberg: *Mord i minne*, chapter entitled "Fascismen i deckaren," (p. 104ff.), Stockholm: Zinderman, 1976. Helen Zahavi: *Dirty Weekend.* London: Methuen, 1991. Anja Snellman: *Pelon maantiede* (Geography of Fear). Helsinki: WSOY, 1995.

p. 249 Quotation. Nina Björk: *Under det rosa täcket: Om kvinnlighetens vara och feministiska strategier.* Stockholm: Wahlström & Widstrand, 1996 p. 151. **Quotation.** Severin: "Inför kvinnlig värnplikt," *Internationalen* 23/1983.

p. 250 Christopher Hitchens: "The author who played with fire," *Vanity Fair*, December 2009; Mario Vargas Llosa: "Lisbeth Salander debe vivir," *El Pas*, September 6, 2009.

p. 252 Stig Larsson: "Det nionde livet," *Sfären*, April 1973.

p. 254 Copyright dispute. See interview with Eva Gabrielsson in *Babel*, March 11, 2009.

p. 255 Fourth book, etc. Letter from the Larssons' lawyer.

p. 256 Offer. "Vi kan ge henne 20 miljoner." *Svenska Dagbladet*, November 1, 2009.

p. 257 No fourth novel. 'Ingen fjärde Stieg Larsson-bok," *Dagens Nyheter*, March 18, 2008.

INTERVIEWS WITH:

Robert Aschberg
Kenneth Ahlborn
Håkan Blomqvist
Jan-Olov Carlsson
Mikael Ekman
Ulla Ekström von Essen
Eva Gedin
Marc de Gouvenain
Magdalena Hedlund
Stig Larsson
Erland Larsson
Joakim Larsson
Kenneth Lewis
Anna-Lena Lodenius
Christopher MacLehose
Ilse Nørr
Daniel Olsson
Erik Pettersson
Daniel Poohl
Andreas Rosenlund
Elin Sennerö

BIBLIOGRAPHY

Ahlmark, Per – m. fl.: *Det eviga hatet: Om nynazism, antisemitism och Radio Islam.* Bonniers och Svenska Kommittén mot anti-Semitism 1993.

Anderson, Scott – Anderson, Jon Lee: *Inside the League.* Dodd, Mead & Co 1986.

Åsbrink, Elisabeth: *Smärtpunkten. Lars Norén, pjäsen Sju tre och morden i Malexander.* Natur & Kultur 2009.

Asimov, Isaac: *Stiftelsetrilogin.* Översättning: Sam J Lundvall. Natur & Kultur 1994.

Baksi, Kurdo: *Min vän Stieg Larsson.* Norstedts 2010.

Berglund, Tobias – Sennerteg, Niclas: *Svenska koncentrationsläger i Tredje rikets skugga.* Natur & Kultur 2009.

Bergström, Lasse: *Bokmärken.* Norstedts 1998.

Björk, Nina: *Under det rosa täcket. Om kvinnlighetens vara och feministiska strategier.* Wahlström & Widstrand 1996.

Blomqvist, Håkan: *Nation, ras och civilisation i svensk arbetarrörelse före nazismen.* Carlsson 2006.

Blomqvist, Håkan: *Socialismens sista sommar. Essäer om 1900-talets förhoppningar och sorger.* Carlsson 2002.

Boëthius, Maria-Pia: *Heder och samvete. Sverige och andra världskriget.* Ordfront 1999.

Boëthius, Ulf: *När Nick Carter drevs på flykten. Kampen mot "smutslitteraturen" i Sverige 1908–1909.* Gidlunds 1989.

Bondestam, Lars: *Eritrea. Med rätt till självbestämmande.* Clavis 1989.

Bratt, Peter: *Med rent uppsåt. Memoarer.* Bonniers 2007.

Broberg, Gunnar – Tydén, Mattias: *Oönskade i folkhemmet. Rashygien och sterilisering i Sverige.* Dialogos 2005.

Brommesson, Douglas: *Från Hanoi till Bryssel. Moralsyn i deklarerad svensk utrikespolitik 1969-1996.* Santérus 2007.

Carlsson, Holger: *Nazismen i Sverige. Ett varningsord.* Trots allt! 1942.

Clinell, Bim: *De hunsades revansch. En resa i fascismens Frankrike.* Ordfront 2003.

Debatten om hedersmord. Feminism eller rasism. Red. Cecilia Englund och Stieg Larsson. Svartvitt och Expo 2004.

Deutscher, Isaac: *Den väpnade profeten.* Översättning: Martin Peterson. *Den avväpnade profeten.* Översättning: Otto Mannheimer. *Den förvisade profeten.* Översättning: Mario Grut. Coeckelberghs Partisanförlag 1971–73.

Ekman, Mikael – Poohl, Daniel: *Ut ur skuggan. En kritisk granskning av Sverigedemokraterna.* Natur & Kultur, 2010.

Elmbrant, Björn: *Dansen kring guldkalven. Så förändrades Sverige av börsbubblan.* Atlas 2005.

Elvander, Nils: *Harald Hjärne och konservatismen. Konservativ idédebatt i Sverige 1865-1922.* Almqvist & Wiksell 1961.

Engdahl, Per: *Fribytare i folkhemmet.* Cavefors 1979.

Enquist, Per Olov: *Ett annat liv.* Norstedts 2008.

Enquist, Per Olov: *Kartritarna.* Norstedts 1992.

Eskilsson, Sture: *Motvind Medvind. Artiklar av Sture Eskilsson 1958–1989 i urval.* Timbro, 1990.

Forsyth, Frederick: *Täcknamn Odessa.* Översättning: Claës Gripenberg. Bonniers 1987.

Forward Ever! Three Years of the Grenadian Revolution. Speeches of Maurice Bishop. Pathfinder Press 1982.

Fridolin, Gustav: *Blåsta. Nedskärningsåren som formade en generation.* Ordfront 2009.

Frimansson, Inger: *God natt min älskade.* Rabén Prisma 1998.

Fukuyama, Francis: *Historiens slut och den sista människan.* Översättning: Staffan Andræ. Norstedts 1992.

Furuland, Lars – Svedjedal, Johan: *Svensk arbetarlitteratur.* Atlas 2006.

Göransson-Ljungman, Kjerstin: *Tjugosju sekundmeter, snö.* Bonniers 1939.

Guillou, Jan: *Ordets makt och vanmakt. Mitt skrivande liv.* Piratförlaget 2009.

Hagerman, Maja: *Det rena landet. Om konsten att uppfinna sina förfäder.* Prisma 2006.

Hansson, Sven Ove: *Till höger om neutraliteten. Bakom fasaden hos näringslivet och moderaterna.* Tiden 1985.

Hill, Ray – Bell, Andrew: *The Other Face of Terror. Inside Europe's Neo-Nazi Network.* Collins 1988.

Högerpopulismen: en antologi om Sverigedemokraterna. Red Håkan A. Bengtsson. Premiss 2009.

Holm, Birgitta: *Sara Lidman – i liv och text.* Bonniers 1998.

Holmberg, John-Henri: *Inre landskap och yttre rymd. Science fictions historia, del 1. Från H. G. Wells till Brian W. Aldiss, del 2. Från J. G. Ballard till Gene Wolfe.* Btj 2002.

Huntington, Samuel P.: *Civilisationernas kamp. Mot en ny världsordning.* Översättning: Katarina Sjöwall Trodden. Atlantis 2006.

Johansson, Alf W.: *Den nazistiska utmaningen. Aspekter på andra världskriget.* Prisma 2006.

Jolin, Christopher: *Vänstervridningen. Hot mot demokratin i Sverige.* Vox/Bernces 1972.

Kapuœciñski, Ryszard: *Kejsaren. En envåldshärskares fall.* Översättning: Britt Arenander. Alba 1985.

Kilander, Åke: *Vietnam var nära. En berättelse om FNL-rörelsen och solidaritetsarbetet i Sverige 1965–1975.* Leopard 2007.

Kjellén, Rudolf: *Politiska essayer. Studier till dagskrönikan II.* Gebers 1915.

Klein, Naomi: *No Logo. Märkena, marknaden, motståndet.* Översättning: Lillemor Ganuza Jonsson och Tor Wennerberg. Ordfront 2001.

Lagergren, Fredrika: *På andra sidan välfärdsstaten. En studie i politiska idéers betydelse.* Brutus Östlings Bokförlag Symposion 1999.

Larsson, Stieg: *Euro-Nat: Sverigedemokraternas internationella nätverk.* Svartvitt och Expo 1999.

Larsson, Stieg: *Flickan som lekte med elden.* Norstedts 2006.

Larsson, Stieg: *Luftslottet som sprängdes.* Norstedts 2007.

Larsson, Stieg: *Män som hatar kvinnor.* Norstedts 2005.

Larsson, Stieg: Överleva deadline. *Handbok för hotade journalister.* Svenska Journalistförbundet 2000.

Larsson, Stieg – Ekman, Mikael: *Sverigedemokraterna—Den nationella rörelsen.* Ordfront 2001.

Larsson, Stieg – Lodenius, Anna-Lena: *Extremhögern.* 2:a rev. uppl. Tiden 1994.

Larsson, Stieg – Poohl, Daniel: *Handbok för demokrater.* Hjalmarsson & Högberg 2004.

Larsson, Stig: *Autisterna.* Alba 1979.

Lidman, Sara: *Gruva.* Bild: Odd Uhrbom. Bonniers 1968.

Lidman, Sara: *Samtal i Hanoi.* Bonniers 1966.

Lindgren, Torgny: *Ormens väg på hälleberget.* Norstedts 1982.

Lindquist, Hans: *Fascism idag. Förtrupper eller eftersläntrare?* Federativs 1979.

Lindqvist, Sven: *Antirasister. Människor och argument i kampen mot rasismen 1750–1900.* Bonniers 1995.

Lindqvist, Sven: *Utrota varenda jävel.* Bonniers 1992.

Lodenius, Anna-Lena: *Gatans parlament. Om politiska våldsverkare i Sverige.* Ordfront 2006.

Lodenius, Anna-Lena – Wikström, Per: *Vit makt och blågula drömmar. Rasism och nazism i dagens Sverige.* Natur & Kultur 1997.

Lööw, Heléne: *Nazismen i Sverige 1929–1979. Pionjärerna, partierna, propagandan.* Ordfront 2004.

Lööw, Heléne: *Nazismen i Sverige 1980-1997. Den rasistiska undergroundrörelsen:musiken, myterna, riterna.* Ordfront 1998.

Lundborg, Herman: *Svensk raskunskap.* Almqvist & Wiksell 1928.

Lundgren, Åke: *Det litterära arvet.* Svenska Turistföreningens årsbok 2001.

Lundqvist, Ulla: *Århundradets barn. Fenomenet Pippi Långstrump och dess förutsättningar.* Rabén & Sjögren 1979.

Mankell, Henning: *Den vita lejoninnan.* Ordfront 1993.

Mankell, Henning: *Mördare utan ansikte.* Ordfront 1991.

Marklund, Liza: *Sprängaren.* Ordupplaget 1998.

Marsdal, Magnus E: *Frp-koden. Hemmeligheten bak Fremskrittspartiets suksess.* Forlaget Manifest 2007.

Mattsson, Pontus: *Sverigedemokraterna in på bara skinnet. Reportage.* Natur & Kultur 2009.

Meningar om mord. *15 uppsatser om deckare, deckarförfattare och deckarhjältar.* Red Jan Broberg. Cavefors 1968.

Moberg, Vilhelm: *Komplotterna. Affärerna Unman och Selling.* Bonniers 1956.

Molin, Karl: *Hemmakriget. Om den svenska krigsmaktens åtgärder mot kommunister under andra världskriget.* Tiden 1982.

Morrison, Maj-Britt: *Jungle West 11.* Tandem Books, 1964.

Nesser, Håkan: *Borkmanns punkt.* Bonniers 1994.

Ofstad, Harald: *Vårt förakt för svaghet. Nazismens normer och värderingar—och våra egna.* Översättning: Cilla Johnson. Prisma 1972.

Östberg, Kjell: *Det är nått visst med en trotskist. Människan i historien och samtiden. Festskrift till Alf W Johansson.* Hjalmarson & Högberg 2000.

Österberg, Carin: *Natur och Kultur. En förlagskrönika 1922–1986.* Natur och Kultur 1987.

Pockettidningen R. *Guld och döda skogar. Rapport från Rönnskärsverken—Sveriges skitigaste industri.* Prisma 1978.

Runcis, Maija: *Steriliseringar i folkhemmet.* Ordfront 1998.

Rydell, Anders – Sundberg, Sam: *Piraterna. De svenska fildelarna som plundrade Hollywood.* Ordfront 2009.

Sastamoinen, Armas: *Hitlers svenska förtrupper.* Federativs 1947.

Sastamoinen, Armas: *Nynazismen.* Tredje upplagan. Federativs 1966.

Schmidt, Michael: *Nynazismens ansikte. En rapport.* Bonnier Alba 1993.

Sjöwall, Maj – Wahlöö, Per: *Den vedervärdige mannen från Säffle.* Norstedts 1971.

Sjöwall, Maj – Wahlöö, Per: *Roseanna.* Norstedts 1965.

Sjöwall, Maj – Wahlöö, Per: *Terroristerna.* Norstedts 1975.

Skidelsky, Robert: *Oswald Mosley.* Papermac 1981.

Snellman, Anja: *Rädslans geografi.* Översättning: Camilla Frostell. Norstedts 2000.

Steele, Beverley A.: *Grenada. A History of Its People.* Macmillan 2008.

Strindbergsfejden. *465 debattinlägg och kommentarer utgivna av Harry Järv,* I-II. Cavefors 1968.

Strömstedt, Margareta: *Astrid Lindgren. En levnadsteckning.* Pan Norstedts 2003.

Sundström, Lena: *Världens lyckligaste folk. En bok om Danmark.* Leopard Förlag 2009.

Svedjedal, Johan: *Ett myller utan mening? Essäer om svenska författarskap.* Red Lars Elleström och Cecilia Hansson. Alba 1990.

Sverigedemokraterna från insidan. *Berättelsen om Sveriges största parti utanför riksdagen.* Red Richard Slätt och Maria Blomquist. Hjalmarson & Högberg 2004.

Tamas, Gellert: *Lasermannen. En berättelse om Sverige.* Ordfront 2002.

Theweleit, Klaus: *Mansfantasier I–II.* Brutus Östlings Bokförlag Symposion 1995.

Vad hände med Sverige i Göteborg? Red Mikael Löfgren och Masoud Vatankhah. Ordfront 2002.

Vestin, Sanna: *Flyktingfällan.* Ordfront 2006.

Vinterhed, Kerstin: *Gustav Jonsson på Skå. Del 1. Visionen. Del 2. Kampen.* Marieberg, 1980.

Wärenstam, Eric: *Fascismen och nazismen i Sverige.* Ny utökad upplaga. Almqvist & Wiksell 1972.

Wendelius, Lars: *Rationalitet och kaos. Nedslag i svensk kriminalfiktion efter 1965.* Gidlunds 1999.

Wijk, Erik: *Orätt. Rättsrötan efter Göteborgshändelserna.* Ordfront 2003.

Zahavi, Helen: *En jävla helg.* Översättning: Barbro Lagergren. Wahlström & Widstrand, 1992.

Zeskind, Leonard: *Blood and Politics. The History of the White Nationalist Movement from the Margins to the Mainstream.* Farrar, Straus & Giroux 2009.

INDEX

Note: Stieg Larsson is abbreviated to SL in parts of the index.